T0319962

A Research Agenda for Sustainable Consumption Governance

Elgar Research Agendas outline the future of research in a given area. Leading scholars are given the space to explore their subject in provocative ways, and map out the potential directions of travel. They are relevant but also visionary.

Forward-looking and innovative, Elgar Research Agendas are an essential resource for PhD students, scholars and anybody who wants to be at the forefront of research.

Titles in the series include:

A Research Agenda for Public Administration
Edited by Andrew Massey

A Research Agenda for Tourism Geographies
Edited by Dieter K. Müller

A Research Agenda for Economic Psychology
Edited by Katharina Gangl and Erich Kirchler

A Research Agenda for Entrepreneurship and Innovation
Edited by David B. Audretsch, Erik E. Lehmann and Albert N. Link

A Research Agenda for Financial Inclusion and Microfinance
Edited by Marek Hudon, Marc Labie and Ariane Szafarz

A Research Agenda for Global Crime
Edited by Tim Hall and Vincenzo Scalia

A Research Agenda for Transport Policy
Edited by John Stanley and David A. Hensher

A Research Agenda for Tourism and Development
Edited by Richard Sharpley and David Harrison

A Research Agenda for Housing
Edited by Markus Moos

A Research Agenda for Economic Anthropology
Edited by James G. Carrier

A Research Agenda for Sustainable Tourism
Edited by Stephen F. McCool and Keith Bosak

A Research Agenda for New Urbanism
Edited by Emily Talen

A Research Agenda for Creative Industries
Edited by Stuart Cunningham and Terry Flew

A Research Agenda for Military Geographies
Edited by Rachel Woodward

A Research Agenda for Event Management
John Armbrecht, Erik Lundberg and Tommy D. Andersson

A Research Agenda for Sustainable Consumption Governance
Edited by Oksana Mont

A Research Agenda for Sustainable Consumption Governance

Edited by

OKSANA MONT

Lund University, Sweden

Elgar Research Agendas

Edward Elgar
PUBLISHING

Cheltenham, UK • Northampton, MA, USA

Published by
Edward Elgar Publishing Limited
The Lypiatts
15 Lansdown Road
Cheltenham
Glos GL50 2JA
UK

Edward Elgar Publishing, Inc.
William Pratt House
9 Dewey Court
Northampton
Massachusetts 01060
USA

A catalogue record for this book
is available from the British Library

This book is available electronically in the **Elgar**online
Social and Political Science subject collection
DOI 10.4337/9781788117814

ISBN 978 1 78811 780 7 (cased)
ISBN 978 1 78811 781 4 (eBook)

Typeset by Servis Filmsetting Ltd, Stockport, Cheshire
Printed and bound by CPI Group (UK) Ltd, Croydon, CR0 4YY

Contents

Figures

Tables

Contributors

Maurie J. Cohen, New Jersey Institute of Technology, USA

Carl Dalhammar, Lund University, Sweden

Koen Frenken, Utrecht University, the Netherlands

Tobias Froese, ESCP Europe Business School, Germany

Doris Fuchs, University of Muenster, Germany

Eva Heiskanen, University of Helsinki, Finland

Max Koch, Lund University, Sweden

Senja Laakso, University of Helsinki, Finland

Matthias Lehner, Lund University, Sweden

Sylvia Lorek, SERI, Sustainable Europe Research Institute, Germany

Florian Lüdeke-Freund, ESCP Europe Business School, Germany

Kes McCormick, Lund University, Sweden

Oksana Mont, Lund University, Sweden

Jenny Palm, Lund University, Sweden

Andrius Plepys, Lund University, Sweden

Stefan Schaltegger, Centre for Sustainability Management (CSM), Leuphana University of Lüneburg, Germany

Juliet Schor, Boston College, USA

Jagdeep Singh, Lund University, Sweden

Nora Smedby, Lund University, Sweden

Arnold Tukker, Institute of Environmental Sciences (CML), Leiden University and Netherlands Organisation for Applied Scientific Research TNO

Acknowledgements

Editing this volume was supported by the project Urban Reconomy, which is funded by a Swedish Research Council for sustainable development (Formas), grant number 211-2014-1440.

We would like to thank Eileen Laurie for her very professional and efficient copy-editing of the volume, which has profoundly improved its quality.

1 Introduction to *A Research Agenda for Sustainable Consumption Governance*

Oksana Mont

1. Sustainable Consumption as a grand challenge and a governance goal

The Industrial Revolution and the pursuit of economic growth have generated both unprecedented societal progress *and* environmental and social externalities that jeopardize the very goal of economic development – well-being – and the very basis on which our society is built – the biophysical system of planet Earth (Rockström et al., 2009). Indeed, three planetary boundaries, that is, genetic diversity, nitrogen and phosphorous flows, have already been breached and two more – land-system change and climate change – are swiftly approaching their limits. The recent International Panel on Climate Change (IPCC) report warns that we have only 12 years to make unprecedented changes in all aspects of our lives, including a reduction of our CO_2 emissions by at least 50% and limiting global warming to 1.5C (IPCC, 2018). The scientists warn that we have run out of time for talks and discussions and that the window for acting against the worst effects of climate change is closing fast (IPCC, 2018). We have entered a critical phase when well-known environmental and social challenges are reaching their tipping points; after these have been crossed, abrupt and irreversible changes in the supporting ecological and societal systems are likely to occur, which will threaten the very survival of our society and indeed us, the human species.

Despite the growing sense of urgency among some actors, global CO_2 emissions are still increasing, and the demand for resources and energy continues to grow. The reason for these increases is because technological solutions such as energy efficiency and climate mitigation efforts are being outpaced by increases in consumption and production levels (IPCC, 2018). This is not surprising as the current economic system celebrates ruthless competition and maximization of wealth accumulation at any (environmental and social) cost (Foxon et al., 2018). Material abundance and prosperity have become beacons of success across the world, and economic growth has been cast as a measure of social progress. However, the benefits of economic growth have not been enjoyed by all: in our unequal world, the eight wealthiest people have the same wealth as the poorest 3.6 billion people (Hardoon, 2017). The global consumer class enjoys access to endless diversity of goods, while less fortunate groups suffer from air, land and water pollution arising from the production of these goods. The costs for global environmental impacts, such as climate change, are disproportionately borne by developing nations and vulnerable people. Thus the concerns about the limits *to* growth, that is, infinite growth on a finite planet, are now combined with concerns about the limits *of* growth, that is, failure to fulfil societal and human development goals (Jackson, 2009; Kallis, 2015).

Many years ago, unsustainable consumption and production patterns and levels were identified as one of the main contributing factors to the grand sustainability challenges (UN, 2015; UNCED, 1992). As early as 1992, the United Nations Conference on Environment and Development in Rio de Janeiro, and the resultant action plan, 'Agenda 21', recognized the importance of addressing unsustainable consumption patterns as a way to resolve the climate change challenge and to foster sustainable development (UNCED, 1992). Sustainable consumption discourse has since become an integral part of many international and national sustainable consumption policies and strategies, including the 10-year framework of programmes (10YFP) on sustainable consumption and production patterns adopted at the Rio+20 Conference in 2002. Many countries developed national policies and measures to reduce the environmental and social impacts of consumption. However, overall consumption-oriented policies have largely failed to become operationalized and translated from international and national commitments into concrete and measurable outcomes at national, local and individual levels (Jackson, 2007).

This failure can be partially explained by the complexity of consumption. Undoubtedly, unsustainable consumption patterns and levels are a grand challenge – a complex and multi-faceted phenomenon that ranges 'from micro- to macro-level perspectives, from the past to the future, from what is to how to obtain what should be, from determining optimal individual choices' to 'attempting to grasp the complete system of production and consumption and its implications for sustainability' (Reisch and Thøgersen, 2015: 13). The complexity is aggravated by unsustainable consumption patterns and levels being embedded and maintained by institutional, structural and behavioural factors. Policymakers are often unwilling to employ strong but less popular regulatory and economic measures to address consumption-related problems, relying mainly on more popular but less effective information-based instruments (Berg, 2011). Paradoxically, though, it is the consumers who have been given the 'power and mandate' to lead the shift to sustainable consumption (Mont et al., 2013), despite a complex web of opposing views and vested interests of diverse actors who shape, depend on and capitalize on unsustainable consumption patterns.

Solutions to the sustainable consumption conundrum cannot be found by single actors who usually face difficulty comprehending and interpreting the challenges, who lack the power and capacity to implement the actions needed and who consequently resort to piecemeal actions. The transition to more sustainable consumption requires a momentous paradigm shift in our society and economy; it calls for working across a broad span of societal actors and disciplinary boundaries on devising and testing unconventional, dynamic and adaptive solutions. To enable the engagement of a variety of actors, the notion of governance may provide a useful approach and an operative space for redefining their role boundaries, for carving out new roles and responsibilities, and for identifying novel ways for their interaction that could enhance and accelerate individual and collective actions towards more sustainable patterns, practices and ultimately levels of consumption.

Governance is 'the patterns of processes by which society handles its problems and shapes its own transformation' (Voß and Kemp, 2006: 8). It concerns '[. . .] all processes of governing, whether undertaken by a government, market, or network, whether over a family, tribe, formal or informal organization, or territory, and whether through laws, norms, power, or language' (Bevir, 2012: 1). It focuses less on the role of state and governmental institutions and more on the processes, activities and practices of governing by societal actors. In this way, governance becomes the result of the interaction, conflicts of interest and power struggles of many societal actors with their diverse world views, problems, aspirations and strategies to achieve them. Governance does not mean an absence of governmental actions, but it does mean active and profound engagement with sustainable consumption agenda by all actors, even those who might not have been associated with sustainable consumption governance before, or who have traditionally taken a passive role in framing and shaping consumption choices.

To help actors to reflect upon and renegotiate their roles in the transformation towards sustainable consumption 'the practice of reflexive governance – a mode of steering that encourages actors to scrutinize and reconsider their underlying assumptions, institutional arrangements and practices' (Hendriks and Grin, 2007: 333) – is promising. The reflexive governance mode acknowledges the complexity of the intertwined economic, technological, environmental and social developments, the vagueness of sustainable consumption goals and the elusiveness of consumer choices. It is based on the idea of continuous learning from the developments by actors involved in governance processes, re-evaluation of actors' convictions and toolboxes, experimenting and testing new strategies and solutions, and engaging in dialogue in pursuit of common understanding. The research community has, therefore, a critical role to play in the transformation and reorientation of the society in a sustainable direction. This book aims to take stock of the extant knowledge on sustainable consumption and to outline research agenda for sustainable consumption governance that could help understand and employ diverse governance processes towards more sustainable consumption patterns, practices and levels, and thereby support transformative system changes to a more sustainable society.

The following section offers a brief overview of the state of the art in sustainable consumption field, highlighting weaknesses and identifying research gaps, followed by a section on the Research Agenda for Sustainable Consumption.

2. Appraisal of the sustainable consumption research field

2.1 Bibliometric analysis

Research on sustainable consumption is about 30 years old. A streamlined biblio-metric analysis reveals that 649 articles containing 'sustainable consumption' in the title have been published since 1980 and registered in SCOPUS (and 3430 articles appear with the same query and during the same period in Google Scholar). One can distinguish three periods in the development of the field. From 1989 to 2002 less than ten papers in total (ranging from one to eight in the SCOPUS database) were published on sustainable consumption per year (between 47 and 70 in Google Scholar). From 2003 to 2009 between 16 and 25 papers were published per year (between 90 and 184 in Google Scholar) and finally from 2010 to 2019 between 35 and 70 papers were published per year (between 200 and 235 in Google Scholar). The number of publications registered in both SCOPUS and Google Scholar is presented in Figure 1.1.

A core group of researchers writing on sustainable consumption comprises about 160 individuals (again judged merely by peer-reviewed articles containing the phrase 'sustainable consumption' in their title) in SCOPUS. Among them Jill Seyfang leads the list of the most prolific scholars with 16 articles, followed by Maurie Cohen, 12; Daniel Fischer, 11; and Oksana Mont, 10. Kersty Hobson, Gert Spaangaren and Arnold Tukker have published eight articles each and Eva Heiskanen, Sylvia Lorek, Ulf Schrader and Patrick Schroeder have published seven articles each.

When analysing subject areas where articles have been published, six main disciplines with a considerably larger number of articles than others can be dis-tinguished (Figure 1.2.): Environmental Science; Business, Management and Accounting; Social Sciences; Economics, Econometrics and Finance; Energy; and Engineering. The diversity of disciplines clearly shows that sustainable consump-tion is not merely a matter for social sciences, but also for other types of sciences

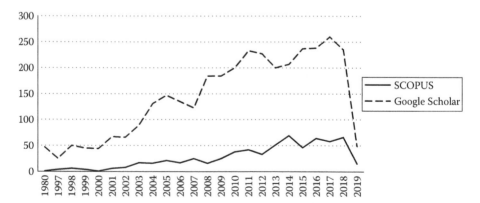

Figure 1.1 Number of articles published per year in SCOPUS and Google Scholar with 'sustainable consumption' phrase in title

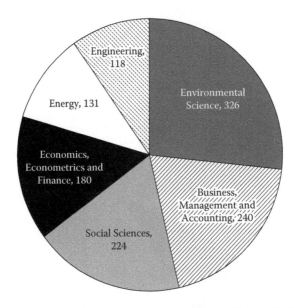

Figure 1.2 Subject areas with the largest number of articles published with 'sustainable consumption' phrase in title

that perhaps deal with different sustainability aspects of consumption, for example, connected to energy, and which mostly probably address sustainable consumption as an integral and inseparable part of sustainable consumption and production (SCP) notion, such as the engineering sciences.

Representing different disciplines, a diversity of academic journals publish on sustainable consumption (Figure 1.3.). The most prolific among them is the *Journal of Cleaner Production* with the high number of 67 articles, followed by the *Journal of Consumer Studies* with only 23 articles and the *Journal of Consumer Policy* with 17 articles.

The increase in the number of published papers over the years may indicate a slowly growing prominence of the topic of sustainable consumption across a number of academic disciplines. However, considering that the total output of academic peer-reviewed publications has increased sixfold between 1980 and 2018 (from 129 473 articles to 770 026), it seems that the numbers actually show a stagnating field of research. Indeed, if we compare the scientific output to the output from another academic fields, for example, transition management, which reached an output of 60 to 100 papers per year within the first ten years of the establishment of the field (Markard et al., 2012) and almost 500 papers during 2018 alone (Köhler et al., 2019), sustainable consumption research does not look like a vibrant research field.

Surprisingly, there is no journal of sustainable consumption that would be an outlet for academic work on sustainable consumption issues. There is a *Sustainable*

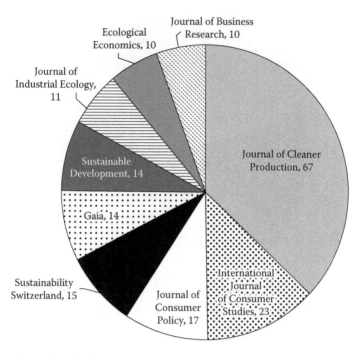

Figure 1.3 Journals with the largest number of articles published with 'sustainable consumption' phrase in title

Production and Consumption journal run by the Institution of Chemical Engineers, which invites interdisciplinary papers including those on consumption-related issues. However, the editorial board of this journal consists largely of engineers, suggesting that the sustainable consumption theme is likely to be treated from a technocratic perspective. The *Journal of Cleaner Production*, which has served as the outlet for research on sustainable consumption for decades, has recently also shown technocratic tendencies. There are many other journals on sustainability, ecological economics and consumer issues that publish articles on sustainable consumption, but there is no single outlet that would represent, position and help consolidate the sustainable consumption academic field.

There is, however, the international Sustainable Consumption Research and Action Initiative – SCORAI – with its associated conferences, events and networks in different regions of the world.

2.2 Research themes and gaps in current knowledge

Sustainable consumption has slowly evolved into a multidisciplinary field of academic research in the past 30 years, spanning disciplines from theory to policy and practice (Middlemiss, 2018). However, up to the present day, sustainable consumption has remained a research field characterized by many emerging

conceptualizations, still developing methodological toolboxes and most importantly lagging behind in practical application and exhibiting a lack of profound
impact on policy and society.

There is still a lack of consensus about what constitutes the field of sustainable
consumption, even though the terminology of sustainable consumption can be
traced back to Agenda 21 from 1992. The term 'sustainable consumption' is an
umbrella term for a diverse set of approaches and conceptualizations, but one can
distinguish three streams: consuming more efficiently, consuming differently or
consuming less. Within the 'consuming more efficiently' stance, the main focus is
on changing consumption patterns by stimulating the provision and consumption
of eco-efficient products (UNEP, 1999). The 'consuming differently' perspective
focuses on finding alternative ways to satisfy consumer needs through renting
and leasing goods for example, rather than owning them. The 'consuming less'
approach propagates the reduction of absolute levels of resource consumption as
the main solution to unsustainable consumption (UNCED, 1992), inevitably leading to criticism of the consumer society (Webb, 2012).

Another way to describe the sustainable consumption field is as a 'research on
existing (often unsustainable) consumption patterns and practices, and studies
reflecting the aspiration of sustainable consumption' (Lorek and Vergragt, 2015:
20). Indeed, the latter reflects the normative stance of the sustainable consumption
field, since it originates in the real world problem of unsustainable consumption
and distribution of resources. Since the aspiration is to solve the wicked problem
of unsustainable consumption, a great diversity of conceptualizations, tools and
approaches are employed from various disciplines. The difficulty is that various
disciplines have a different understanding of what constitutes the problem of sustainable consumption, what its origins are and what the solutions to the problem
look like. Interdisciplinary research is emerging and will be much needed in the
future that aims to find possibilities for cross-fertilization between disciplines.

Following on from the two understandings of sustainable consumption one could
distinguish two intellectual stances in sustainable consumption research, which are
often called weak and strong sustainability. Weak sustainability embraces solutions
to unsustainable consumption patterns that are sought within the technological
or systemic-rational paradigm, that is, solving problems by innovating production processes and products (McMeekin and Southerton, 2012) and stimulating
the provision and consumption of eco-efficient products by increasing the environmental awareness of consumers through eco-labels and consumer campaigns.
Supporting this view is the idea of a sovereign consumer who has the power,
capacity and freedom to make rational choices that contribute to or drive the
change to sustainability by generating demand for green products and thereby
creating greener markets (European Commission, 2008). The role for policy in
weak sustainability is to facilitate consumers' choices by correcting market failures
through, for example, information provision and by internalizing external – for
example, environmental and social – costs, which private individuals might not

account for (Mont and Dalhammar, 2005). Essentially consumer sovereignty has been used by policymakers as an excuse not to act for fear of intervening in the private life of citizen-consumers and, at the same time, place responsibility for the transition to sustainability onto consumers' shoulders (Mont et al., 2013). This kind of 'hands-off' position from governments treats consumer choices merely as individual choices, failing to account for institutional, social and other influences on individuals' behaviour. Indeed individuals often find themselves 'locked-into' unsustainable institutions, infrastructures and contexts, even if they would like to change their consumption patterns and practices (Sanne, 2002). These 'lock-ins' are at least partially responsible for the multiple gaps between consumer knowledge and attitudes, on the one hand, and actual behaviours on the other, as well as between consumer actions and their impacts (Csutora, 2012). There is growing evidence that the technological or systemic-rational approaches of weak sustainability are insufficient for bringing about sustainable consumption (Le Quéré et al., 2015) due to the 'rebound effects' at individual (Hertwich, 2005) and societal levels (Herring and Sorell, 2009) and because attaining sustainable consumption patterns, and especially levels, requires changes in the social fabric of society (Jackson, 2009). Framing sustainable consumption as a way of reaching weak sustainability helps powerful actors with vested interests to short-sightedly maintain the status quo of our unsustainable economic and social systems. Focusing on technocratic solutions has helped avoid asking critical questions about the scale of resource consumption – how much is enough and how are the benefits of economic growth to be distributed in a socially just way?

At the same time, support is growing for much more powerful measures that could bring about strong sustainability, measures that not only aim to change production and consumption patterns but also consumption levels; measures that are paramount for reaching sustainable development within planetary limits (Costanza, 2006). Advocates of strong sustainability see the need to achieve an absolute reduction in the aggregate levels of resource consumption and associated environmental impacts (Jackson, 2009). Recent additions to the field include more specific definitions of real sustainable consumption that explicitly engage with the notion of real net reductions in global material consumption (Fedrigo and Hontelez, 2010) and that aim to 'reverse the depletion of natural capital, repair the rapid unravelling of the global biosphere, and produce more prosperity at lower levels of overall consumption' (Fuchs et al. 2016: 298). Strong sustainability challenges the dominant way of producing, consuming and living by advocating lower consumption volumes for the present generations. A small but growing stream of research models alternative ways of organizing our economy that could sustain society under conditions of slower economic growth (Victor, 2010; Viktor, 2008) or reduced consumption levels while meeting key quality of life criteria (Druckman and Jackson, 2010). At the same time, better conceptual clarity is needed when a reduction in absolute levels of different parameters is discussed in different studies: gross domestic profit (GDP), consumption, work-time, radical and physical degrowth (van den Bergh and Kallis, 2012). Achieving absolute reduction unavoidably necessitates a discussion of what constitutes the good life, prosperity and human progress and how to ensure intra-

and intergenerational justice when defining strong sustainability (D'Alisa et al., 2015). The notions of strong sustainability and degrowth are emotionally charged, since many actors associate them with images of lost wealth and freedom of choice, stagnation, decreased access to welfare, and reduction in overall levels of well-being (Mont et al., 2013; van den Bergh, 2011). At the same time, there is a growing stream of academic research that contests the straightforward links between economic growth (expressed as aggregate income) and happiness (expressed as average happiness) (Easterlin, 1974) even though it continues to be a subject for heated debate, (Easterlin and Angelescu, 2009; Stevenson and Wolfers, 2008). Some research points to the possibility of a double dividend, when changes in consumption patterns may bring about both environmental and social benefits (Jackson, 2005; Jackson, 2009). Strong sustainability position acknowledges the critical role of societal actors in the transformation, going beyond the traditional triad of policymakers, businesses and civil society, to include other actors who might not always have been prominent in the sustainable consumption landscape, but who undoubtedly have critical roles to play in the reorientation of consumption practices, patterns and levels, such as cities, social media, prosumers and insurance companies. Here, however, understanding the dynamics of power and taking responsibilities for action becomes critical (Fuchs et al., 2016) and deserves further research.

Although the conceptualizations of the two perspectives have gained considerable traction in the sustainable consumption field, some authors find this dichotomy problematic, since it reduces the ongoing complex debate to two antagonistic perspectives, both of which have their limitations and weaknesses (Geels et al., 2015). The weak sustainability position – *system optimization* – is criticized for falling short of delivering the needed reductions of resource consumption at the scale and speed required and for perpetuating the 'business-as-usual' development with slight optimization (Alfredsson et al., 2018). The strong sustainability perspective – *system reorientation* – on the other hand, is conceptually still in its infancy but has already been labelled as politically unacceptable (D'Alisa et al., 2015). Perhaps a way out of this deadlock is to explore ways of consuming differently that would require *system transformation* and accelerating the uptake and mainstreaming of alternative solutions while more robust scientific knowledge is being created to support planned reorientation of society towards slower economic growth or, when feasible, degrowth. Some academics suggest that socio-technical transitions and changes in social practices belong in this category (Geels et al., 2015), since they aim to transform social and technical domains simultaneously. I would argue that alternative consumption models, for example, peer-to-peer sharing and alternative business models (e.g. the circular economy), have much in common with the sectorial level socio-technical transitions or socially and technically embedded practices, since they focus on meso-level transformations. As suggested by Vergragt (2013: 124) we need to 'foster new forms of business ownership, emphasize local and informal economies (self-provisioning, collaborative consumption, local currencies, time banks, product-to-service alternatives and others) . . .' Importantly, understanding processes that govern the transformation to these new forms of consuming and provisioning have not been explicitly explored in sustainable consumption literature. Future research can make use of several theories from a variety of disciplines, such as governance theory, institutional theory, actor-network theory and stakeholder theory when studying governance and institutionalization processes of new consumption and business models, practices and transformations. Valuable lessons and inspiration can also be found in such mid-range theories as social practice theory (Shove et al., 2012) and transition theory (Geels et al., 2015), especially since they offer insights for mainstreaming, scaling up and accelerating social and technical transformations. To facilitate and speed up such meso-level transformations, research is needed to improve our understanding of how the alternatives are embedded in, influenced by and influence the material, cultural, social and political landscape.

3.   Research agenda for sustainable consumption governance

To address some of the aforementioned gaps in current knowledge, we propose a research agenda for sustainable consumption governance. The goal of such a research agenda is to facilitate knowledge creation for societal impact, that is, novel conceptualizations and insights, out-of-box solutions and methods that could help combat consumption-related environmental and social problems. Each chapter in this book emphasizes the need for research to develop and implement much more powerful solutions, decisions and actions leading towards sustainable consumption at different levels and by different governing actors. Thus, the research agenda should also help explore novel ways for stakeholder engagement and for encouraging reflexive modes of governing that could help improve the sustainability of consumption in the context of increasingly ambiguous roles and dispersed power among actors. This book represents a collective perspective of a broad group of researchers on diverse strategies, concepts and measures that are emerging as potential pathways towards more sustainable consumption governance: in both theory and practice. It is also a way to give voice to the actors and agency that we believe have critical roles to play in addressing the collective problem of unsustainable consumption.

The book is divided into three main parts, each with three or four chapters that consider different aspects of sustainable consumption governance. Part I describes the background to the sustainable consumption research field and identifies limitations and weaknesses in the current understanding of consumption-related impacts and in sustainable consumption governance overall. Part II introduces alternative systems of provisioning and consuming by exploring the sharing economy, prosumerism and the role of business models in shaping sustainable consumption. Part III critically examines the modern landscape of sustainable consumption policies and new governance approaches as well as roles of alternative governors of sustainable consumption, including cities.

Chapter 2 by Sylvia Lorek and Doris Fuchs offers a historical overview of academic and political discourse about sustainable consumption in the past 30 years. It provides a systematic and contrasting account of differences and simi-larities between weak and strong sustainable consumption (SSC), which serves as a foundation for discussing implications for a research agenda. The authors advocate SSC governance and discuss the need for broad changes in society when SSC is the aim. The latter includes changes in the economy, infrastructures serving our daily habits, the dominant culture and often unsustainable lifestyles, as well as the institutions and power relationships that drive them. The authors introduce a novel approach – consumption corridors – to governing consump-tion patterns and levels and discuss its benefits as an instrument in pursuit of SSC. They call for further research on design and implementation of consump-tion corridors.

Chapter 3 by Max Koch discusses growth strategies and consumption patterns in transition, taking a historical perspective from Fordism to finance-driven capital-ism. The author applies a combination of the Regulation approach and Bourdieusian sociology and reflects that consumption-oriented purchase decisions are neither 'spontaneous' nor 'individual', but influenced by structural factors such as social class and state strategies, of which neither consumers nor consumption industries are usually aware. The chapter also argues that the Regulation approach is compat-ible with Bourdieusian sociology; more specifically, Bourdieu's concept of 'habitus' as an alternative to rational choice theories as well as a bridge between 'objective' social structures, including patterns of inequality and consumption and 'subjective' lifestyles. The introduction of the Regulation approach and Bourdieusian cultural sociology provides a combined concept for the analysis of societal consumption patterns within wider capitalist growth strategies. This is subsequently applied to a comparison of the two main growth strategies after World War II: Fordism and finance-driven capitalism. Future research should be dedicated to unifying frag-mented proposals for 'eco-social policies' and formulating a coherent strategy for the economic, political and ecological restructuring of advanced countries.

Chapter 4 by Arnold Tukker addresses a requirement for sustainable consumption governance – a clear understanding of how consumption of specific categories of goods and services in specific countries causes environmental impacts in global value chains. One of the main challenges for analysing the impacts of consump-tion is associated with the state and features of assessment methods. This chapter first offers a comprehensive analysis of extant methods for assessing consump-tion impacts and then proceeds to identify and discuss the priority consumption areas of households: food, housing and individual mobility, and their subgroups. Determining variables for the environmental footprints of household consumption are then identified where income, the numbers of dwellers per household, house size and the electricity mix are among the most important explanatory variables of the impacts of household consumption. Suggestions for future research include meas-ures for improved monitoring of how consumption drives environmental impacts.

Chapter 5 by Andrius Plepys and Jagdeep Singh presents key challenges associated with a systematic sustainability evaluation of access-based consumption models.

Starting with a causal loop diagram representing various reported and potential impacts of a generic sharing system, the authors provide a comprehensive picture of main direct and indirect social, economic and environmental implications of the sharing economy. They also discuss the limitations in sustainability evaluations of the sharing economy, including non-transparency about methods as well as unclear system boundaries and assumptions made. An overview of the strengths and weaknesses of different modelling approaches employed for analysing the effects of sharing economy is provided. Car sharing is used as an example for demonstrating an input–output-based sustainability assessment. Implications for modelling impacts from changes in consumption patterns and from changes in production sectors are discussed. Future research directions include suggestions for improving the existing national accounting frameworks to accommodate the specifics of the emerging sharing economy, better measurements of labour inputs and annual income in the sharing economy and improving resolution and geographical and sectoral coverage of the multiregional input–output tables.

Part II explores the role of business models in shaping sustainable consumption and critically examines alternative systems of provisioning and consuming – the sharing and prosumer economy.

Chapter 6 by Florian Lüdeke-Freund, Tobias Froese and Stefan Schaltegger explores the role of business models in shifting towards more sustainable consumption patterns and levels. The main ideas discussed in this chapter relate to the role of business models in supporting SSC, different sustainability strategies and how sustainable business model patterns can become a means to design better production–consumption systems. These ideas can serve as a starting point for more comprehensive and balanced debates about how companies, that is, the major designers of modern production–consumption systems, can contribute to SSC. The authors ask readers to go beyond the often heard calls for efficiency and sufficiency business models, which too often ignore the fact that neither sustainability strategies nor business models unfold in a vacuum. Hence, it is important to consider multiple sustainability strategies and multiple business model design options simultaneously. The authors, therefore, call for approaches that consider both multiple sustainability strategies and multiple business model patterns in order to create better production–consumption systems that could help humanity to navigate an increasingly narrowing 'strong sustainable consumption corridor'.

Chapter 7 by Matthias Lehner discusses the idea of the prosumer, implications of the concept for consumption trends in the future, and how it could be of significance for the discussion on sustainable consumption governance. The author suggests that there are two types of prosumption: the one in which people engage for pleasure, and the other in which people participate out of economic necessity, and that these two types of prosumption have different implications for sustainable consumption governance. A key aspect of this discussion is time (as opposed to money) as a measure of the possible impact of the maker movement on society. The chapter builds on the idea that a higher level of engagement with an object deriving from prosumption brings significant costs for the prosumer; not in monetary terms but in an equally scarce resource today: time. The author argues that this could lead to a refocusing of consumption from the fast consumption of mass products to extended consumption of high-quality products and that this could be the main contributor to more sustainable consumption. Several research directions are outlined aiming to better understand the actual impact of prosumption on overall consumption levels.

Chapter 8 by Koen Frenken and Juliet Schor introduces and examines the vibrant and contested field of practice and academic research – the sharing economy. The chapter starts by providing a thorough overview of the knowledge base related to the sharing economy, which helps identify three key features of the sharing economy: consumer-to-consumer interaction, temporary access and physical goods. These features also play a critical role in helping the authors distinguish the sharing economy from other forms of platform economy, including the product-service economy, the second-hand economy and the on-demand economy. The authors unveil economic and historical reasons for the emergence of the sharing economy and explore the economic, social and environmental sustainability impacts of sharing economy platforms. They conclude that indirect sustainability effects are still largely unknown. The chapter ends with reflections on current and future regulations for the sharing economy. The authors see future research focus on the diversity of platforms in terms of their governance, scalability and impacts.

Part III discusses policies and alternative governors of sustainable consumption.

Chapter 9 by Carl Dalhammar presents the kaleidoscope of policies for sustainable consumption. While much of the early policy-related consumption research focused on pricing and consumer information, effective policies have been hard to implement. Even if some policies have been implemented, there is little evidence of any significant effect. One explanation for the limited progress is that far too much focus has been, and is still, devoted to individual choices of consumers in the market when instead we need collective action to move forward. Another explanation is that often stronger steering is required, including policies that rely more on coercion, restrictions of choice, and strong economic incentives, rather than encouragement and voluntariness. The chapter then moves on to analyse specific policies for the sharing and circular economies. Some inherent complexities and contradictions found in the visions and proposed policies of these concepts are discussed and problematized in the context of sustainable consumption governance. The chapter discusses one promising new policy development in Europe: incentivizing longer product lifetimes as a strategy to save resources. These policies may constitute a 'game changer' in the long run if they can affect consumers and markets. Future research is needed to identify and design new policies and policy packages that have real 'leverage' and could lead to greater systemic change.

Chapter 10 by Eva Heiskanen and Senja Laakso addresses the question of whether unsustainability can be edited out from consumption in the journey from information provision to nudging and beyond. The authors begin by introducing the most commonly used methods to steer consumption towards these targets – from the provision of information to nudging and interventions based on a social practice perspective – along with examples and policy implications. The chapter illustrates the journey from what can be called the 'mainstream paradigms in pro-environmental consumer-oriented change attempts' (Keller et al., 2016: 77), to the critique of these approaches. The authors also present the newest ideas on how to make consumption practices more sustainable by nudging consumers and designing better choice architectures that help consumers change their behaviour according to their rational interests. They argue that to edit out unsustainable consumption patterns on a large scale we need to look beyond the individual consumer and individual instances of unsustainable consumption, to historical, structural and cultural factors shaping consumer society. The authors see research needs in exploring policy practices that prevent policymakers from making decisions more aligned with SSC.

Chapter 11 by Jenny Palm, Nora Smedby and Kes McCormick introduces and analyses cities as sustainable consumption governors. In a rapidly urbanizing world, the role of cities in enhancing sustainable consumption patterns is increasing, so the progressive governance agenda requires cities to engage with issues of lifestyle and consumption. When addressing sustainable consumption challenges, cities need to adopt working methods and approaches to include multiple stakeholders in their governance processes. Most likely, cities will use both traditional forms of authority and new partnerships or processes to achieve effective and efficient governance. For example, collective ownership is being discussed as a way to mobilize participation from the local community and ideas of decentralized structures and democratized technical infrastructures are being debated. The authors discuss how local governments need to deal with different trends when taking a meta-governor role in developing sustainable consumption patterns. Finally, the chapter analyses conflicts in literature and in practice, related to how different forms and structures of governance processes contribute to sustainable cities. Future research should develop methods for evaluating different governance modes of cities and to explore how and when the infrastructure and planning of cities should change in order to facilitate sustainable consumption and the sharing economy.

Chapter 12 by Maurie J. Cohen addresses post-ownership sustainable consumption governance and the onset of post-consumerism. The chapter starts with an excursion into history, looking at the developments in consumption and expansion of wage-based employment that created a middle-class lifestyle, which is now waning for many reasons. The livelihoods of less affluent households have become precarious because of irregular participation in waged employment and rising economic insecurity. Households are struggling to reproduce familiar consumerist routines and are instigating social experiments in order to trial alternative provisioning arrangements. The demise of mass consumer lifestyles and the emergence of post-consumerism have significant and challenging implications for sustainable consumption governance. The equity dimensions of sustainable consumption take on equal importance with the biophysical impacts of resource use. This process of change also highlights the need for policies to nurture and support the cultivation of small-scale experiments and to aid social learning that helps diversity provisioning opportunities. It facilitates novel business models, promotes relationships based on solidarity through cooperativism, and enables community-based modes of self-help and the rediscovery of communal forms of prosumption. Also required is the political resolve to restrain patterns of outsized acquisition, while creating a system of public finance capable of investing in new institutional infrastructures.

Acknowledgements

This work was supported by the project Urban Reconomy, which is funded by a Swedish Research Council for sustainable development (Formas), grant number 211-2014-1440.

References

Alfredsson, E., M. Bengtsson, H.S. Brown et al. (2018), 'Why achieving the Paris Agreement requires reduced overall consumption and production', *Sustainability: Science, Practice and Policy*, **14** (1), 1–5.

Berg, A. (2011), 'Not roadmaps but toolboxes: Analysing pioneering national programmes for sustainable consumption and production', *Journal of Consumer Policy*, **34** (1), 9–23.

Bevir, M. (2012), *Governance: A Very Short Introduction*, Oxford: Oxford University Press.

Costanza, R. (2006), 'Limits to growth: The 30-year update', *Ecological Economics*, **59** (3), 397–9.

Csutora, M. (2012), 'One more awareness gap? The behaviour–impact gap problem', *Journal of Consumer Policy*, **35** (1), 145–63.

D'Alisa, G., F. Demaria and G. Kallis (eds) (2015), *Degrowth: A Vocabulary for a New Era*: Abingdon, UK: Routledge.

Druckman, A. and T. Jackson, (2010), 'The bare necessities: How much household carbon do we really need?', *Ecological Economics*, **69** (9), 1794–804.

Easterlin, R.A. (1974), 'Does economic growth improve the human lot? Some empirical evidence', in P.A. David and M.W. Reder (eds), *Nations and Households in Economic Growth: Essays in Honour of Moses Abramowitz*, New York and London: Academic Press, pp. 89–125.

Easterlin, R. A. and L. Angelescu (2009), 'Happiness and growth the world over: Time series evidence on the happiness-income paradox', Discussion Paper No. 4060, Institute for the Study of Labor, Bonn.

European Commission (2008), 'Communication from the Commission to the Council and the European Parliament on the Sustainable Production and Consumption and Sustainable Industrial Policy Action Plan', Brussels: European Commission.

Fedrigo, D. and J. Hontelez (2010), 'Sustainable consumption and production', *Journal of Industrial Ecology*, **14** (1), 10–12.

Foxon, C. I., S. Lorek, H. Mallee et al. (2018), *The Political Economy of Sustainable Consumption and Production*, Kyoto: The Research Institute for Humanity and Nature.

Fuchs, D., A. Di Giulio, K. Glaab et al. (2016), 'Power: The missing element in sustainable consumption and absolute reductions research and action', *Journal of Cleaner Production*, **132** (September), 298–307.

Geels, F.W., A. McMeekin, J. Mylan et al. (2015), 'A critical appraisal of Sustainable Consumption and Production research: The reformist, revolutionary and reconfiguration positions', *Global Environmental Change*, **34**, 1–12.

Hardoon, D. (2017), 'An economy for the 99%: It's time to build a human economy that benefits everyone, not just the privileged few', Briefing paper, Oxfam, accessed 25 February 2018 at https://policy-practice.oxfam.org.uk/publications/an-economy-for-the-99-its-time-to-build-a-human-economy-that-benefits-everyone-620170.

Hendriks, C.M. and J. Grin (2007), 'Contextualizing reflexive governance: The politics of Dutch transitions to sustainability', *Journal of Environmental Policy & Planning*, **9** (3–4), 333–50.

Herring, H. and S. Sorell (2009), *Energy Efficiency and Sustainable Consumption: The Rebound Effect*, Basingstoke, UK: Palgrave Macmillan.

Hertwich, E.G. (2005), 'Consumption and the rebound effect: An industrial ecology perspective', *Journal of Industrial Ecology*, **9** (1–2), 85–98.

IPCC [International Panel on Climate Change] (2018), 'Global warming of 1.5° C. Summary for policymakers', IPCC, Switzerland.

Jackson, T. (2005), 'Live better by consuming less? Is there a "double dividend" in sustainable consumption?', *Journal of Industrial Ecology*, **9** (1–2), 19–36.

Jackson, T. (2007), 'Sustainable consumption', in G. Atkinson, S. Dietz, E. Neumayer and M. Agarwala (eds), *Handbook of Sustainable Development*, Cheltenham, UK and Northampton, MA, USA: Edward Elgar Publishing, pp. 254–70.

Jackson, T. (2009), *Prosperity without Growth: Economics for a Finite Planet*, London: Earthscan.

Kallis, G. (2015), 'Social limits of growth', in G. D'Alisa, F. Demaria and G. Kallis (eds), *Degrowth: A Vocabulary for a New Era*, New York and London: Routledge, pp. 137–40.

Keller, M., B. Halkier and T.A. Wilska (2016), 'Policy and governance for sustainable consumption at the crossroads of theories and concepts', *Environmental Policy and Governance*, **26** (2), 75–88.

Köhler, J., F.W. Geels and F. Kern et al. (2019), 'An agenda for sustainability transitions research: State of the art and future directions', *Environmental Innovation and Societal Transitions*. Available at https://doi.org/10.1016/j.eist.2019.01.004.

Le Quéré, C., R. Moriarty, R.M. Andrew et al. (2015), 'Global carbon budget 2015', *Earth System Science Data*, **7** (2), 349–96.

Lorek, S. and P. Vergragt (2015), 'Sustainable consumption as a systemic challenge: inter-and transdisciplinary research and research questions', in L.A. Reisch and J. Thøgersen (eds), *Handbook of Research on Sustainable Consumption*, Cheltenham, UK and Northampton, MA, USA: Edward Elgar Publishing, pp. 19–32.

Markard, J., B. Truffer and R. Raven (2012), 'Sustainability transitions: An emerging field of research and its prospects', *Research Policy*, **41** (6), 955–67.

McMeekin, A. and D. Southerton (2012), 'Sustainability transitions and final consumption: Practices and socio-technical systems', *Technology Analysis & Strategic Management*, **24** (4), 345–61.

Middlemiss, L. (2018), *Sustainable Consumption: Key Issues*, Abingdon, UK: Routledge.

Mont, O. and C. Dalhammar (2005), 'Sustainable consumption: At the cross-road of environmental and consumer policies', *International Journal of Sustainable Development*, **8** (4), 258–79.

Mont, O., E. Heiskanen, K. Power et al. (2013), *Improving Nordic Policymaking by Dispelling Myths on Sustainable Consumption*, Nordic Council of Ministers, Stockholm, accessed 20 February 2019 at http://norden.diva-portal.org/smash/get/diva2:702825/FULLTEXT01.pdf.

Reisch, L.A. and J.B. Thøgersen (eds) (2015), *Handbook of Research on Sustainable Consumption*, Cheltenham, UK and Northampton, MA, USA: Edward Elgar Publishing.

Rockström, J., W. Steffen, K. Noone et al. (2009), 'A safe operating space for humanity', *Nature*, **461** (7263), 472–6.

Sanne, C. (2002), 'Willing consumers or locked-in?', *Ecological Economics*, **42** (1–2), 273–87.

Shove, E., M. Pantzar and M. Watson (2012), *The Dynamics of Social Practice: Everyday Life and how it Changes*, London: Sage.

Stevenson, B. and J. Wolfers (2008), 'Economic growth and subjective well-being: Reassessing the Easterlin paradox', Working Paper 14282, National Bureau of Economic Research, Cambridge.

UN [United Nations] (2015), 'Sustainable Development Goals', accessed 21 February 2019 at http://www.un.org/sustainabledevelopment/sustainable-consumption-production.

UNCED [United Nations] (1992), 'Agenda 21', paper presented at The Earth Summit: The United Nations Conference on Environment and Development, Rio de Janeiro.

UNEP [United Nations Environment Programme] (1999), 'Changing consumption and production patterns', available at https://www.un.org/press/en/1999/19990423.ENDEV509.html.

van den Bergh, J.C. (2011), 'Environment versus growth – a criticism of "degrowth" and a plea for "a-growth"', *Ecological Economics: The Journal of the International Society for Ecological Economics*, **70** (5), 881–90.

van den Bergh, J.C. and G. Kallis (2012), 'Growth, a-growth or degrowth to stay within planetary boundaries?', *Journal of Economic Issues*, **46** (4), 909–20.

Vergragt, P. (2013), 'A possible way out of the combined economic-sustainability crisis', *Environmental Innovation and Societal Transitions*, **6**, 123–5.

Victor, P. (2008), *Managing without Growth: Slower by Design, Not Disaster*, Cheltenham, UK and Northampton, MA, USA: Edward Elgar Publishing.

Victor, P. (2010), 'Questioning economic growth', *Nature*, **468** (7322), 370–71.

Voß, J.-P. and R. Kemp (2006), 'Sustainability and reflexive governance: Introduction', in J.-P. Voß, D. Bauknecht and R. Kemp (eds), *Reflexive Governance for Sustainable Development*, Cheltenham, UK and Northampton, MA, USA: Edward Elgar Publishing, pp. 3–30.

Webb, J. (2012), 'Climate change and society: The chimera of behaviour change technologies', *Sociology*, **46** (1), 109–25.

PART I

Pre-Conditions for Sustainable Consumption Governance

2 Why only strong sustainable consumption governance will make a difference

Sylvia Lorek and Doris Fuchs

1. The concept of weak and strong sustainable consumption (governance)

This chapter delineates academic and political debates and developments on different concepts of sustainable consumption and makes the case for the necessity of strong sustainable consumption governance as well as the benefits of consumption corridors as an instrument for achieving strong sustainable consumption. Sustainable consumption has been on the international political agenda for about three decades now (United Nations 1992; 2002; 2015b). As articulated in 'Agenda 21' (United Nations, 1992), sustainable consumption encompasses resource consumption, labour conditions and impacts on the social and ecological environment that originate from the production processes of the goods and services we consume. Yet over the last 30 years, the concept of sustainable consumption has been largely characterized as the promotion of 'more sustainable' products, services and behaviours (Fuchs and Lorek, 2005). 'More sustainable' in this context means improvements in eco-efficiency, that is, a reduction in resource consumption per consumption unit gained through improvements in production processes or efficiency friendly designs. It can also yield (in theory) a higher income for small-scale farmers or workers through the implementation of fair trade prices. These improvements are commonly described as win–win scenarios as they supposedly generate both environmental and economic benefits.

Improving consumption efficiency can be a prerequisite for achieving sustainable consumption. However, existing limits on the Earth's resources and its capacity to serve as a sink for pollutants indicate that efficient consumption is a weak version of sustainable consumption. As research on the rebound effect has documented, achievements based on efficiency alone are frequently outweighed by a growth in consumption volumes (Greening et al., 2000; Steinberger et al., 2010). This implies that, in order to provide sufficient conditions for sustainable consumption, efficient consumption needs to be accompanied by reductions in the consumption levels of the global consumer class, which in turn require changes in infrastructures and in the politico-economic drivers of consumption (Kharas, 2010). The concept of strong sustainable consumption captures this understanding (Fuchs and Lorek, 2005; Hobson, 2013; Lorek and Fuchs, 2013; Spangenberg, 2014).

The chapter proceeds in three steps. First, it sets the context in terms of current ecological challenges and the history of involvement of different actors in (global) sustainable consumption governance. The chapter then deconstructs prevailing misconceptions about sustainable consumption and discusses the implications of societal norms, the role of the notion of limits or the norm of sufficiency. The concluding section proposes consumption corridors as a useful instrument in pursuit of strong sustainable consumption.

2.   Challenges to planetary boundaries and sustainable consumption governance

2.1   How (un)sustainable is our consumption?

Research on the planetary boundaries, climate change and peak everything (Rockström et al., 2009; Heinberg, 2010; Steffen et al., 2015) has been raising the alarm for more than a decade. A major study – '2020. The climate turning point' – provided evidence that the more time passes, the more drastic the turnaround in current unsustainable trends will need to be (Revill et al., 2017). The three years between 2017 and 2020 have been identified as crucial to safeguarding our climate (Figueres et al., 2017).

And yet, even these analyses neglect the important link to consumption, focusing on six milestones: a global transition to renewable energy sources, zero emission transport, decarbonized infrastructure, land restoration to replace deforestation, decarbonized heavy industry, and strong investment in climate action by the finance sector. These milestones downplay the fact that income and associated consumption are the primary greenhouse gas (GHG) emission drivers and that greater infrastructure investment requires a significant share of the available carbon budget. Therefore, political action plans also have to include policies aimed at actively reducing aggregate consumption volumes and their associated energy and material use (Alfredsson et al., 2018).[1]

On the international political agenda, sustainable consumption has been considered under the acronym SCP (sustainable consumption and production); first during the Marrakech Process (United Nations Environment Programme/United Nations Department of Economic and Social Affairs, 2008) and through the 10-Year Framework of Programmes for Sustainable Consumption and Production (SCP), since 2012, both programmes under the leadership of United Nations Environment Programme. Contemporaneously, we note societal debates on the ecological effects of consumption and associated shifts in mindsets (Cohen, 2013). Indeed, there are many positive trends in sustainable consumption today. The general increase in the awareness of climate change and other sustainability issues is palpable, not least due to the massive communication campaigns around the UN Sustainable Development Goals (United Nations, 2015b). The media has also given some attention to the widening of economic disparity and resulting increases in inequity (mainly within countries). Furthermore, there is a clear increase in the consumption of specific types of more sustainable products, such as energy-efficient household appliances (Newall, 2017) or organic food (Soil Association, 2018).

Food waste has received increasing political attention (Stewart, 2009) and stimulated a range of improvements, such as environmentally sound packaging and the organized distribution of leftover food (SAVE FOOD Initiative, 2017). Rising acceptance of vegetarian and vegan lifestyles indicates that there is an increasing awareness of and demand for strong sustainable consumption (Cherry, 2015). There have also been positive developments in human mobility. For instance, participation in car sharing initiatives is rising, as are sales in electric vehicles. One beneficial development is the decreasing interest of younger people in car ownership as a status symbol (Klein and Smart, 2017).

Nevertheless, these 'positive' developments are only a small part of the picture (Fuchs, 2017). In terms of mobility, for instance, the identified trends do not mean that we can identify an overall improvement in the sustainability of travelling patterns. Not only sales of electric cars but also those of specifically diesel cars and SUVs have increased (Fuchs, 2017). Similar trends exist with respect to kilometres per person travelled. Air travel, in particular, has increased over the last decade – especially among the younger generation (Luzecka, 2016).

In addition to more frequent travel (for example, weekend trips), ICT (information and communication technologies) equipment has also become a status symbol (van Wee, 2015). Its ecological and social impact is also substantial. ICT not only changes the way people communicate and interact, but it is also associated with socially and ecologically unsustainable mining, is characterized by inbuilt obsolescence and creates hazardous waste. On the positive side, ICT has enabled the rise of collaborative consumption: the peer-to-peer-based activity of sharing access to goods and services, coordinated through community-based online services (Hamari et al., 2016).

Sharing, in general, has attracted significant attention as a potentially sustainable consumption activity. It foregoes attachment to individual ownership of commodities – the central feature of a materialistically oriented economy (Heinrichs and Grunenberg, 2012). However, the fast and widespread commercialization of sharing via platforms such as Airbnb and Uber has led to major regulatory and political disputes. Some sharing companies can be characterized as applying predatory or even exploitative practices. Therefore, we need to distinguish between non-profit and for-profit initiatives. Non-profit sharing organizations are potentially powerful tools for building a social movement centred on genuine practices of sharing and cooperation (Schor, 2016). Yet, realizing this potential will require the democratization of the ownership and governance of such platforms and/or the diffusion of alternative non-market-based platforms.

2.2   (Global) sustainable consumption governance and its participants

International policy actors have pursued some relevant activities to steer consumption away from an unsustainable direction over the past decade. The '10-Year Framework of Programmes on Sustainable Consumption and Production' (10YFP) came into force after the Rio+20 conference in 2012 (United Nations, 2015a). It is coordinated by the United Nations Environment Programme (UNEP) and originally consisted of six thematic programmes: sustainable public procurement, consumer information, sustainable tourism, sustainable lifestyles and education, sustainable buildings and construction, and sustainable food systems. However, while all of the programmes explicitly aim to enhance decoupling, the activities they emphasize mainly aim at encouraging and enabling more conscious (for instance, more resource-efficient) consumption choices without reducing overall consumption, that is, implementing weak consumption governance (Bengtsson et al., 2018).

The Sustainable Development Goals (SDGs), adopted by the UN General Assembly in 2015 (United Nations, 2015a) and hailed as a milestone in global sustainable development policy, include SDG 12: 'Ensure sustainable consumption and production patterns' – the result of successful lobby by UNEP and other actors. A closer look, however, reveals the political compromise that this goal represents. The first target is to implement the 10YFP on SCP at national level and progress towards this is to be measured in terms of the number of countries with a national SCP action plan. Given the absence of a specific template for such an action plan, many plans focus on national green growth development strategies aiming to meet growth targets in a more sustainable way. Half of the remaining targets included in SDG 12 (measured by twelve indicators) aim at increasing knowledge and awareness, implementing corresponding policies, and strengthening research and development. Only four of the eleven targets have more ambitious overarching goals in terms of achieving absolute improvements in the sustainability of consumption.' A closer look at the indicators, however, shows that they fall short of the targets since they measure progress in relative rather than absolute terms (Bengtsson et al., 2018).[3] In addition to SDG 12, SDG 8, which focuses on decent work and economic growth, refers back to 10YFP, especially in its target 8.4: 'to improve global resource efficiency in consumption and production and endeavour to decouple economic growth from environmental degradation'. Again, the focus is on efficiency gains, which represent weak sustainable consumption governance. In sum, neither the 10YFP nor the SDGs envision a turn towards strong sustainable consumption (Spangenberg, 2017).

A more meaningful step towards making the impacts of unsustainable consumption more visible is the greater application of a consumption perspective in statistical accounting, by the European Environment Agency, for example (European Environment Agency, 2013). This perspective focuses attention on the fact that resource use and GHG emissions along the production process need to be accounted for in the countries in which the products and services are consumed and not where they are produced. Thus, this could provide a basis for strong sustainable consumption governance. However, the data gathered have yet to be used by relevant political actors.

At the level of *national policies*, the understanding and interpretation of sustainable consumption varies substantially between countries. Only a small number of countries have developed a dedicated national SCP framework programme or action plan. Ministries active in SCP policymaking at national level and who set the tone and direction include: environment, agriculture, energy, industry and transport. Accordingly, energy, food, agriculture, and buildings and construction play a role in the action plans, flanked by environmental protection or conservation in general. Some examples are: 'More from less – wisely' in Finland (Finnish Ministry of the Environment, 2013), the 'National Programme for Sustainable Consumption' in Germany (German Federal Ministry for the Environment, Nature Conservation, Building and Nuclear Safety, 2018) and the 'Strategy for Sustainable Consumption' in Sweden (Government Office of Sweden, 2016). More frequently, however, national governments address aspects of SCP in their framework policies at the general level, with a focus either on sustainable development, green growth/green economy or national environmental action plans. Some have included programmes relevant for SCP in more than one strategy. An analysis of environmental laws and regulations within EU member states (Slezák, 2017) further reveals an 'implicit framework' of policies with relevance to SCP at the level of strategic planning. The new EU member states, in particular, address aspects of SCP in their thematic programmes in the context of environment and energy, or in the ones addressing rural development (Slezák, 2017). In various countries, national institutional and/ or multi-stakeholder mechanisms for SCP have been established. They most commonly involve stakeholder groups including governmental and public institutions, non-governmental organizations (NGOs) and foundations, academic institutions and research centres. In terms of policy areas, a focus – at least within Europe – appears to be on green public procurement/sustainable public procurement (GPP/ SPP); waste management and waste prevention (including food waste); organic/ ecological agriculture; information provision (including European, regional and national eco-labelling); Corporate Social Responsibility (CSR); eco-design, life cycle analysis and eco-innovations; and urban mobility (Slezák, 2017). Furthermore, policymakers appear to assume that improvements will come from knowledge transfer, learning and information sharing, communication, and awareness raising, in addition to the development of standards, guidelines and labels relevant to SCP.

In general, then, national (and regional) policy mainly promotes weak sustainable consumption. Efforts echo the 'buy sustainable' recommendations (European Commission, 2012), highlighting the principle of consumer sovereignty (Akenji, 2014). EU legislation on eco-design and energy labelling, for instance, might be an effective tool for improving the energy efficiency of products. The main objective of the legislation, however, is to support industrial competitiveness and innovation by raising the environmental performance of products throughout the Internal Market (European Commission, 2016). Yet, the sustained promotion of these products maintains the myth that technological solutions are sufficient for achieving sustainability. It distracts from the need to tackle challenging issues, for example, the prevailing culture of consumerism and materialism that is closely linked to resource use and environmental impacts. Policymakers are often concerned that meaningful consumption policies are too controversial to propose, even where there is strong public interest in improving the sustainability of consumption patterns. Policy is never neutral, but shapes social norms and values in society (Mont et al., 2013). Currently, this 'shaping' continues to predominantly foster a tendency towards more unsustainable development.

Thus an assessment of international and national policy developments reveals the great challenges ahead if we want to induce fundamental and rapid changes in consumption levels: long-term or systemic perspectives are required as well as changes to inadequate legislation and frameworks including necessary reforms to tax codes, subsidies and infrastructures (Slezák, 2017).

Do other actors fill the gap left by international and national policy with respect to strong sustainable consumption governance? Earlier analyses have shown this is not the case (Fuchs and Lorek, 2005; Lorek and Fuchs, 2013). Indeed, the vast majority of *business* actors are still entrenched in an economic model based on (ever-increasing) mass production and consumption. Not surprisingly, these actors have little, if any, interest in promoting strong sustainable consumption. At the same time, however, business actors, in particular transnational corporations, exercise more political power than ever (Fuchs, 2013; Gumbert and Fuchs, 2018). These actors are enabled by significant asymmetries in material resources with regard to civil society and the public sector, and also because of the continued hegemony of neoclassical economic thinking and the 'growth imperative'. Creating (or keeping) jobs continues to be the dominant argument, even in contexts with an environmental or social approach to sustainability. While the Agenda 2030 preamble flags people, planet, prosperity, peace and partnership as the guiding principles for sustainable development (United Nations, 2015a), actual debates still focus on the triple bottom line: people, planet, and profit (Elkington, 1994; 2018).

Similarly, many NGOs shy away from politically costly messages that communicate the need to reduce consumption. They also tend to promote ecologically superior purchases rather than no purchases. This may not be surprising to the extent that NGOs depend on membership for survival. Efforts by political parties, such as the Green Party in Germany, to promote speed limits or vegetarian days at public canteens in the interest of saving ecological resources have had a high political cost in terms of lost votes (Spengler, 2018).

In contrast, *research* on sustainable consumption has experienced remarkable growth since 2005, with an increasing number of publications, citations in journals and special issues of journals in evidence. Indeed, Liu et al. (2017) document the evolution of sustainable consumption research from being focused primarily on behaviour and single-interest issues towards more comprehensive and systemic assessments, with a broad range of topics in the worldwide research arena. This gradual shift towards analysing systems for sustainable consumption (and production) in fact reflects strong sustainable consumption aspects. This part of the literature highlights that achieving truly sustainable consumption levels requires fundamental changes in the economy and in the infrastructures serving our daily habits, in the dominant culture and in unsustainable lifestyles, as well as in the institutions and power relationships which drive them (Vergragt et al., 2014; Fuchs et al., 2016).

Beside research explicitly anchored in the sustainable consumption discourse, other research communities clearly address elements of this debate. Noteworthy examples include research on social innovation (see Backhaus et al., 2018) and degrowth (D'Alisa et al., 2014). The former does not necessarily challenge dominant institutions, as it tends to reproduce prevailing approaches based upon political consumerism, rather than fundamental rethinking of policy, and economic and social organization (McFarland and Wittmayer, 2018). The latter, however, explicitly considers limits and delves into the development of relevant structures – from mental to political – for ensuring a good life with limited resources (D'Alisa et al., 2014).

The 2010s have also seen the rise of various networks on SCP research, all trying to connect to other stakeholder communities and to contribute to policy and action. In preparation for the Rio+20 conference, the Global Research Forum on Sustainable Production and Consumption (GRF-SCP) was set up to strengthen the community of researchers and practitioners engaged in research on the worldwide transition to sustainable production and consumption systems. This network is closely related to policy processes at global level. So far, its global conferences have tackled issues such as dialogues between global and regional research on SCP (Lorek et al., 2012), prerequisites for a global transition to sustainable lifestyles (GRF-SCP, 2014), the circular economy (GRF-SCP, 2017), and transforming production and consumption (GRF-SCP 2019). A further network is the Sustainable Consumption Research and Action Initiative (SCORAI). It consists of professionals working at the interface of material consumption, human well-being, and technological and cultural change. SCORAI explicitly aims to foster a transition beyond the currently dominant consumer society. Exchange on specific content (especially via the lively e-mail list), thought-provoking workshops, a video series and a map of sustainable consumption teaching are part of SCORAI's formats. Another global initiative is a Knowledge–Action Network on Systems of Sustainable Consumption and Production (KAN-SSCP) within the Future Earth organization. The network aims to strengthen collaboration between communities of researchers and practitioners that are currently focused on either production or consumption. In working groups ranging from SCP in cities, via SCP in global value chains, to the political economy of SCP, the network has set up a research and engagement plan that extends almost as far as 2030 (KAN SSCP, 2018). The plethora of research networks on sustainable consumption, however, also reveals a problem. It highlights a wealth of research activity vying for attention and influence, but also fragmentation. It remains to be seen whether the current level of noise and momentum created by research on strong sustainable consumption will result in real change. Relevant research networks have come and gone before, for example, the SCORE research network on sustainable consumption, and many other fruitful but temporary undertakings.

Thus far, we can only conclude that political and societal efforts in pursuit of strong sustainable consumption remain weak. One important dimension stifling efforts by civil society and governments are current norms and ideas dominant in many countries. Accordingly, the following section will discuss and deconstruct some of these norms and suggest different perspectives on less 'attractive' ones.

3.   Guiding the path to strong sustainable consumption governance

3.1   Unveiling misconceptions

Two major misconceptions regarding sustainable consumption are widespread. One is that lots of small individual changes will produce significant results. In other words, if we can get individuals to commit to improvements in their consumption habits at little cost in terms of finance or convenience and perhaps even resulting in financial benefits, such as turning off lights when leaving a room, the quantity of such actions taken will make a considerable difference in overall energy consumption. Furthermore, individuals will, over time, automatically proceed from such small steps to greater steps as they became more aware of the ecological impacts of their consumption habits.

Unfortunately, research has found these perspectives to lack empirical support. The sum of small individual changes tends to result in insufficient aggregate improvements, and a procession from small to large changes by individuals is certainly not automatic and is highly improbable. On the contrary, individuals frequently overestimate the impact of the small steps taken and perceive a reduced need for greater ones. Mont et al. therefore argue that, while small changes and mass movements may make a difference, it is essential to underline that large changes are also necessary. Policymakers as well as civil society should therefore emphasize a dual approach: acknowledge the relative importance of the small changes that individuals can make in their lives and encourage them to participate in the necessary large-scale changes as engaged citizens (Mont et al., 2013).

At the turn of the millennium, research had identified food (meat and dairy consumption), housing (heating/cooling and the living area/person) and mobility (individual car mobility and air traffic) as the most important consumption clusters (Lorek and Spangenberg, 2001). A stronger focus on these clusters in communication and regulation is needed urgently. While the tremendous impact of meat and dairy products is recognized, the importance of shrinking the average per capita dwelling area remains confined to debates in few (academic) circles working for example, on sufficiency (Bierwirth, 2015; Thomas et al., 2017; Cohen, 2018; Lorek,

2018). Air traffic is recognized as a problem, but current policy practices further support its expansion.

The second misconception often shines through in the claim 'I cannot afford sustainability'. Weak sustainable consumption governance with its focus on efficiency improvements in products has meant that sustainable lifestyles often are perceived as something that can be bought, indeed, which have to be bought, like the energy retrofitting of buildings, A(+++) appliances, organic food and e-cars. These commodities are indeed frequently only available at high (or higher) prices.

As pointed out above, however, purchasing 'greener' products by itself does not constitute a sustainable lifestyle. The reduction in energy use gained by a general switch to more efficient products would translate into a substantially reduced ecological footprint and thus a sustainable lifestyle for only a very few households belonging to the global consumer class. Sustainability in consumption requires a far more comprehensive approach than buying specific items. Indeed, a substantial body of research now confirms that higher income levels almost uniformly correlate with less sustainable lifestyles – regardless of how many sustainable items the households has purchased or how 'green' the attitudes of the household members are (Moser and Kleinhückelkotten, 2017). In addition to the rebound effect (Wallenborn, 2018), researchers have identified the action–impact gap as a cause here, along with the well-researched attitude–action gap. Overall, lifestyles on lower budgets often turn out to be much more sustainable. The implications of this insight are ambivalent, however. A resource-low lifestyle not based on a voluntary decision but caused by poverty, for example, can be in conflict with the social aspects of sustainability. This issue remains largely undiscussed.

3.2   Overcoming an obsession: Letting go of the 'better life' in favour of a 'good life'

Over the past decades, if not centuries, the pursuit of a good life has come to be reinterpreted as the pursuit of a better life. Indeed, the idea of the need to pursue and invest in one's potential to live a better life is continuously carried forth like a mantra, by advertising, entertainment formats and in politics. The Brundtland Commission's definition of sustainable development manifested the vision of 'the better life' as the heart of the sustainability debate (Brundtland, 1987). This 'carrot' of promising a better life has proven very successful even in sustainability debates, despite its contradictory implications. While the good life entails elements of stability and contentedness, the search for the better life necessarily includes discontent, as there is always something more to strive for.

Two forces contribute to the societal preoccupation with the pursuit of a better life: first, the power structures in the political economy and second, and especially, the constant media promotion of a message that 'happiness is around the corner'. Consumers are bombarded daily with suggestions for improving their lives and themselves by purchasing new products. The proponents of this message strictly stay in the 'more' and 'growth' philosophy, within which only slightly more sustainable consumerist alternatives are acceptable (Lorek and Fuchs, 2013).

A better recognition and cultivation of *contentedness* (in German: *Zufriedenheit*) could take a tremendous amount of pressure from global resource demand. *Zufriedenheit* describes the deep inner feeling that things are good and enough just as they are. However, constant marketing and powerful media explicitly aim to persuade people that they are not content since content people might choose to leave the rat race for the 'good' life instead. There has been research and action on how to support the flourishing of *Zufriedenheit* (for example, Kasser 2002), but examination of this needs to be expanded considerably (for example, Lorek and Fuchs, 2013).

3.2   Discovering the appeal of limits and sufficiency

Over the last decades, sustainable consumption has been pursued mainly through the greater efficiency of new technologies, as noted above. Efficiency is represented as the silver bullet in the fight against high resource and energy use. But energy efficiency is specifically and intentionally not about conservation. Larger, more powerful, more functional products are given the label 'efficient' simply by using less energy than other equally large, powerful, functional products (Calwell, 2010). Efficiency labelling is based on measuring efficiency per unit of volume (for example, cubic metres in the case of refrigerators), even though the product itself might be much larger than the previous models that in total consumed much less electricity – a highly misleading measurement approach.

In consequence, a stronger approach than relative efficiency is slowly attracting interest: sufficiency. Sufficiency implies upper limits for resource consumption but also goes far beyond this. An article by Spengler (2016) on the 'two types of enough' explains that while the envisioned sufficient lifestyles need to offer *enough* for everyone to live a dignified life, as called for by justice theory, there is an *enough* in the sense of a maximum identified in environmental science. With this clear awareness of limits, sufficiency becomes an antithesis to the 'higher, further, faster, more' orientation that drives the current economic system. If sufficiency were established as an organizing principle of society, it could replace the growth paradigm, offering an opportunity to overcome current distributional dynamics and reap the benefits of a more equitable society (Spangenberg, 2018). Conceived in this way, sufficiency could steer technology and its innovative potential to help efficiency measures achieve their full potential while simultaneously avoiding rebound effects (Lorek, 2018).

Academic and societal debate thus has to focus on: (1) how to identify upper and lower limits, (2) how to reach the sufficiency space between these limits, and (3) how to arrange lifestyles worth living within that space. Various authors are currently developing concepts that aim to answer these questions by integrating insights from social science in a more strategic way. Among them are 'consumption corridors' (Di Giulio and Fuchs, 2014; Fuchs, 2017), 'contract and converge' (Vadovics et al., 2012), the 'doughnut economy' (Raworth, 2017) and 'Living Well within Limits' (Steinberger, 2017).

4.   Implications for research (and practice): Consumption corridors

Based on the notions of a 'good life' and limits, scholars have developed the concept of sustainable consumption corridors. In our view, this concept holds the most promise for operationalizing and implementing strong sustainable consumption governance: it focuses squarely on consumption in its simultaneous pursuit of social justice and ecological sustainability. Accordingly, this concluding section delineates the concept of consumption corridors and presents ideas on ways of pursuing their design and implementation.

The consumption corridors concept starts from the assumption that the purpose of consumption is to enable individuals to live a good life that meets their needs, rather than promoting growth or absorbing surplus production (Di Giulio et al., 2012). The focus here is on 'objective' or 'protected' needs, those fundamental needs that are associated with being human and opportunities for living a good life (Defila et al., 2018). Furthermore, following an anthropological approach, the concept of consumption corridors assumes that humans have universal needs that are independent of cultural contexts. Moreover, it posits that an ethical obligation exists to provide all humans with the possibility of fulfilling such needs, regardless of whether they make use of them. Such needs must be distinguished from subjective desires. The substantive core of needs, in turn, is adaptable to contexts of time and space. It is crucial, moreover, to distinguish needs from 'satisfiers' (products, services, infrastructures or institutions necessary for meeting needs) and resources (needed to provide and use satisfiers).

In order to have an opportunity to fulfil their needs individuals will need to have access to a minimum level of resources for consumption. Guaranteeing such a minimum consumption level for all individuals in a world of limited resources translates into the necessity of upper limits to consumption. In other words, maximum consumption limits need to be set at the level beyond which consumption by one individual or group would not compromise other individuals' abilities to meet their needs and thus achieve minimum consumption levels (Blättel-Mink et al., 2013; Di Giulio and Fuchs, 2014; Fuchs, 2017). Together maximum and minimum consumption limits define consumption corridors, that is, the space in which sustainable consumption is possible and in which individuals are free to design their lives and consumption according to their own preferences. Thus, consumption corridors address simultaneously planetary boundaries and issues of intragenerational and intergenerational justice.

To design such consumption corridors, societies first would need to engage in deliberative processes to reach consensus on needs and appropriate satisfiers for those needs that were relevant to their context. Translating these satisfiers into resources, in turn, would pave the way towards an identification of minimum consumption levels. In principle, this exercise is not all that different from current political practices of identifying consumption baskets in the context of welfare policies. Important distinctions, however, are clear differentiation between needs and satisfiers, and also societal deliberation; these could be starting points for the design of consumption corridors. Taking into account these minimum consumption limits in terms of resources and scientific knowledge about planetary boundaries would then allow the determination of maximum consumption levels.

Clearly, the design and implementation of consumption corridors is a challenging task. It is likely to be associated with societal contestation since strong sustainable consumption in general and consumption corridors in particular require a redistribution of global resources. Consumption corridors are a worthwhile endeavour, however, as a world of sustainable consumption corridors would allow all individuals living now and in the future to live not a better life, but a good one.

NOTES

1 At the same time, it is important to acknowledge, of course, that improving the quality of life of billions of people in the developing world requires increased consumption of energy and materials (O'Neill et al., 2018).

2 See 12.2, 12.4, 12.6, 12.C (available at https://unstats.un.org/sdgs/indicators/Global%20Indicator%20Framework%20 after%202019%20refinement_Eng.pdf).

3 See 12.2.1, 12.2.2, 12.3.1, 12.4.2, 12.5.1, 12.C.1 (https://unstats.un.org/sdgs/indicators/Global%20Indicator%20Fra mework%20after%202019%20refinement_Eng.pdf).

References

Akenji, L. (2014), 'Consumer scapegoatism and limits to green consumerism', *Journal of Cleaner Production*, **63**, 16–23.

Alfredsson, E., M. Bengtsson, H.S. Brown et al. (2018), 'Why achieving the Paris agreement requires reduced overall consumption and production', *Sustainability: Science, Practice and Policy*, **14** (1), 1–5.

Backhaus, J., A. Genus, S. Lorek et al. (eds) (2018), *Social Innovation and Sustainable Consumption: Research and Action for Societal Transformation*, Abingdon, UK: Routledge.

Bengtsson, M., E. Alfredsson, M. Cohen et al. (2018), 'Moving beyond resource efficiency: Transforming systems of sustainable consumption and production for achieving the sustainable development goals', *Sustainability Science*, **13** (6), 1533–47.

Bierwirth, A. (2015), 'Strategische Entwicklung eines zukunftsfähigen Wohnraumangebots–ein Suffizienz-Szenario', *uwf UmweltWirtschaftsForum*, **23** (1–2), 49–58.

Blättel-Mink, B., B. Brohmann, R. Defila et al. (2013), *Konsum-Botschaften – Was Forschende für die gesellschaftliche Gestaltung nachhaltigen Konsums empfehlen*, Stuttgart: Hirzel.

Brundtland, G.H. (1987), *Our Common Future: World Commission on Environment and Development*, Oxford: Oxford University Press.

Calwell, C. (2010), 'Is efficient sufficient? The case for shifting our emphasis in energy specifications to progressive efficiency and sufficiency', Report to the European Council for an Energy Efficient Economy (ECEEE), Stockholm: ECEEE Secretariat.

Cherry, E. (2015), 'I was a teenage vegan: Motivation and maintenance of lifestyle movements', *Sociological Inquiry*, **85** (1), 55–74.

Cohen, M. (2013), 'Collective dissonance and the transition to post-consumerism', *Futures*, **52** (August), 42–51.

Cohen, M. (2018), 'Sustainable consumption and new conceptions for sufficient home size', World Social Science Forum, Fukuoka, Japan, 25–8 September.

D'Alisa, G., F. Demaria and G. Kallis (2014), *Degrowth: A Vocabulary for a New Era*, Abingdon, UK: Routledge.

Defila, R., A. Di Giulio and C.R. Schweizer (2018), 'Two souls are dwelling in my breast: Uncovering how individuals in their dual role as consumer-citizen perceive future energy policies', *Energy Research and Social Science*, **35** (January), 152–62.

Di Giulio, A., B. Brohmann, J. Clausen et al. (2012), 'Needs and consumption – a conceptual system and its meaning in the context of sustainability', in R. Defila, A. Di Giulio and R. Kaufmann-Hayoz (eds), *The Nature of Sustainable Consumption and How to Achieve it. Results from the Focal Topic "From Knowledge to Action – New Paths towards Sustainable Consumption"*, Munich: Oekom, pp. 45–66.

Di Giulio, A. and D. Fuchs (2014), 'Sustainable consumption corridors: Concept, objections, and responses', *GAIA*, **23** (1), 184–92.

Elkington, J. (1994), 'Towards the sustainable corporation: Win-win-win business strategies for sustainable development', *California Management Review*, **36** (2), 90–100.

Elkington, J. (2018), '25 years ago I coined the phrase "Triple bottom line". Here's why it's time to rethink it', *Harvard Business Review*, 25 June.

European Commission (2012), 'A new European consumer agenda – boosting confidence and growth by putting consumers at the heart of the Single Market', Press Release, (COM(2012) 225 final), Brussels: European Commission – DG Health and Consumers.

European Commission (2016), 'Communication on the Eco-Design Workplan 2016–2019', accessed 21 December 2018 at http://ec.europa.eu/DocsRoom/documents/20375.

European Environment Agency (2013), 'European Union CO2 emissions: Different accounting perspectives, EEA Technical Report 20/2013', Copenhagen: European Environment Agency.

Figueres, C., H.J. Schellnhuber, G. Whiteman et al. (2017), 'Three years to safeguard our climate', *Nature News*, **546** (7660), 593.

Finnish Ministry of the Environment (2013), *More from less – wisely*, Helsinki: Finnish Ministry of the Environment.

Fuchs, D. (2013), 'Theorizing the power of global companies', in J. Mikler (ed.), *The Handbook of Global Companies*, Hoboken: Wiley-Blackwell, pp. 77–95.

Fuchs, D. (2017), 'Consumption corridors as a means for overcoming trends', in C. Bala and W. Schuldzinski (eds), 'The 21st century consumer: Vulnerable, responsible, transparent? Proceedings of the international conference on consumer research 2016', Düsseldorf: Verbraucherzentrale NRW e.V.

Fuchs, D., A. Di Giulio, K. Glaab et al. (2016), 'Power: What is missing in consumption and absolute reductions research and action', *Journal of Cleaner Production*, **132** (September), 298–307.

Fuchs, D. and S. Lorek (2005), 'Sustainable consumption governance – a history of promises and failures', *Journal of Consumer Policy*, **28**, 261–88.

German Federal Ministry for the Environment, Nature Conservation, Building and Nuclear Safety (2018), *National Programme on Sustainable Consumption – From Sustainable Lifestyles towards Social Change*, Berlin: German Federal Ministry for the Environment, Nature Conservation, Building and Nuclear Safety (BMUB).

Government Office of Sweden (2016), *Strategy for Sustainable Consumption*, Stockholm: Swedish Ministry of Finance.

Greening, L., D.L. Greene and C. Difiglio (2000), 'Energy efficiency and consumption – the rebound effect – a survey', *Energy Policy*, **28** (6), 389–401.

GRF-SCP (2014), 'Global transitions to sustainable production and consumption systems', Global Research Forum on Sustainable Production and Consumption, GRF International Conference Shanghai, 8–11 June.

GRF-SCP (2017), 'Sustainable lifestyles, livelihoods and the circular economy', Global Research Forum on Sustainable Production and Consumption, GRF International Conference Brighton, 27–29 June.

GRF-SCP (2019), 'Transforming Production and Consumption: Bridging Sustainability Research with Policy and Practice', Global Research Forum on Sustainable Production and Consumption, 4th GRF International Conference Hong Kong, 26-29 June.

Gumbert, T. and D. Fuchs (2018), 'The power of corporations in global food sector governance', in Andreas Nölke and Christian May (eds), *Handbook of the International Political Economy of the Corporation*, Cheltenham, UK and Northampton, MA, USA: Edward Elgar Publishing.

Hamari, J., M. Sjöklint and A. Ukkonen (2016), 'The sharing economy: Why people participate in collaborative consumption', *Journal of the Association for Information Science and Technology*, **67** (9), 2047–59.

Heinberg, R. (2010), *Peak Everything: Waking up to the Century of Declines*, Gabriola Islands: New Society Publishers.

Heinrichs, H. and H. Grunenberg (2012), *Sharing Economy: Auf dem Weg in eine neue Konsumkultur?*, Lüneburg: DEU.

Hobson, K. (2013), '"Weak" or "strong" sustainable consumption? Efficiency, degrowth, and the 10-Year Framework of Programmes', *Environment and Planning C: Government and Policy*, **31** (6), 1082–98.

KAN SSCP (2018), 'Future Earth Knowledge-Action Network on Systems of Sustainable Consumption and Production – Research and Engagement Plan', accessed 9 January 2019 at http://www.futureearth.org/asiacentre/sscp-kan.

Kasser, T. (2002), *The High Price of Materialism*, Cambridge, MA: MIT Press.

Kharas, H. (2010), 'The emerging middle class in developing countries', Paris: OECD Development Centre Working Papers.

Klein, N.J. and M.J. Smart (2017), 'Millennials and car ownership: Less money, fewer cars', *Transport Policy*, **53**, 20–29.

Liu, Y., Y. Qu, Z. Lei et al. (2017), 'Understanding the evolution of sustainable consumption research', *Sustainable Development*, **25** (5), 414–30.

Lorek, S. (2018), 'Identification of promising instruments and instrument mixes to promote energy sufficiency', EUFORIE – European Futures for Energy Efficiency, Deliverable 5.5.

Lorek, S., J. Barber and K. Onthank (eds) (2013), 'Global and regional research on sustainable consumption and production systems: Achievements, challenges and dialogues', Workshop Report of the Global Research Forum on Sustainable Production and Consumption, June 13–15, 2012, Rio de Janeiro, Brazil.

Lorek, S. and D. Fuchs (2012), 'Strong sustainable consumption governance – precondition for a degrowth path?', *Journal of Cleaner Production*, **38**, 36–43.

Lorek, S. and J.H. Spangenberg (2001), 'Indicators for environmentally sustainable household consumption', *International Journal of Sustainable Development*, **4** (1), 101–20.

Luzecka, P. (2016), '"Take a gap year!" A social practice perspective on air travel and potential transitions towards sustainable tourism mobility', *Journal of Sustainable Tourism*, **24** (3), 446–62.

McFarland, K. and J. Wittmayer (2018), 'Hitting a policy wall: The transformative potential and limitations of community pick-up point schemes', in J.A. Backhaus, A. Genus, S. Lorek, E. Vadovics and J. Wittmayer (eds), *Social Innovation and Sustainable Consumption: Research and Action for Societal Transformation*, Abingdon, UK: Routledge, pp. 72–85.

Mont, O., E. Heiskanen, K. Power et al. (2013), *Improving Nordic Policymaking by Dispelling Myths on Sustainable Consumption*, Copenhagen: Nordic Council of Ministers.

Moser, S. and S. Kleinhückelkotten (2017), 'Good intents, but low impacts: Diverging importance of motivational and socioeconomic determinants explaining pro-environmental behavior, energy use, and carbon footprint', *Environment and Behavior*, **50** (6), 626–56.

Newall, S. (2017), '12 best sustainable fashion brands for women', *The Independent*, accessed 9 January 2019 at https://www.independent.co.uk/extras/indybest/fashion-beauty/womens-clothing/best-sustainable-fashion-brands-women-clothing-ethical-eco-friendly-affordable-london-luxury-a7982316.html.

O'Neill, D.W., A.L. Fanning, W.F. Lamb et al. (2018), 'A good life for all within planetary boundaries', *Nature Sustainability*, **1** (2), 88.

Raworth, K. (2017), *Doughnut Economics: Seven Ways to Think Like a 21st-Century Economist*, London: Chelsea Green Publishing.

Revill, C., V. Harris, S. Rahmsdorf et al. (eds) (2017), '2020. The climate turning point', 'Mission 2020', accessed 21 December 2018 at http://www.mission2020.global/wp-content/uploads/2020-The-Climate-Turning-Point.pdf.

Rockström, J., W. Steffen, K. Noone et al. (2009), 'A safe operating space for humanity', *Nature*, **46** (1) 472–5.

SAVE FOOD Initiative (2017), 'SAVE FOOD Congress' 2017, Food and Agricultural Organization of the United Nations and Messe Düsseldorf, 4 May.

Schor, J. (2016), 'Debating the sharing economy', *Journal of Self-Governance and Management Economics*, **4** (3), 7–22.

Slezák, J. (2017), 'Governmental policies and initiatives to promote Sustainable Consumption and Production (SCP) in the pan-European region', background paper to the UNEP Global Report on National SCP Policies and Initiatives, Zürich: SERI internal paper.

Soil Association (2018), *Organic Market Report 2018*, accessed 20 December 2018 at https://www.soilasso ciation.org/certification/trade-news/2018/organic-has-reached-its-highest-sales-ever-at-over-22b.

Spangenberg, J.H. (2014), 'Institutional change for strong sustainable consumption: Sustainable consumption and the degrowth economy', *Sustainability: Science, Practice and Policy*, **10** (1), 62–77.

Spangenberg, J.H. (2017), 'Hot air or comprehensive progress? A critical assessment of the SDGs', *Sustainable Development*, **25** (4), 311–21.

Spangenberg, J.H. (2018), 'Sufficiency: A pragmatic, radical visionary approach', in R. Mastini (ed.), *Sufficiency – Moving beyond the Gospel of Eco-Efficiency*, Brussels: Friends of the Earth Europe.

Spengler, L. (2016), 'Two types of "enough": Sufficiency as minimum and maximum', *Environmental Politics*, **25** (5), 921–40.

Spengler, L. (2018), *Sufficiency as Policy: Necessity, Possibilities and Limitations*, Baden-Baden: Nomos Verlag.

Steffen, W., K. Richardson, J. Rockström et al. (2015), 'Planetary boundaries: Guiding human development on a changing planet', *Science*, **347** (6223).

Steinberger, J. (2017), 'Living Well within Limits', accessed 21 December 2018 at https://lili.leeds.ac.uk.

Steinberger J., F. Krausmann and N. Eisenmenger (2010), 'Global patterns of materials use: A socioeconomic and geophysical analysis', *Ecological Economics*, **69** (5), 1148–58.

Stewart, T. (2009), *Waste – Uncovering The Global Food Scandal*, New York: W.W. Norton and Company.

Thomas, S., L.-A., Brischke, J. Thema et al. (2017), 'Energy sufficiency policy: How to limit energy consumption and per capita dwelling size in a decent way', Proceedings of the ECEEE 2017 summer study on energy efficiency – consumption, efficiency and limits.

United Nations (1992), 'Agenda 21'; Results of the World Conference on Environment and Development, United Nations, New York.

United Nations (2002), 'Johannesburg Plan of Implementation', World Summit on Sustainable Development, United Nations, New York.

United Nations (2015a), 'Transforming our world: The 2030 Agenda for Sustainable Development', Resolution 70/1, adopted by the General Assembly on 25 September 2015, (Document A/RES/70/1), United Nations, New York.

United Nations (2015b), *Sustainable Development Goals*, New York: United Nations, accessed 21 December 2018 at https://www.un.org/sustainabledevelopment/sustainable-development-goals.

United Nations Environment Programme/United Nations Department of Economic and Social Affairs (2008), 'The Marrakech Process', accessed 20 October 2018 at http://esa.un.org/marrakechprocess.

Vadovics, E., S. Milton and the Converge Project Consortium (2012), *Equity within Limits in Theory and Practice*, Budapest: Green Dependent Institute.

van Wee, B. (2015), 'Peak car: The first signs of a shift towards ICT-based activities replacing travel? A discussion paper', *Transport Policy*, **42**, 1–3.

Vergragt, P., L. Akenji and P. Dewick (2014), 'Sustainable production, consumption, and livelihoods: global and regional research perspectives', *Journal of Cleaner Production*, **63**, 1–12.

Wallenborn, G. (2018), 'Rebounds are structural effects of infrastructures and markets', *Frontiers in Energy Research*, **6** (99).

3 Growth strategies and consumption patterns in transition: From Fordism to finance-driven capitalism

Max Koch

1. Introduction

Two centuries of capitalist growth in Western societies have coincided with significant increases in objective and subjective well-being. Yet these increases have come at a price: the thresholds for specific biophysical processes such as climate, biodiversity and the nitrogen cycle being approached or crossed (Steffen et al., 2015). Attempts to decouple gross domestic product (GDP) growth absolutely from the ecological footprints of production and consumption have not been successful to date (Pichler et al., 2017). Since the material welfare standards enjoyed by rich countries cannot be generalized to the rest of the planet, these countries would thus need to review their production and consumption patterns and 'degrow' to make their economies and societies compatible with planetary limits (D'Alisa et al., 2014; Koch and Mont, 2016; Spash, 2017). Indeed, if planetary boundaries are to be taken seriously, only the satisfaction of basic human needs, and not much more, could be assured in the rich countries for the time being (Koch et al., 2017). This chapter seeks to contribute to an institutional understanding of consumption governance through an analysis of how consumption practices are linked to production norms in specific capitalist growth strategies.

Theorizing consumption – including in growth-critical discourses – is at times hampered by what Shove (2010) referred to as the 'ABC formula', where A stands for attitude, B for behaviour and C for choice. In such approaches, social inequality, power structures and the ways in which these are perceived tend to be neglected, while the responsibility for sustainable consumption is shifted onto individuals and private households. This obviously applies more to what Lorek and Fuchs (2013) refer to as 'weak' rather than 'strong sustainable consumption', which explicitly contributes to 'degrowth' thinking. Yet not even the latter formulation systematically considers the structural links between capitalist growth economy and consumption patterns. This chapter suggests that a combination of the regulation approach and Bourdieusian sociology could contribute to providing the required analytical tools. In particular, it attempts to reflect the fact that acts of consumption are neither 'spontaneous' nor 'individual', but rather are influenced by the imperatives of wider strategies of capitalist growth and by structural factors such as social inequality and state strategies – which consumers and consumption industries are normally unaware of. In fact, growth-oriented contemporary production and consumption patterns tend to be perceived as the 'natural' state (Koch, 2018).

This chapter first introduces the regulation approach as an institutional attempt to link analyses of production patterns to those of consumption. The focus will be on the institutional particulars of how *longues durées* of capitalist growth take the form of compatible commodity streams of production and consumption. Second, the chapter argues that the regulation approach is compatible with Bourdieusian sociology of consumption. Bourdieu's concept of 'habitus', in particular, can be used as an analytical bridge between 'objective' social structures, including patterns of inequality, and allegedly 'subjective' and 'individual' lifestyles and cultural practices. Taken together, the regulation approach and Bourdieu's cultural sociology provide a novel analytical tool for the understanding of consumption patterns within wider capitalist growth strategies. Third, this concept will be applied to a comparison of the two main growth strategies after World War II: Fordism and finance-driven capitalism. The conclusion summarizes the argument and delineates future research avenues.

2. The regulation approach

Structural contradictions between the capitalist growth economy and the ecological system must remain within certain limits so that the legitimacy and maintenance of the overall social order are not fundamentally undermined. Tensions and contradictions between these two take on different forms, presenting themselves as continuous development or as rupture, depending on diverse types of institutional regulation (Koch, 2012; Paterson and Laberge, 2018). An institutional attempt to link analyses of production patterns to those of consumption has been proposed by the regulation approach, which – at least in the Parisian version – continues key insights from Marx's *Critique of Political Economy*, such as 'modes of production' and 'social formations', and complements them with 'intermediary concepts' ('accumulation regime' and 'mode of regulation'). These concepts express the largely non-variable conditions of agents involved in the relations of production and exchange, as well as the historical changes that these relations undergo during different phases of capitalist growth (Boyer and Saillard, 2002). While the abstract features of capitalism are seen as largely transhistorical, both crises in the accumulation process and phases of expanded production are addressed in the context of their institutional embedding. The regulatory settings required for continued and expanded capital accumulation are socially, culturally and politically constructed and contested within a myriad of societal struggles, in which relations both within and between social classes play a prominent role. The notion of 'intermediary concepts', in particular, emphasizes that the articulation of a given social formation in time and space corresponds to particular structural features and institutional forms. 'Accumulation regimes' are associated with certain historical phases and development paths or growth strategies, which take the form of compatible commodity streams of production and consumption, reproduced over a long period of time. They differ historically, for example, as to whether intensive or extensive, export-oriented or import-oriented forms dominate, or vice versa. All accumulation regimes are associated with a specific industrial paradigm, a dominant principle of division of labour, an energy regime and a corresponding 'mode of consumption'.

In contrast to neoclassical economics, consumption is not viewed as an isolated or behavioural phenomenon – as the result of autonomous individual choices – but within its social genesis and context. Aglietta (1987: 154) conceptualizes consumption as 'an organized set of activities, which – while predominantly private – became subject to a general logic of the reconstitution of energies expended in social practices and the preservation of abilities and attitudes implied by the social relations'. What and how much we buy and consume is of the greatest relevance for ecological issues such as the carbon cycle, since these decisions are normally bound to matter and energy transformations that more often than not necessitate the burning of fossil fuels. The regulation approach insists – contradicting the predominant notion of *Homo economicus* in the neoclassical perspective – that purchase decisions or the 'demand side' of economics are neither 'formally rational' nor 'autonomous', but instead are greatly influenced by structural factors such as income inequality and corporate sales strategies. This approach agrees with socio-logical and anthropological research that point out that purchasing things is not in the first place about the goods themselves but rather about the symbolic messages that purchase acts express and mediate (Boyer, 2008).

A 'mode of regulation' comprises an ensemble of social networks as well as rules, norms and conventions, which together facilitate the seamless reproduction of an accumulation regime. The term 'mode of regulation' stresses the fact that capital-ism does not reproduce itself only upon the basis of the immanent logic dealt with Marx's *Capital*, for example, but that its stabilization also requires institutional forms: these comprise the wage relation or 'wage-labour nexus' (Bertrand, 2002); the enterprise form; the nature of money (Guttmann, 2002); the state; and inter-national regimes (Aglietta, 2002). Critical geographers have complemented these institutional forms with a notion of geographic scales, which determine the main spatial boundaries within which structural coherence is sought (Brenner, 2004). Regulationists view the institutional forms that help stabilize capitalist development during particular growth periods as the hard-won products of social struggles and diverse and often contradictory interests. Regulation in its concrete forms is, hence, not simply the product of the strategies of the dominant classes, which themselves are divided by different competitive interests, but always reflect a degree of com-promise with dominated groups. Modes of regulation and patterns of governance vary considerably depending on the nature of such institutional compromises.

3.   Bourdieu's sociology of consumption

Regulationists and Bourdieu share the basic hypothesis that 'life in society is made possible by the way in which institutions are constructed, just as economic activity is organized by the mode of *régulation*' (Boyer, 2008: 348). Hence, both object to what Bourdieu (2005: 7) calls the 'scholastic bias' in economics and social sciences. This bias consists in the tendency to construct increasingly abstract models 'which leads the scholar to project his thinking into the minds of the active agents and to see (his own representations) as underlying their practice'. Far from being an anthropological constant, the ascendancy of an aptitude for rational behaviour in production and consumption is, for example, the result of long historical processes, during which it was inscribed in people's social and cognitive structures, practical patterns of thinking, perception and action. Regulationist research has furthermore turned to Bourdieu's concept of 'habitus' as an alternative to the theory of rational choice, and as an analytic bridge between 'objective' social structures, including patterns of inequality and consumption, and allegedly 'subjective' lifestyles. As an internalized product of the social structures that conditioned it, habitus supplies us with a sensibility towards these structures and the options they include and exclude. This *amor fati* supplies a sort of social orientation, by which the occupants of a given position in social space are guided towards socio-cultural practices that suit them and befit the occupants of their social position.

Bourdieu's sociology of consumption demonstrates that there are few things less 'individual' than taste or consumptive practices. The latter are instead socially conditioned and maintained by dominant groups to enforce their distance or distinction from the sphere of material necessity and, hence, from other societal groups. Understood as 'social necessity made second nature' (Bourdieu, 1984: 476), taste becomes an efficient weapon in the social struggle about resources. In matters ranging from food and drink, cosmetics and newspapers to art and music, taste and distinction define and delineate the 'high' from the 'low', the sacred from the profane, and the legitimate from the illegitimate. The cultural space is subdivided into a range of fields such as cinema, theatre or computer games, which are themselves constituted by specific power relations, strategies and interests, in which an actor's coordinates are a reflection of his or her economic, cultural and social 'capital'. In the sphere of consumption, different class cultures develop different tastes, so that even the perception and appropriation of one and the same cultural product by different classes follows different social patterns and yields different amounts of symbolic capital. In *Distinction*, Bourdieu empirically demonstrates the correspondence between socio-economic positions, education levels and taste. Both dominating and dominated groups live in specific social circumstances that condition them to develop and 'prefer' lifestyles that are homologous with those positions. Legitimate cultural practices such as museum attendance, theatregoing, recreational reading of 'the classics', the development of interests in cinematic genres and directorial styles, foreign travel and a liking for avant-garde music have become largely reserved for the dominant class.[1]

Fields within the space of consumption resemble other societal fields, that is, the rules of the game reflect power relations within which 'cultural capital', both in its institutionalized and embodied forms, serves as a currency to classify the actors and their practices into a hierarchy of lifestyles. Yet cultural or symbolic goods differ from material goods in that one can consume them only to the extent that one understands their meaning, and requires adequate schemes of appreciation and understanding – a capability, however, that is unequally distributed across social space. Class-specific socialization in families and the school system ensures that a disproportional number of those attaining high educational credentials will enjoy a relationship of comfortable familiarity with the legitimate culture. This process of 'cultivation' through which cultural capital is accumulated begins in the family, and takes the form of an investment of money and time (either of hired specialists or the parents' own time), which, if successful, returns dividends in school, university, social contacts and the marriage and job markets.

In essence, in the sphere of consumption, social differences are reproduced and even appear as natural since 'legitimate' taste is the farthest from the sphere of necessity. Due to this objective distance, consumption appears to be built upon an 'ethos of ease', of 'casualness, grace, facility, elegance, freedom, in a word, natural-ness' (Bourdieu, 1984: 339). As mentioned before, purchasing things for individual consumption is not, in the first place, about the goods themselves, but rather about the symbolic message that the act of purchase conveys. Both the acquisition and possession of use values symbolize much of our social standing in society, our identity and our sense of belonging. If, however, the rate of production of new, fashionable and desirable goods is high and accelerating, continuous efforts must be made by all social agents to re-establish or improve their original social posi-tion and to distance themselves from other people. Yet there is always the danger of vulgarization, of devaluation through emulation and generalization of certain cultural practices that once held an aura of legitimacy. This process accelerates the never-ending cycles of the avant-garde's definition of taste and the mainstream's 'keeping-up' strategies. This cycle plays into the hands of diverse culture indus-tries, yet contradicts the principal reproductive needs of the Earth as an ecological system, because, all other things being equal, increases in commodified consump-tion are accompanied by greater matter and energy throughputs, which lead to environmental degradation.

4.   From Fordism to the finance-driven growth strategy

The regulation approach refers to a historical situation, in which a regime of accumulation including the consumption norm and the mode of regulation are sufficiently complementary as a 'growth strategy' or a 'mode of development' to secure an extensive period of economic expansion and social cohesion. The stability of such a growth model is further enhanced when shared values and norms help to bring about a 'common-sense' value system subscribed to by members of all social classes. The correspondence between growth strategy and ideology frames and gives meaning to people's day-to-day beliefs and social practices – including cultural practices – thereby providing relatively high levels of social inclusion. Fordism and finance-driven capitalism are the most recent historical examples of such growth strategies.

4.1 Fordism

Fordist production techniques initially emerged in the United States in the 1920s and subsequently became the cornerstone of a new accumulation regime in a range of countries including in Western Europe, Australia and Japan. This regime was stabilized by a mode of regulation that enabled a high level of demand for mass-produced and standardized goods such as cars, radios, televisions, washing machines and refrigerators for example, by means of Keynesian social and economic policies. The growth of the Fordist production–consumption nexus was due to the availability of cheap fossil fuels such as oil, and the corresponding environmental consequences (Koch, 2012). At the same time, the demand for (fossil) mineral resources turned many developing countries into 'extraction societies' – and this structurally undermined their ability to benefit from the economic growth associated with the Fordist accumulation regime. It is not coincidental that the increase in greenhouse gas emissions and climate change after World War II coincided with the growth in and generalization of the Fordist production and consumption norm in the Western world and the simultaneous establishment of an international division of labour in industrialized and extraction societies.

Unlike the 1930s, when solvent consumers were scarce, during the era of post-war reconstruction, there was stable and expanding demand for both consumer goods and the means of production to build them. Since most Western European households did not yet own durable goods such as household appliances, mass production could become the technological basis for the rapid generalization of their consumption. The turnover of fixed capital was accelerated by the continuing increase in the number of products, which reduced the costs of individual products. Profits were supported by consumer demand that, in turn, was based on increasing real wages, which were usually determined by collective agreements and tied to expected growth in productivity. Wage labourers working in a factory could be mobilized in trade unions relatively easily. Their rising negotiation power was not only reflected in systems of company level co-determination, but was increasingly recognized in society in general, leading to forms of centralized collective bargaining either at industry or national level in most Western European countries (Boyer and Saillard, 2002). Fast growth rates in GDP and productivity meant real wages rose and employment moved towards full capacity. High levels of domestic demand promoted full employment and led to an unparalleled investment boom in Western Europe.

The lowered price of industrial products raised the purchasing power of wage labourers, thus increasing both employers' profits and employees' real wages. The state benefited from this favourable situation and used the growing income from taxation for the expansion of a welfare state system, which, in turn, guaranteed a minimum standard of living and material consumption for those who did not – for whatever reason – participate in the labour market. The introduction and generalization of Fordism qualitatively adapted the conditions under which the worker's individual reproduction took place and loosened the 'ties of family, or bonds of neighbourhood proximity or supplementary activity' that had linked them to a 'non-capitalist environment' (Aglietta, 1987: 153–4). With the enormous reduction of prices in essential consumer goods, the conditions for what Burghart Lutz (1989) called the 'internal takeover' (*innere Landnahme* in the German original) of ever more spheres of life by capitalism: the participation of wage earners in commodified forms of consumption, which – hitherto monopolized by the dominant classes – signified a substantial improvement in their material standard of living. However, taking out mortgages and consumer loans made the wage labourer's existence further dependent on continuing participation in the work process and made rebellious behaviour against the dominant production and consumption model increasingly difficult to afford.

The spheres of work and non-work became closely linked in novel ways; two areas of peoples' private lives came to be particularly affected by the Fordist consumption norm: housing and the rise of a suburban lifestyle based on individual mobility. Standardized housing 'put an end to [the] unhygienic and unsafe interiors' that had characterized pre-Fordist housing among the working class, and 'permitted the installation of household appliances that saved domestic labour' (Aglietta, 1987: 160). Housing became also a symbol of status since housing could be bought rather than simply rented. Mass-produced prefabricated housing reduced costs to a point where, extended over the overall term of payment, it was, as Aglietta observed, less of a 'burden on the working-class wage of the 1950s than were the rents extorted by landlords of the inter-war years' (Aglietta, 1987: 160). Yet the rationalization of housebuilding brought with it a parcellation of households so that traditional 'proletarian' working class milieus were gradually replaced by a homeowner culture. The new homes were either flats or, in the case of the upwardly mobile, semi-detached or detached family homes with functionally differentiated 'departments' for eating, sleeping, and children (Hirsch and Roth, 1986).

Bourdieu uses the French housing market in the heyday of Fordism as an example of the increasing links between the spheres of production and consumption and, at the same time, provides a fundamental critique of the neoclassical notion of viewing individual consumption acts or purchasing goods as 'individual choices'. In *The Social Structures of the Economy* Bourdieu (2005) empirically demonstrates that economic choices such as whether to buy or to rent or whether to buy an old house or a new one are far from 'individual' or even 'natural', but, instead, depend on the socially constituted economic dispositions of the agent (the 'demand' side), and on the supply of dwellings. Contrary to neoclassical economic theory, which treats both supply and demand as 'unconditioned givens', Bourdieu (2005: 15) argues that they are both shaped, more or less directly, by state socio-economic and, especially, housing policies. Though the extent of state activity in social housing differed from country to country, it nevertheless played – and continues to play – a crucial role in determining the conditions for owning, renting, constructing, and defining regulations on taxation and the qualitative standards of housing. In the French case, state housing policy became more oriented towards homeownership from the 1960s, resulting in a diminishing supply of accessible rented property and thus redirecting a section of potential tenants towards ownership. Among homeowners, social differences based on economic and cultural capital were reproduced in the process.

Defining living in cities as blighted, and in rural areas as backward, New Deal programmes in the USA intended to produce a society of almost inconceivable homogeneity by modifying the physical landscape through the creation of new environments 'fit for life and the living'. Suburbanization led to increasing demand for geographic mobility, and this, in turn, began to undermine local, municipal and neighbourhood relationships. Workers' housing estates and working-class areas, with the once typical atmosphere of practical solidarity were displaced and gradually replaced by dormitory towns. Suburbanization was thus tantamount to an extension of the Taylorist time–space matrix to the individual or private sphere: as more and more people no longer lived where they worked, inner cities became deserted immediately after shopping hours. Alongside electric power, which made the benefits of city life available in suburban areas, it was the car and individual mobility that enabled the decentralization of the population intended in New Deal programmes. While in pre-Fordist periods, suburbanization had been constrained by the need for public transport and had congregated along tram and railway lines, the spread of cars 'enabled urbanites to flee inner cities and settle wherever there were roads' (Marcus and Segal, 1989: 269). Public and collective transport systems were among the main casualties of this development. Public transport vehicles that generated economies of scale by carrying many passengers on regular routes at scheduled times were faced with fewer passengers due to cars.

Still another factor that helped to make production and consumption norms compatible was that many services and activities that had been done at home were now commercialized and bought and sold on markets. For example, the use of dishwashers and washing machines replaced manual washing, vegetables were now bought in shops and supermarkets instead of being grown in kitchen gardens. Ready meals often replaced home-cooked meals. At the same time, the relative importance of personal services was reduced in the overall employment system and instead became a recruiting ground for industrial employment. The percentage of wage labour within all types of economic activity increased to the same extent that services and products took the form of commodities: dependent employment and the corresponding income increasingly became the requirement for the acquisition of indispensable goods and services.

In summary, the expansion of the Fordist mode of consumption took place against a background of the dismantling of traditional social situations and lifestyles, and was characterized by suburbanization, the modified role of the family as a socialization agency, increased individual geographic and social mobility, as well as by an increase in state regulation in areas such as welfare, social protection and education. Despite the fact that 'objective' social differences, particularly those of class, were not evened out in this process, the combination of reduced working hours, made possible due to the enormous increase in labour productivity, and the increasing strength of organized labour were perceived as a 'surge in individualization' away from traditional collective networks (Beck, 1992). This surge, however, also featured elements of social isolation and societal disintegration, which were accompanied by the beginnings of what Hirsch and Roth (1986: 58) identified as 'precarious subjectivity'. Social homogenization and individualization in combination with the emergence of forms of everyday culture such as television, which brought together masses of people who had previously led different, class- and group-specific lifestyles, crucially contributed towards a decrease in the subjective perception of class.

Even though quantitative levels of consumption remained stratified, the Fordist consumption norm was nevertheless generalized to the entire society as a comprehensive normative orientation. Hirsch and Roth followed from this that both mental structures and social forms of interaction came to be moulded by the consumption of commodities that were themselves produced in capitalist ways. The promise of a constantly growing amount of use values partially compensated for the humiliations suffered by individuals in Taylorist work processes and in other areas of life regulated by bureaucratic structures. Self-perceptions of individual fulfilment and identity became increasingly dependent on the possibilities and the degree of participation in the expanding standards of mass consumption (Hirsch and Roth, 1986: 59). Pre-Fordist collective orientation was gradually removed, and the 'capitalist spirit' began to encompass the entire working class. Yet in contrast to the Calvinist period – when work itself was seen as a fulfilment and perceived as a sign of being part of the 'elect', and consumption was reduced to the absolute minimum (Weber, 1958) – work was now largely perceived as an alienating activity that had to be compensated for by unlimited commodified consumption.

4.2   Finance-driven capitalism

Regulationists have accounted for the tensions inherent in the Fordist consumption norm by indicating that the compensation provided by the consumption of commodities in order to alleviate the sufferings of the production sphere can never be complete. Instead of ensuring personal 'emancipation', when the continuous consumption of ever more commodities asserted itself during the Fordist period, it was sometimes perceived as even greater heteronomy with corresponding losses in individual autonomy and self-determination. At the same time, it became obvious to some that mass consumption systematically produced negative external effects – for example, in the form of traffic jams, environmental problems and disasters, and the degradation of cities – which began to compromise the use values of beloved consumption goods such as the car. Increasing numbers of people began to question the imperatives of Fordist growth and to form ecological movements and later green parties that brought together many of the fragmented political groups from the student revolts of the late 1960s. During the same time period, new women's movements broke with the patriarchal division of labour and thereby weakened one of the cornerstones of the Fordist mode of regulation and societalization: the nuclear family and the male breadwinner model. This, in turn, led to changes in demands for state support, particularly from single-parent families and elderly people. Finally, these changes were accompanied by the readjustment of the spatial arrangements of Fordism: issues of housing, for example, became relevant since single households were concentrated in urban areas that often had been abandoned by the middle classes. The trend towards suburbanization was partially reversed as a result. However, disruptive experiences with the Fordist mode of societalization and consumption caused only a minority to question their lifestyles. Most people simply increased their work efforts in order to achieve even higher incomes to acquire yet more commodities and to improve their chances in the competition of positional – that is, not arbitrarily – augmentable goods. The spiral of consumption and production continued to accelerate in the post-Fordist period.

A growing number of political economists such as Boyer (2000), Stockhammer (2008) and Krugman (2009) have argued that a new accumulation regime began to emerge after the 1970s that is characterized by transnationalized production and the liberalization of international capital flows inter alia. 'Financialization' covers a range of phenomena, including the deregulation of the financial sector and the liberalization of global capital flows, significant increases in financial transactions and the proliferation and profitability of new financial instruments and investors such as hedge funds. In addition to the growing influence of financial capital as opposed to industrial capital, the new growth strategy was also built on a structural weakening of organized labour vis-à-vis capital in general. Stockhammer (2008) theorizes these processes in terms of a shift from a 'management–labour' to a 'shareholder–management' balance. Reductions in real wages in the Western world were temporarily compensated by the facilitation of access of the working class to loans and other financial instruments.

While the Fordist mode of consumption was largely built upon the purchase of durable consumer goods, subsequent waves of commodified consumption, which restructured increasingly more areas of life, involved information and communication technologies such as the Internet. Entire new industries opened up in the 'entertainment' business, for example, as new generations of home computers, laptops, iPods and smartphones were launched on the market at ever-shorter intervals. 'Shopping', be it in malls or online, took on a new quality; in contrast to the post-war period when many of the purchased goods had essential use values (for washing, clothing, mobility, and so on), post-Fordist consumption patterns transcended the sphere of necessity. Following on from Bourdieu, consumer researchers and social psychologists presume that we develop an attachment to the things we own, which causes us to perceive material possessions as part of our 'extended self' (Belk, 1988, cited in Jackson, 2009: 64). Some of these possessions are 'fleeting' (Jackson, 2009: 64), that is, 'they burn with novelty momentarily and are extinguished as suddenly something else attracts our attention'. Others are more durable, sometimes providing a 'sanctuary for our most treasured memories and feelings'. In an increasingly secular world, individual choices of what is 'sacred' and what is 'profane' are usually no longer made in religious terms – as Durkheim (2001) observed a century ago – but upon the grounds of what Jackson (2009: 64) calls a new materialism that functions as a substitute for religious consolation.

On top of financialization via the indebtedness of private households, in the case of the Western working classes, the demand problem for further commodified private consumption was addressed by exporting the Western consumption norm to other parts of the world including Asia and Latin America. After import substitution ended, the markets of many developing countries were flooded with new media images and foreign consumer goods as a result. 'Western' lifestyles were promoted in advertising and the media, since the markets for consumer goods were not as saturated in the 'emerging economies' of China, India or Brazil whose relative weight and general significance in the world economy has grown over the last decades. Income levels rose for increasing percentages of these populations so that more people could afford consumption patterns previously associated with Western societies. Social structures and lifestyles evolved quickly as a result. Consumption patterns of the emerging urban middle classes started to differ qualitatively from those of the lower classes. The relative weight of necessity items such as food decreased in middle-class households, 'while discretionary spending (such as on recreation and education, transport and communication, housing and utilities, or household and personal items)' (Reusswig and Isensee, 2009: 132) increased. In a similar way to developments in the 1950s and 1960s in the USA and Western Europe, more Chinese people started to acquire the classic 'Fordist' consumer durables such as televisions, private cars and their modern counterparts (PCs, iPods, and so on) and, less often, a family property in suburban areas (Zhang et al., 2009: 145). This is being complemented by other originally Western cultural practices such as tennis or golf. At the same time, attitudes towards beauty contests, fashion shows, sexual behaviour and eating habits started to change and approximate Western patterns (Dittrich, 2009).

The significant relative price reduction for consumer goods for middle-class households and the rapid speed at which consumer markets in Asia and, to a lesser extent, Latin America have developed make it justifiable to speak of a 'second wave' of internal takeover of more and more areas of life by capitalism, following on from the first Fordist wave, particularly in Western Europe. Indeed, at no other point in time have so many people in the world participated in consumption patterns that used to be the privilege of elites. Developing countries, especially in Asia, are not just the 'factory of the world' due to the transfer and offshoring of industrial production from high labour cost countries to cheap labour cost locations. As in Western Europe after World War II, developing countries have become increasingly attractive as purchasers of 'Western' products. This popularization and generalization of consumption practices, previously the monopoly of the few, has rather obvious ecological downsides. Apart from requiring that ever-increasing quantities of the planet's finite natural resources are used for the production of consumer goods, thereby accelerating the greenhouse effect, the spread and intensification of the Western consumption norm has also significantly increased the mobility of many people. The explosion in the number of cars and the increased use of aeroplanes are important contributing factors to the high and growing levels of greenhouse gas emissions. Indeed, the dependence on massive quantities of fossil fuels is a structural feature that Fordism and finance-driven capitalism have in common.

Since the heyday of Fordism, this has led to increasing greenhouse gas emissions and the worsening of related environmental issues in most regions of the world.

5. Conclusion and further research

Consumption is too often misunderstood as the autonomous act of rationally acting sovereign individuals, while the close links between the social structures of production and consumption are not systematically considered. I have here suggested a regulation theoretical view which, in combination with an application of Bourdieusian sociology, can help understand the interlinking of the two spheres. As in all capitalist economies, these are shaped by the growth imperative. Relatively prosperous periods (*longues durées*) of capitalist growth emerge where both consumption and production norms expand in parallel. Concrete adjustments of the two norms vary and differ from one historical growth strategy to the next. The rather strong links between the growth imperative, institutional forms, and production and consumption norms suggest that the feasibility of achieving environmental sustainability via governance forms that exclusively focus on consumption – that is, without at the same time addressing the growth imperative and the sphere of production – is limited. Bourdieu in particular demonstrates that acts of consumption – via taste and distinction – tend to reproduce patterns of social inequality that, in turn, have their origin in the concrete forms of the capitalist division of labour.

From the theoretical point of view taken in this chapter, it would seem that the structural preconditions for any significant limitation to conspicuous consumption are simultaneously attempts to reduce structural inequality and reforms of the division of labour of communal, state and individual property: thus markets would play a significantly lesser role than currently. In this situation it is encouraging that scholars have started to discuss 'eco-social policies', which aim to address both social inequality and environmental sustainability issues. Such policies could help bring about a redistribution of work, wealth and pollution rights, and stimulate alternative forms of consumption in policy areas such as macroeconomic steering, minimum and maximum incomes, carbon rationing, the role of commons and the cooperative economy, as well as alternative monetary systems.[2] Proposals such as a maximum limit on income and wealth policies may facilitate a shift from a growth-oriented production and consumption regime towards one based on the stability of biophysical parameters. However, many of these, partially far-reaching, policy proposals have been developed in an isolated way by different groups without much contact. Future research should be dedicated to complementing and unifying these as yet fragmented proposals and to formulating a coherent strategy for the economic, political and ecological restructuring of rich countries.

Regulation theory and its core concepts such as 'institutional forms' have hitherto been successfully applied to understanding the links between production and consumption norms in the context of capitalist growth. Yet in the continuing absence of any empirical indication for an absolute decoupling of GDP growth, resource use and carbon emissions, future research could ask what kind of institutional forms may facilitate a planned degrowth process where monetary growth is deprioritized and biophysical indicators prioritized, and at the end of which human needs for everyone now and in the future are met within environmental limits. This applies especially to the role of money where local currencies may need to play a much more important role than today, and to that of international regimes and scale where a range of regulatory responsibilities may need to be upgraded to global levels. On the one hand, global governance networks would need to delineate thresholds for matter and energy throughput for production and consumption in accordance with natural science expertise. On the other hand, these would determine the room for manoeuvre within which national and local economies could evolve. Kothari (2018: 254), for example, suggests the assignment of 'a minimal set of matters' to the global level, while the bulk of decision-making would 'go to the most local level feasible' where he assumes that diverse approaches to meeting collective goals are most 'accepted and encouraged'.

A final institutional form to consider in relation to a degrowth transition is that of the state. The new division of labour across scales outlined above would in all likelihood mean a lesser role and a stricter regulation of market forces than currently. Without denying the allocative efficiency of markets altogether, these would nevertheless operate in much narrower limits given the primacy of global sustainability and intergenerational justice. Instead, a 'steering state' would at various levels be *primus inter pares* in a mixed economy and a governance network of public, collective, communal and private actors. New combinations of state and common ownership may be developed in relation to the governance of socio-natural resources such as energy and water. A concept that appears to be promising in this context and which could guide future research is that of a 'communal' or 'plurinational' state, with which Kothari (2018) analyses various experiences from Asian and Latin American countries where common values and visions of well-being from indigenous peoples, local communities and civil society have enriched policymaking on national levels.

NOTES

1 For a more recent application of Bourdieu's sociology of culture, see Bennett et al. (2009)

2 For thematic overviews of eco-social policies, see Büchs and Koch (2017: 112–23) and Gough (2017: 194–209).

References

Aglietta, Michel (1987), *A Theory of Capitalist Regulation: The US Experience*, 2nd edn, London: Verso.

Aglietta, Michel (2002), 'The international monetary system', in Robert Boyer and Yves Saillard (eds), *Regulation Theory: The State of the Art*, London: Taylor and Francis, pp. 64–72.

Beck, Ulrich (1992), *Risk Society: Towards a New Modernity*, London and New Delhi: Sage.

Bennett, Tony, Mike Savage, Elizabeth Silva et al. (2009), *Culture, Class, Distinction*, Abingdon, UK: Routledge.

Bertrand, Hughes (2002), 'The wage-labour nexus and the employment system', in Robert Boyer and Yves Saillard (eds), *Regulation Theory: The State of the Art*, London: Taylor and Francis, pp. 80–86.

Bourdieu, Pierre (1984), *Distinction: A Social Critique of Judgement and Taste*, Cambridge, MA: Harvard University Press.

Bourdieu, Pierre (2005), *The Social Structures of the Economy*, Cambridge: Polity.

Boyer, Robert (2000), 'Is a finance-led growth regime a viable alternative to Fordism? A preliminary analysis', *Economy and Society* **29** (1), 111–45.

Boyer, Robert (2008), 'Pierre Bourdieu, a theoretician of change? The view from regulation theory', in Alexander Ebner and Nikolaus Beck (eds), *The Institutions of the Market: Organizations, Social Systems, and Governance*, Oxford: Oxford University Press, pp. 348–98.

Boyer, Robert and Yves Saillard (eds) (2002), *Regulation Theory: The State of the Art*, London: Taylor and Francis.

Brenner, N. (2004), 'Urban governance and production of new state spaces in Western Europe, 1960–2000', *Review of International Political Economy* **11** (3), 447–88.

Büchs, Milena and Max Koch (2017), *Postgrowth and Wellbeing: Challenges to Sustainable Welfare*, Basingstoke, UK: Palgrave Macmillan.

D'Alisa, Giacomo, Federico Demaria and Giorgos Kallis (eds) (2014), *Degrowth: A Vocabulary for a New Era*, Abingdon, UK: Routledge.

Dittrich, Christoph (2009), 'The changing food scenario and the middle classes in the emerging megacity of Hyderabad, India', in Hellmuth Lange and Lars Meier (eds), *The New Middle Classes: Globalizing Lifestyles, Consumerism and Environmental Concern*, Dordrecht, Heidelberg, London and New York: Springer, pp. 269–80.

Durkheim, Emile (2001), *The Elementary Forms of the Religious Life*, Oxford: Oxford University Press.

Gough, Ian (2017), *Heat, Greed and Human Need: Climate Change, Capitalism and Sustainable Wellbeing*, Cheltenham, UK and Northampton, MA, USA: Edward Elgar Publishing.

Guttmann, Robert (2002), 'Money and credit in regulation theory', in Robert Boyer and Yves Saillard (eds), *Regulation Theory: The State of the Art*, London: Taylor and Francis, pp. 57–63.

Hirsch, Joachim and Roland Roth (1986), *Das neue Gesicht des Kapitalismus: Vom Fordismus zum Postfordismus*, Hamburg: VSA.

Jackson, Tim (2009), *Prosperity without Growth? The Transition to a Sustainable Economy*, London: Sustainable Development Commission.

Koch, Max (2012), *Capitalism and Climate Change: Theoretical Discussion, Historical Development and Policy Responses*, Basingstoke, UK: Palgrave Macmillan.

Koch, Max (2018), 'The naturalisation of growth: Marx, the regulation approach and Bourdieu', *Environmental Values*, **27** (1), 9–27.

Koch, Max and Oksana Mont (eds) (2016), *Sustainability and the Political Economy of Welfare*, Abingdon, UK: Routledge.

Koch, Max, Hubert Buch-Hansen and Martin Fritz (2017), 'Shifting priorities in degrowth research: An argument for the centrality of human needs', *Ecological Economics*, **138**, 74–81.

Kothari, A., (2018), 'Towards radical alternatives to development', in Hartmut Rosa and Christoph Henning (eds), *The Good Life beyond Growth: New Perspectives*, London: Routledge, pp. 251–62.

Krugman, Paul (2009), *The Return of Depression Economics and the Crisis of 2008*, New York and London: W.W. Norton and Company.

Lorek, Sylvia and Doris Fuchs (2013), 'Strong sustainable consumption governance – precondition for a degrowth path?', *Journal of Cleaner Production*, **38**, 36–43.

Lutz, Burghart (1989), *Der kurze Traum immerwährender Prosperität*, Frankfurt and New York: Campus.

Marcus, Alan and Howard Segal (1989), *Technology in America: A Brief History*, San Diego and New York: Harcourt Brace Jovanovich.

Paterson, Matthew and Xavier P. Laberge (2018), 'Political economies of climate change', *WIREs Climate Change*, **9** (2), e506.

Pichler, Melanie, Anke Schaffartzik, Helmut Haberl and Christoph Görg (2017), 'Drivers of society-nature relations in the Anthropocene and their implications for sustainability transformations', *Current Opinion in Environmental Sustainability*, **26**, 32–6.

Reusswig, Fritz and Andre Isensee (2009), 'Rising capitalism, emerging middle-classes and environmental perspectives', in Hellmuth Lange and Lars Meier (eds), *The New Middle Classes: Globalizing Lifestyles, Consumerism and Environmental Concern*, Dordrecht, Heidelberg, London and New York: Springer, pp. 119–42.

Shove, Elizabeth (2010), 'Beyond the ABC: Climate change policy and theories of social change', *Environment and Planning, A* **42**, 1273–85.

Spash, Clive (ed.) (2017), *Routledge Handbook of Ecological Economics: Nature and Society*, Abingdon, UK: Routledge.

Steffen, Will, Katherine Richardson, Johan Rockström et al. (2015), 'Planetary boundaries: Guiding human development on a changing planet', *Science*, **347** (6223).

Stockhammer, Englebert (2008), 'Some stylized facts on the finance-dominated accumulation regime', *Competition and Change*, **12** (2), 184–202.

Weber, Max (1958), *The Protestant Ethic and the Spirit of Capitalism*, Abingdon, UK: Routledge.

Zhang, Yaoqi, Jinyang Deng, Suman Majumdar et al. (2009), 'Golfing in China', in Hellmuth Lange and Lars Meier (eds), *The New Middle Classes: Globalizing Lifestyles, Consumerism and Environmental Concern*, Dordrecht, Heidelberg, London and New York: Springer, pp. 143–58.

4 Quantifying environmental impacts of consumption: Implications for governance

Arnold Tukker

1. Introduction

Ultimately, all production is driven by consumption. It is hence final consumption by humanity that drives the environmental impacts of production. In the past, global trade was just a small part of the economic production within a country. At that time, the monitoring of carbon and other emissions and resource extraction at country level was reasonably representative of the environmental pressures caused by consumption in each country. However, in recent decades, growth in international trade has outpaced the growth of global gross domestic product (GDP). It is no longer sufficient to analyse the impacts of production at national level (Peters et al., 2011; Wiedmann et al., 2011). Consumption in one country drives production in value chains spanning many others. This creates a complex, global web of activities impacting the environment in multi-faceted ways (Tukker and Dietzenbacher, 2013). For proper governance of sustainable consumption, it is essential to understand how consumption of specific categories of goods and services in specific countries (and ideally by specific consumer groups) drive environmental impacts in global value chains.

Against this background, this chapter will review how final consumption drives environmental pressures, identify the priority areas, and address crucial consumption drivers. We start by reviewing methods for analysing the impacts of consumption, then look at priority consumption areas and the main drivers. This is followed by proposals for methods to analyse the relation between consumption and the impacts of production can be made more reliable and robust before ending with conclusions and governance implications.

2. Approaches for assessing impacts of consumption

To deal with the assessment of environmental pressures in trade, practitioners use two broad approaches (see Tukker et al., 2016). The first is the *coefficient* approach and has been frequently applied with regard to water and land use (Hoekstra and Chapagain, 2007; Moran et al., 2009). This approach uses the detailed trade statistics of, for example, the UN Comtrade Database (United Nations, 2014–17) and FAOSTAT, the statistical system of the Food and Agricultural Organization of the United Nations (Food and Agricultural Organization of the United Nations, n.d.), the former, for instance, covering over 5000 products traded between countries. This means that water or land use per kilogramme or the monetary value of a product imported from the country of export can be analysed, detailing the water and land use embodied in imports. National statistics give information on national water and land use, and also enable the calculation of the water and land use embodied in exports. The net water and land use of each product can be estimated from the water and land use of national production and of imports and exports.

This example focuses on land and water pressures for a reason: agricultural products are the main drivers for land and water use. These tend to be produced in the country of export and do not have supply chains with major water and land use impacts. This approach, however, neglects water and land use related to other imported products, which, according to Hubacek and Feng (2016), can lead to relevant errors in consumption-based accounts for land, to give one example. A significant drawback of the coefficient approach is that it assumes that an imported product was manufactured solely in the country of export, thus neglecting the current situation where many products are created in value chains that span several countries, each with its own coefficients for emissions and resource use. Figure 4.1 provides a stylized example. The imports of country C from B are 110 units. A coefficient approach would estimate the emissions and resource use per unit production in country B, and allocate this number multiplied by 110 units to country C. In reality, however, of the 110 units that country C imports no less than 100 units of added value are created in country A, and only 10 units in Country B. Thus most of the emissions and resource use in the country C imports take place in country A, even though all country C imports come from country B. Particularly for non-agricultural products, which tend to have complex value chains, the coefficient approach does not give an appropriate answer on how consumption in country C drives carbon and other emissions and resource use elsewhere in the world.

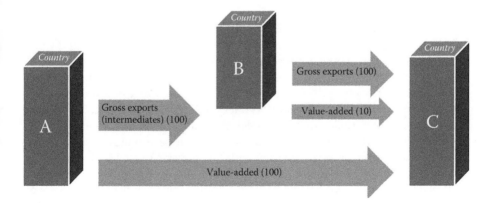

Figure 4.1   Gross exports and trade in value added

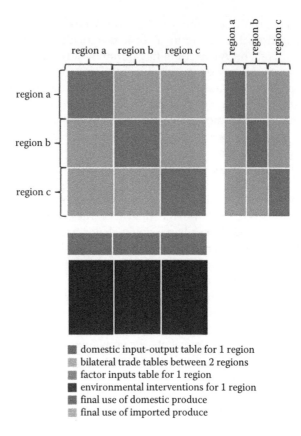

Figure 4.2   Example of MR EE SUT/IOT with three regions

Therefore, practitioners have developed a second method, making use of Multi-Regional Environmentally Extended Supply and Use/Input-Output Tables' (MR EE SUT/IOT, e.g. Tukker et al., 2016).

Figure 4.2 shows a typical MR EE SUT/IOT with a country's total economy where production is divided into a few dozen industry sectors and consumption divided into a few dozen product (and service) groups. Figure 4.2 depicts how much of these specific products (output), for example cars, is produced by each industry sector, expressed in euros. It also shows for each industry sector how many other products are required to achieve this production (input), for example, the amount of steel, glass, plastics, electricity and electronics the car industry in that country needs to produce its output of cars. Furthermore, for each industry, the primary resource use and emissions ('environmental extensions') can be identified, for example, land use by agricultural sector, or CO_2 emissions by electricity production sector. Thus the ways in which the economy is interconnected can be analysed. One example is the final use of cars by consumers; here the production value contributed by the car industry, the steel industry and so on, can be analysed. But

---

Box 4.1 METHODS FOR ASSESSING POLLUTION AND RESOURCE USE EMBODIED IN TRADE

1. Using emission and resource use coefficients for foreign countries derived with Life Cycle Inventories (LCIs) in combination with trade data on imported products (Schoer et al., 2013).
2. Applying the 'Domestic Technology Assumption' (DTA), that is, assuming that imported products are produced with the same technologies as domestically produced products (Wood and Dey, 2009).
3. Applying the DTA corrected for purchasing power parities, or relative prices of imports compared to European production (Tukker et al., 2013a).
4. Using emission and resource coefficients for foreign countries derived with Environmentally Extended Input Output (EE IO) data for these countries, taking into account bilateral trade only (Lenzen et al., 2004).
5. Using available environmental Global Multi-Regional Input Output (GMRIO) databases at face value, and calculating footprints of a country with such a GMRIO (Tukker et al., 2016).
6. Using official data for a specific country for which environmental footprints need to be calculated, and adjusting and rebalancing an existing GMRIO by implementing the aforementioned country specific data in it. This is also called a 'single-country national accounts consistent (SNAC) footprint' (Edens et al., 2015).
7. Using official data for a specific country for which footprints are calculated, but using the full environmental GMRIO model only to calculate pollution and resources in imports rather than creating a new GMRIO adjusted to this specific country.

---

since we also know the emissions and primary resource extraction per monetary unit (euros or US dollars) for each industry, we can now estimate the total primary resource extraction and life cycle emissions for the total consumption of cars in that country (see Eurostat, 2008; Miller and Blair, 2009). The example above is for one country only, and as indicated, imports and exports in the current global economy are substantial.

Practitioners have sought various solutions to this problem (for an overview, see Tukker et al. 2018a), summarized in Box 4.1.

The simplest approach is using a national input–output table and assuming that the pollution and resource use of imported products is identical to that of nationally produced products (DTA). A slightly more sophisticated approach is to correct for relative prices of domestically produced and imported products (price-corrected domestic technology assumption). However, these two approaches do not account for country-specific intensities for emissions and resource use by production sector. To address this, a multi-regional input–output approach must be used. It is necessary to create EE SUT/IOT data for the most important world economies and to identify the trade flows between the specific sectors of all these countries (Peters et al., 2012; Tukker et al., 2013b). The result is the aforementioned MR EE SUT/IOT, which gives a detailed picture of all linkages between production and consumption in the global economy. Figure 4.2 provides an example with three regions.

Table 4.1   Characteristics of existing GMRIOs

No.	Name	Characteristics and references
1	Eora	Sector detail varying from 25 to 500; about 180 countries (Lenzen et al., 2012a; 2012b; 2013)
2	EXIOBASE	200 products, 160 industries, 48 countries/regions (Tukker et al., 2009; 2013b; Wood et al., 2014; 2015; Stadler et al., 2017)
3	WIOD	35 sectors, 40 countries plus 1 Rest of World (Dietzenbacher et al., 2013)
4	GTAP-MRIO	57 sectors, 140 countries/regions (Peters et al., 2011)
5	ICIO (Inter-country Input-Output table)	34 sectors, 64 countries/regions (OECD, 2015). Researchers used OECD IO data to build an early GMRIO called GRAM: 48 sectors, 53 countries/region (Wiebe et al., 2012a, 2012b; Bruckner et al., 2015)

Source: Tukker and Dietzenbacher, 2013; Tukker et al., 2018a; 2018b.

Creating MR EE IO databases is, however, labour intensive, even if this is done via automation (Wood et al., 2015) or virtual laboratory environments (Lenzen et al., 2014). Only a handful of such databases have been constructed (Table 4.1). While MR EE IO databases have drawbacks like an aggregated sector classification, and assume that economic flows are a reasonable representation of physical flows (Weisz and Duchin, 2006), their strength is their inherent consistency at global level. All direct emissions of greenhouse gases (GHG) and primary extraction/use of water, land and materials, as well as the number of jobs and added value created by industries are, by definition, directly related to the final consumption of products – these cannot be 'lost' in the calculations. The MR EE IO approach is now the method of choice to assess how final consumption, via value chains, drives emissions and resource use per economic sector per country.

3.   Drivers and priorities of environmental impacts of household consumption

3.1   Introduction

We now turn to the assessment of the impacts of consumption and related priority areas. One of the first reviews of such analyses was done in the context of the environmental impacts of products (EIPRO) project funded by the EU and published as a special issue of the *Journal of Industrial Ecology* (Tukker, 2006). This review will be expanded below with more recent work.[1] Most studies focus on energy use, CO_2 emissions or GHG emissions. We first review these results as well as other indicators that not all studies reviewed have covered (such as land use, water use, etc.).

3.2   Priority consumption categories[2]

Table 4.2 shows results of energy-related indicators (expanded from Tukker and Jansen (2006). Final consumption categories have been reclassified and aggregated to over ten COICOP (Classification of Individual Consumption According to Purpose) categories. It should be noted that most studies focused on total final consumption, that is, combining household consumption, government consumption and sometimes also exports.[3]

Table 4.2 shows a clear pattern (Hertwich, 2005). Food, housing (including electrical appliances) and individual transport dominate the use of energy, CO_2 emissions and GHG emissions. In all studies each of these categories tends to contribute between 15% and 30% of the total impacts, and add up to 70% or more of the total. Deviations from this pattern are due to methodological issues. Nemry et al. (2002) and Labouze et al. (2003), for example, have low contributions of food due to the fact that food was either not included or since methane emissions, particularly relevant in the production of rice and animal husbandry, were neglected. Consequently, the relative contribution of housing and transport in their work may have been overestimated. We further see that in the study of Palm et al. (2006). Here, transport is relatively low since this is a specific sector for all household-related energy use. Finally, Peters and Hertwich's study (2006) gives a relatively high contribution of transport to the overall CO_2 emissions of household consumption, while overall emissions per capita in Norway are relatively low, largely thanks to abundant hydroelectric power. Furthermore, Nijdam and Wilting (2003) have a relatively high contribution from recreation, largely because this category includes package holidays, which in other studies would be classified under transport.

The conclusion that food, housing and transport drive some 70% of the impacts of final consumption has consistently been confirmed by later studies including a 2010 review of the International Resources Panel (Weber and Matthews, 2008b; Kerkhof et al., 2009; Hertwich et al., 2010; Huysman et al., 2016; Tukker et al., 2016; Ivanova et al., 2017). Tukker and Jansen (2006) also analysed which subgroups within the areas of food, mobility and housing were relevant. In the case of food, this was meat and meat products (including poultry); milk, cheese, and related products; other non-animal food products; and expenditures in restaurants. For housing, this concerned heating equipment, cooking equipment, and hot water generation equipment (particularly due to their energy use); (electrical) energy-using products; and housing construction. Finally, for transport, relevant subcategories are private car travel (highly dominant); air travel services; train travel services; and travel related to package holidays.

Tukker and Jansen (2006) also looked at other impact indicators, such as resource extraction and water use and land use. Again, the same categories of food, housing and transport were responsible for over 70% of the impacts driven by final consumption. The relative importance differs however by final consumption category. Water use and particularly land use are mainly driven by food consumption. For resource use, housing, transport and food have more equal contributions.

Table 4.2 Contribution per COICOP category to energy-related impact indicators in different studies

COICOP		1	2		4	5	6	7	8	9	10
Study	% of total expenditure in EU25 Tukker and Jansen (2006)	Collins et al. (2006)	Dall et al. (2002)	Labouze et al. (2003)	Moll and Acosta (2006)	Jansen and Thollier (2006)	de Vries and te Riele (2006), Nijdam and Wilting (2003)	Palm et al. (2006)	Peters and Hertwich (2006)	Huppes et al. (2006)	Druckman and Jackson, 2008
Geographical focus	EU25	Cardiff	Denmark	EU15	Germany	Belgium	Netherlands	Sweden	Norway	EU25	UK
Indicator		Footprint	Energy	GWP	Energy	GWP	GWP	CO2	CO2	GWP	CO2
Main approach		Top-down/ hybrid	Bottom-up	Bottom-up	Top-down	Bottom-up	Top-down	Top-down	Top-down	Top-down	Top-down
CP01–02 Food	19.3%	20.6%	26.2%	7.0%**	13.0%	3.6%**	22.1%	7.7%	12.2%	31.0%	15%
CP03 Clothing	3.1%	0.8%	1.3%	3.3%	2.2%	1.3%	6.5%	0.7%	10.3%	2.4%	11%
CP04–05 Housing	25.1%	30.2%	40.8%	58.8%	54.3%	53.5%	33.4%	29.1%	23.0%	23.6%	27%
CP06 Health	3.9%	0.3%	n/a***	n/a	1.8%	0.3%	0.3%	1.0%	1.1%	1.6%	8%
CP07 Transport	14.1%	21.9%	19.5%	29.6%	18.3%	32.9%	17.3%	15.5%	35.9%	18.5%	9%
CP08 Communication	4.0%	0.5%	n/a	0.0%	n/a	2.9%	0.0%	1.7%	2.1%	2.1%	1%
CP09 Recreation	9.1%	10.2%	7.2%	0.0%	8.1%	n/a	15.1%	0.5%	0.5%	6.0%	26%
CP10 Education	1.4%	0.4%	n/a	n/a	1.8%	n/a	0.7%	0.3%	0.1%	0.5%	2%
CP11 Restaurants	9.6%	10.8%	n/a	n/a	n/a	n/a	2.8%	1.8%	1.3%	9.1%	See CP09
CP12 Miscellaneous	10.3%	4.4%	5.1%	1.3%	0.4%	5.4%	1.8%	6.6%	13.1%	5.2%	–
Other Refined petroleum products / Direct household energy*								35.0%			–
TOTAL	100%	100%	100%	100%	100%	100%	100%	100%	100%	100%	100%

Notes:

* Palm et al (2006) reported energy use by households as a separate category. To be distributed over housing and transport.

** Nemry et al (2002) did not include food in their study; this value is related to packaging for food. Labouze et al. (2003) under-estimated the impacts of food for a variety of reasons in their work; see Tukker and Jansen (2006).

*** n/a: not visible as a specific category in the underlying study

3.3   Determining variables

Various authors have analysed the determining variables that explain high or low environmental footprints of household consumption (e.g. Lenzen et al., 2006; Tukker et al., 2010; Ivanova et al, 2015; 2017). Literature tends to agree on such determining variables. These are listed here, largely following the earlier text of Tukker et al. (2010), expanded with factors mentioned by Ivanova et al. (2017), who compared the per capita carbon emissions of consumption at detailed regional level in Europe, and carried out a quantitative correlation analysis between such factors and carbon emissions.

- *Income*: Environmental impacts rise with household income since increasing affluence enables consumers to use more energy and to acquire larger volumes of material goods. In general, luxury goods generate smaller additional impacts per monetary unit compared to goods designed to meet basic needs (Druckman and Jackson, 2008; Weber and Matthews, 2008b; Kerkhof et al., 2009). Some literature suggests that consumption-based impacts may rise proportionally more than with income (Baiocchi et al., 2010).
- *Household size*: Per capita environmental impacts vary inversely with household size. People living under the same roof share energy-using appliances and cohabitants tend to require less individual living space (and related heating and cooling demands) than single household occupants (Weber and Matthews, 2008b). A generally positive correlation exists between household size and emissions in absolute terms, however. These analyses lead to two important observations – growing populations and decreasing household sizes both lead to increases in emissions (Liu et al., 2003; Wilson and Boehland, 2005).
- *Location*: Urban residents are typically responsible for fewer overall environmental impacts than people living in suburbs or rural communities. First, urban dwellings are generally smaller and, due to higher building densities, have less exposed surface area than suburban homes. Second, suburbanites and rural residents usually have high automobile dependency (Ewing and Cervero, 2001; Sanne, 2002; Jackson, 2003).
- *Automobile ownership*: Given that mobility is responsible for a substantial proportion of the environmental impacts that emanate from household consumption, people who use public transport on a regular basis generally have smaller footprints. An important caveat, however, is that public transport tends to be less expensive than automobile ownership. Spending this saved income can lead to significant rebound effects (Ornetzeder et al., 2008). Ivanova et al. (2015) mention that access to forests and semi-natural areas may help foster low-carbon leisure activities (walking, skiing, etc.) but could also lead to higher use of natural resources.
- *Food consumption patterns*: Vegetarians and consumers who eat locally harvested, seasonal, or organic food generally have lower per capita environmental impacts than individuals who rely on more customary diets (Garnett, 2008; Weber and Matthews, 2008a; Tukker et al., 2011). The assessment becomes

more complicated when local fruit and vegetables produced in energy-inten-
sive greenhouses are compared with the 'food miles' accrued by field-grown
alternatives from distant locations (Blanke and Burdick, 2005; Pretty et al.,
2005).

- *Social and cultural differences*: Going back at least as far as the work of
  Erickson (1997), researchers have recognized the variation that exists in
  energy consumption across countries of similar incomes. Although some of
  this variability can be attributed to population density, infrastructure, and so
  forth, it is also important to recognize how different social and cultural pre-
  dispositions temper prevalent understandings pertaining to the use of energy
  and materials (Marechal, 2009).
- *Geographic location and housing type*: Residents of climatically extreme
  regions who have low-quality, poorly insulated homes tend to have compara-
  tively high environmental impacts. The situation is more complicated than a
  simple case of relatively warmer or cooler climates, however. One also needs
  to account for the vastly different policy circumstances created by housing
  stock that is predominantly owner-occupied versus renter-occupied as well
  as factors related to how different information technologies (feedback) and
  energy-control devices (e.g. thermostats) can differently affect household
  energy consumption without changes in price or other policy parameters
  (Wood and Newborough, 2007; Burgess and Nye, 2008).
- *Tertiary education*: According to Chancel and Piketty (2015), education and
  social status could lead to individual preferences, both of which can result in
  more or less emission intensive lifestyles.
- *Electricity mix*: Households usually have limited influence on the average electricity mix that is offered in a country. Countries such as Sweden and Norway
  that rely heavily on hydroelectric power (also nuclear in Sweden) tend to have
  lower carbon emissions per capita than other developed nations.

Income appears to have the highest explanatory factor, explaining 29% of household
emissions. As well as the electricity mix, heating degree days are another important
factor. Impacts related to expenditure on clothing, mobility and manufactured
products appear to be rather income inelastic. Higher members per household
reduces impact; additional rooms per household increases impact; higher education levels increases impact, particularly due to food consumption (higher animal
protein consumption). The differentiation between urban and rural regions appears
to be insignificant except for mobility.

4.   Discussion: improved monitoring of how consumption drives environmental impacts

The sections above demonstrate a clear consensus about the most important
consumption categories that drive the impact of household consumption, as well
as their determining variables. Virtually all studies single out food (meat, dairy,
followed by the rest), housing (heating, cooling, electrical equipment and construc-

tion) and transport (private car driving, followed by public transport and air travel) as the priorities. There is robust agreement that factors such as income, the numbers of dwellers per household, house size, and the electricity mix are among the most important explanatory variables of the impacts of household consumption. Such top-level insights provide a good basis for a governance agenda in support of sustainable consumption. Some suggestions will be made in the conclusions.

Having said this, a sustainable consumption governance agenda is also supported by the availability of sound monitoring mechanisms. These enable the analysis of the effectiveness of governance interventions and how behavioural change, via changes in expenditure patterns, may lead to lower impacts along global value chains. In principle, time series of the (global) MRIO models discussed in this chapter allow such monitoring. If we have knowledge of expenditure patterns by income group or consumer type, in particular, it would be possible to see how changes in impacts of consumption relate to changes in expenditure patterns, income level, efficiency gains in production processes, structural economic change, or change in source country of imported products. This, however, relies on the availability of more detailed consumption expenditure data by income group globally (see Ivanova et al., 2017), and creating more robust GMRIO databases while ensuring these are updated annually. Currently, environmental footprints of consumption calculated with different MRIO databases still vary significantly. Interestingly, differences in the emission and resource extraction data per country appear to be a dominant factor in calculated differences in footprints. The solution for this problem is obvious: the harmonization of databases used to compile extensions like CO_2 and other emissions, resource extractions, water and land use. The next important factor contributing to uncertainty is the estimation of a country's GDP as a percentage of global GDP, in addition to the structure of the MRIO of a specific country as captured in a specific GMRIO. The least important factor, surprisingly, appears to be the estimation of global trade relations (see Owen, 2017; Tukker et al., 2018b). This leads to the following suggestions for improved monitoring of how consumption drives (global) environmental impacts:

1. Harmonize the most important factors contributing to uncertainty in GMRIO databases as listed above.
2. Create an institutional context in which GMRIO databases are regularly updated, instead of those being currently developed by short-term academic projects without permanent funding.
3. Ensure that GMRIO databases have sufficient detail for monitoring the shift towards sustainable consumption. First, product and sector detail is relevant for calculating sound water, material, and land footprints. Consumption items like beef with high footprints and beans with low footprints should be visible, for example, and illustrating the impact of diet change is also important (Lenzen, 2011; de Koning et al., 2015; Tukker et al., 2018b). Second, consumption expenditure patterns by income category and consumer type should ideally be available to monitor the influence of income and life-style changes.

Tukker et al. (2018b) suggest the following roadmap for such improvements.[4] In the short term, basic harmonization of existing GMRIO databases constructed by scientists could be realized as follows. First, harmonized databases for extensions should be developed or used, such as the resource extraction database recently developed by the UN International Resources Panel (IRP). Here, particularly work on water, land and emission extensions remains to be done. It is likely that such simple measures could reduce the differences in calculations of footprints of nations with different databases by over 50%.

A further step towards a higher level of credibility of GMRIO databases could be made as follows: the Organisation for Economic Co-operation and Development (OECD) produces currently the ICIO GMRIO, which has a (too) high level of aggregation of 30 sectors, with the aim of performing footprint analyses. Using procedures developed for EXIOBASE and Eora, ICIO GMRIO could be detailed to an appropriate level for footprint analyses, and combined with the common environmental extension databases.[5] This would lead to a GMRIO database with an appropriate level of detail, but in which important elements (the structure at the level of 30 sectors globally and extensions) are harmonized and endorsed by important organizations such as the OECD and UN IRP.

Finally, the problem that even such a GMRIO database overrides national accounts data can be overcome by applying the SNAC or 'simplified SNAC' procedure described in Box 4.1. This simplified SNAC procedure can be applied for all countries that have limited 'feedback emissions' (i.e. emissions and resource use in their exports that also appear in their imports via global value chains). This is the case for almost all countries except China and the USA. If a semi-standardized GMRIO were available and combined with available national accounts data, the calculation of country footprints would be a rather straightforward exercise.

In the long term, bodies such as the UN Statistical Division, World Bank, OECD, Eurostat and National Statistical Institutes (NSIs) should be provided with the resources to make national accounts, and particularly the importing and exporting of data, consistent at the global level at regular time intervals, ideally yearly. The World Bank already has set up a detailed consumption expenditure database by income group for some 160 low- and medium-income countries. Ideally this database would be expanded to all countries globally and annually updated (World Bank, 2017). Unlike researchers, such official organizations (particularly NSIs) have access to data of unprecedented quality and detail and, in principle, are in the best position to provide high-quality statistics that at the same time are consistent at global level. From the experience of compiling the existing GMRIO databases, they could identify the most pressing inconsistencies at international level as input to the continuous improvement processes already applied in their regular data inventory and reconciliation work.

5. Conclusions

This chapter has reviewed the findings of studies in the last 10 to 15 years that have analysed how final consumption drives environmental impacts along global value chains. Since trade – and with this, embodied emissions and resource use – has exploded in recent decades, monitoring environmental impacts of consumption at national level is insufficient. Impacts of consumption of product category x in country y can take place largely abroad. Global Multi-Regional Input Output Tables (GMRIO) have become the method of choice for monitoring the relation between final consumption by country and product and environmental impacts along global value chains.

Work thus far shows convincingly that housing (cooling and heating), food consumption (meat and dairy followed by the rest), mobility (car and air transport) and the use of electrical appliances dominate impacts of consumption. Income and household size are among the most important indirect drivers of impacts of consumption. This provides a number of obvious leverage points for the reduction of the impacts of consumption: stimulate carbon neutral housing, discourage low-density use of houses, make the energy system carbon neutral, stimulate low-meat and low-dairy diets, make cities compact and provide alternative mobility options for car ownership (e.g. public transport, e-bikes), minimize energy use of appliances via product policy and stimulate low-impact expenditures in general while potentially stimulating a good quality of life without significant growth in future income. For policymakers, the main message of this chapter is hence that governance approaches stimulating sustainable consumption could be focused on such solutions.

GMRIO databases with appropriate detail are an excellent tool to monitor the effectiveness of governance approaches that stimulate sustainable consumption and lifestyles. For this purpose, existing GMRIO databases should be harmonized, particularly with regard to environmental extensions, to reduce uncertainty in current footprint assessments. Furthermore, GMRIO databases should be regularly updated, ideally by providing resources to international organizations or collaborative NSIs. Finally, monitoring of expenditures on specific products and services by country ideally is differentiated by income category or consumer type, following the example of the World Bank consumption database (World Bank, 2017). Such an infrastructure would make it possible to assess changes in the impact of consumption by income category by country as well as the factors that drive such changes such as changes in consumption patterns, changes in income, efficiency improvements in production, or structural changes in the economy including trade patterns. For scientists and statistical professionals, the main message is hence to embark on further work on the monitoring system outlined here, while policymakers taking sustainable consumption governance seriously need to acknowledge that resources must be made available to enable such an effort.

NOTES

1 The choice of adding additional studies is only arbitrary. The field of environmental footprint analyses has exploded and a great number of papers are now available (e.g. Hoekstra, 2010). It is not the purpose of this chapter to provide a complete review, but merely to provide main indications of the priority areas.
2 This section summarizes and expands upon Tukker and Jansen (2006)
3 The data of Collins et al. (2006) deal only with household expenditure. Palm et al. (2006) concentrate all energy-related household emissions in a specific energy-related emissions sector in their IO table.
4 The text below largely follows the concluding section of Tukker et al. (2018a)
5 In this, we assume the ICIO database is using also harmonized data that ensure the GDP or final demand in a country is a sound representation of the percentage of global GDP, another factor that can influence footprint calculations significantly.

References

Ahmad N. and J. Ribarsky (2014), 'Trade in value added, jobs and investment', paper prepared for the 33rd IARIW General Conference, Rotterdam, the Netherlands, 24–30 August 2014.

Baiocchi, G., J. Minx and K. Hubacek (2010), 'The impact of social factors and consumer behavior on CO_2 emissions in the UK: A panel regression based on input-output and geo-demographic consumer segmentation data', *Journal of Industrial Ecology*, **14** (1), 50–72.

Blanke, M. and B. Burdick (2005), 'Food (miles) for thought: Energy balance for locally-grown versus imported apple fruit', *Environmental Science and Pollution Research*, **12** (3), 125–7.

Bruckner, Martin, Günther Fischer, Sylvia Tramberend et al. (2015), 'Measuring telecouplings in the global land system: A review and comparative evaluation of land footprint accounting methods', *Ecological Economics*, **114**, 11–21.

Burgess, J. and M. Nye (2008), 'Re-materialising energy use through transparent monitoring systems', *Energy Policy*, **36** (12), 4454–9.

Chancel L. and T. Piketty (2015), 'Carbon and inequality: from Kyoto to Paris', Paris School of Economics, accessed 22 November 2018 at http://piketty.pse.ens.fr/files/ChancelPiketty2015.pdf.

Collins, A., A. Flynn, T. Wiedmann et al. (2006), 'The environmental impacts of consumption at a sub-national level: The ecological footprint of Cardiff', *Journal of Industrial Ecology*, **10** (3), 9–24.

Dall, O., J. Toft, and T. T. Andersen (2002), 'Danske husholdningers miljøbelastning' ['Environmental pressure from Danish households'], Arbejdsrapport 13, Copenhagen: Ministry of Environment.

de Koning, A., M. Bruckner, S. Lutter et al. (2015), 'Effect of aggregation and disaggregation on embodied material use of products in input–output analysis', *Ecological Economics*, **116** (2015), 289–99.

de Vries, J. and H. te Riele (2006), 'Playing with hyenas: Renovating environmental product policy strat-egy', *Journal of Industrial Ecology*, **10** (3), 111–27.

Dietzenbacher, E., B. Los, R. Stehrer et al. (2013), 'The construction of world input–output tables in the WIOD project', *Economic Systems Research*, **25** (1), 71–98.

Druckman, A. and T. Jackson (2008), 'Household energy consumption in the UK: A highly geographi-cally and socio-economically disaggregated model', *Energy Policy*, **36** (8), 3177–92.

Edens, B., R. Hoekstra, D. Zult et al. (2015), 'A method to create carbon footprint estimates consistent with national accounts', *Economic Systems Research*, **27**, 1–18.

Erickson, R. (1997), *Paper or Plastic? Energy, Environment, and Consumerism in Sweden and America*, Westport, CT: Praeger.

Eurostat (2008), *Eurostat Manual of Supply, Use and Input-Output Tables*, Luxembourg: Office for Official Publications of the European Communities.

Ewing, R. and R. Cervero (2001), 'Travel and the built environment', *Transportation Research Record*, **1780**, 87–113.

Food and Agriculture Organization of the United Nations (n.d.), FAO Statistical Database, accessed 17 February 2019 at http://www.fao.org/faostat/en/#home.

Garnett, T. (2008), 'Cooking up a storm: Food, greenhouse gas emissions, and our changing climate', Guildford, UK: Centre for Environmental Strategy, University of Surrey.

Hertwich, E. (2005), 'Life cycle approaches to sustainable consumption: A critical review', *Environmental Science and Technology*, **39** (13), 4673–84.

Hertwich E.G., E. van der Voet, S. Suh et al. (2010), *Assessing the Environmental Impacts of Consumption and Production: Priority Products and Materials*, Paris: UNEP.

Hoekstra, A.Y. and A.K. Chapagain (2007), 'Water footprints of nations: Water use by people as a function of their consumption pattern', *Water Resources Management*, **21** (1), 35–48.

Hoekstra, R. (2010), 'Towards a complete database of peer-reviewed articles on environmentally extended input-output analysis', paper prepared for the 18th International Input–Output Conference, 20–25 June, Sydney, Australia.

Hubacek, K. and K. Feng (2016), 'Comparing apples and oranges: Some confusion about using and interpreting physical trade matrices versus multi-regional input-output analysis', *Land Use Policy*, **50**, 194–201.

Huppes, G., A. de Koning, S. Suh et al. (2006), 'Environmental impacts of consumption in the European Union: High-resolution input–output tables with detailed environmental extensions', *Journal of Industrial Ecology*, **10** (3), 129–46.

Huysman, Sofie, Thomas Schaubroeck, Malgorzata Goralczyk et al. (2016), 'Quantifying the environmental impacts of a European citizen through a macro-economic approach, a focus on climate change and resource consumption', *Journal of Cleaner Production*, **124**, 217–25.

Ivanova D., K. Stadler, K. Steen-Olsen et al. (2015), 'Environmental impact assessment of household consumption', *Journal of Industrial Ecology*, **20**, 526–36.

Ivanova, Diana, Gibran Vita, Kjartan Steen-Olsen et al. (2017), 'Mapping the carbon footprint of EU regions', *Environmental Research Letters*, **12** (5), 054013.

Jackson, L. (2003), 'The relationship of urban design to human health and condition', *Landscape and Urban Planning*, **64** (4), 191–200.

Jansen, B. and K. Thollier (2006), 'Bottom-up life-cycle assessment of product consumption in Belgium', *Journal of Industrial Ecology*, **10** (3), 41–55.

Kerkhof, Annemarie C, Sanderine Nonhebel and Henri C. Moll (2009), 'Relating the environmental impact of consumption to household expenditures: An input–output analysis', *Ecological Economics*, **68**, 1160–70.

Labouze, E., V. Monier, Y. Le Guern et al. (2003), 'Study on external environmental effects related to the lifecycle of products and services', final report version 2, European Commission, Paris.

Lenzen, M. (2011), 'Aggregation versus disaggregation in input output analysis of the environment', *Economic Systems Research*, **23** (1), 73–89.

Lenzen M., L.L. Pade and J. Munksgaard (2004), 'CO2 multipliers in multi-region input–output models', *Economic Systems Research*, **16**, 391–412.

Lenzen M., M. Wier, C. Cohen et al. (2006), 'A comparative multivariate analysis of household energy requirements in Australia, Brazil, Denmark, India and Japan', *Energy*, **31**, 181–207.

Lenzen, M., K. Kanemoto, D. Moran et al. (2012a), 'Mapping the structure of the world economy', *Environmental Science and Technology*, **46**, 8374–81.

Lenzen, M., D. Moran, K. Kanemoto et al. (2012b), 'International trade drives biodiversity threats in developing nations', *Nature*, **486**, 109–12.

Lenzen, M., D. Moran, K. Kanemoto et al. (2013), 'Building EORA: A global multi-region input–output database at high country and sector resolution', *Economic Systems Research*, **25**, 20–49.

Lenzen, M., T. Geschke, T. Wiedmann et al. (2014), 'Compiling and using input–output frameworks through collaborative virtual laboratories', *Science of the Total Environment*, **485–6** (1), 241–51.

Liu, J., G. Daily, P. Ehrlich et al. (2003), 'Effects of household dynamics on resource consumption and biodiversity', *Nature*, **421** (6922), 530–33.

Marechal, K. (2009), 'An evolutionary perspective on the economics of energy consumption: The crucial role of habits', *Journal of Economic Issues*, **43** (1), 69–88.

Miller, R. and P.R Blair (2009), *Input–Output Analysis: Foundations and Extensions*, 2nd edn, Cambridge: Cambridge University Press.

Moll, S. and J. Acosta (2006), 'Environmental implications of resource use: Environmental input–output analyses for Germany', *Journal of Industrial Ecology*, **10** (3), 25–40.

Moran, D.D., M.C. Wackernagel, J.A. Kitzes et al. (2009), 'Trading spaces: Calculating embodied ecological footprints in international trade using a product land use matrix (PLUM)', *Ecological Economics*, **68** (7), 1938–51.

Nemry, F., K. Thollier, B. Jansen et al. (2002), 'Identifying key products for the federal product & environment policy', final report, Namur/Mol, Belgium: Federal Services of Environment Department on Product Policy, Institut Wallon de Développement Economique et Social et d'Aménagement du Territoire ASBL/Vlaamse Instelling voor Technologisch Onderzoek.

Nijdam, D.S. and H. Wilting. (2003), 'Milieudruk consumptie in beeld' ['A view on environmental pressure on consumption'], RIVM rapport 7714040004, Bilthoven, the Netherlands: National Institute for Public Health and the Environment (RIVM).

OECD [Organisation for Economic Co-operation and Development] (2015), OECD Inter-Country Input–Output (ICIO) Tables, accessed 2 February 2018 at https://www.oecd.org/sti/ind/inter-country-input-output-tables.htm.

Ornetzeder, M., E. Hertwich, K. Hubacek et al. (2008), 'The environmental effect of car-free housing: A case in Vienna', *Ecological Economics*, **65** (3), 516–30.

Owen, A. (2017), *Techniques for Evaluating the Differences in Consumption-Based Accounts: A Comparative Evaluation of Eora, GTAP and WIOD*, Cham, Switzerland: Springer International.

Palm, V., A. Wadeskog and G. Finnveden (2006), 'Swedish experience using environmental accounts data for integrated product policy (IPP) issues', *Journal of Industrial Ecology*, **10** (3), 57–72.

Peters, G.P. and E.G. Hertwich (2006), 'The importance of imports for household environmental impacts', *Journal of Industrial Ecology*, **10** (3), 89–109.

Peters, G.P., J.C. Minx, C.L. Weber et al. (2011), 'Growth in emission transfers via international trade from 1990 to 2008', *Proceedings of the National Academy of Sciences*, **108** (21), 8903–88.

Peters, G.P., S.J. Davis and R.M. Andrew (2012), 'A synthesis of carbon in international trade', *Biogeosciences*, **9** (8), 3247–76.

Pretty, J., A. Ball, T. Lang et al. (2005), 'Farm costs and food miles: An assessment of the full cost of the UK weekly food basket', *Food Policy*, **30** (1), 1–19.

Sanne, C. (2002), 'Willing consumers—or locked-in? Policies for a sustainable consumption', *Ecological Economics*, **42** (1–2), 273–87.

Schoer, K., R. Wood, I. Arto et al. (2013), 'Estimating raw material equivalents on a macro-level: Comparison of multi-regional input–output analysis and hybrid LCI-IO', *Environmental Science and Technology*, **47** (24), 14282–9.

Stadler, K., R. Wood, M. Simas et al. (2017), 'EXIOBASE3 – developing a time series of detailed environmentally extended multi-regional input–output tables', *Journal of Industrial Ecology*, **22** (3), 502–15.

Tukker, A. (2006), 'Identifying priorities for environmental product policy', *Journal of Industrial Ecology*, **10** (3), 1–4.

Tukker, A. and E. Dietzenbacher (2013), 'Global multiregional input–output frameworks: An introduction and outlook', *Economic Systems Research*, **25** (1), 1–19.

Tukker, A. and B. Jansen (2006), 'Environment impacts of products: A detailed review of studies', *Journal of Industrial Ecology*, **10** (3), 159–82.

Tukker, A., E. Poliakov, R. Heijungs et al. (2009), 'Towards a global multi-regional environmentally extended input–output database', *Ecological Economics*, **68** (7), 1928–37.

Tukker A., M.J. Cohen, K. Hubacek et al. (2010), 'The impacts of household consumption and options for change', *Journal of Industrial Ecology*, **14**, 13–30.

Tukker A., R.A. Goldbohm, A. de Koning et al. (2011), 'Environmental impacts of changes to healthier diets in Europe, *Ecological Economics*, **70** (10), 1776–88.

Tukker, A., A. de Koning, R. Wood et al. (2013a), 'The price corrected domestic technology assumption – a method to assess pollution embodied in trade using primary official statistics only', *Environmental Science and Technology*, **47** (4), 1775–83.

Tukker, A., A. de Koning, R. Wood et al. (2013b), 'EXIOPOL – development and illustrative analyses of a detailed global MR EE SUT/IOT', *Economic Systems Research*, **25** (1), 50–70.

Tukker, A., T. Bulavskaya, S. Giljum et al. (2016), 'Europe's environmental footprints in a global context: A structural deficit in resource endowments', *Global Environmental Change*, **40**, 171–81.

Tukker, A., S. Giljum and R. Wood (2018a), 'Recent progress in assessment of resource efficiency and environmental impacts embodied in trade', *Journal of Industrial Ecology*, **22** (83), 489–501.

Tukker, Arnold, Arjan de Koning, Anne Owen et al. (2018b), 'Towards robust, authoritative assessments of environmental impacts embodied in trade – current state and recommendations', *Journal of Industrial Ecology*, **22** (3), 585–98.

United Nations (2014–17), UN Comtrade Database, accessed 2 February 2015 at https://comtrade.un.org.

Weber, C. and S. Matthews (2008a), 'Food miles and the climate impacts of freight transportation in American food consumption', *Environmental Science and Technology*, **42** (10), 3508–13.

Weber, C. and S. Matthews (2008b), 'Quantifying the global and distributional aspects of American household carbon footprint', *Ecological Economics*, **6** (6), 379–91.

Weisz, H. and F. Duchin (2006), 'Physical and monetary input–output analysis: What makes the difference?', *Ecological Economics*, **57** (3), 534–41.

Wiebe, K.S., M. Bruckner, S. Giljum et al. (2012a), 'Calculating energy-related CO2 emissions embodied in international trade using a global input-output model', *Economic Systems Research*, **24**, 113–39.

Wiebe, K.S., M. Bruckner, S. Giljum et al. (2012b), 'Carbon and materials embodied in the international trade of emerging economies – a multiregional input–output assessment of trends between 1995 and 2005', *Journal of Industrial Ecology*, **16**, 636–46.

Wiedmann, T., H.C. Wilting, M. Lenzen et al. (2011), 'Quo Vadis MRIO? Methodological, data and institutional requirements for multi-region input–output analysis', *Ecological Economics*, **70** (11), 1937–45.

Wilson, A. and J. Boehland (2005), 'Small is beautiful: U.S. house size, resource use, and the environment', *Journal of Industrial Ecology*, **9** (1–2), 277–88.

Wood, G. and M. Newborough (2007), 'Energy-use information transfer for intelligent homes: Enabling energy conservation with central and local displays', *Energy and Buildings*, **39** (4), 495–503.

Wood R. and C.J. Dey (2009), 'Australia's carbon footprint', *Economic Systems Research*, **21** (3), 243–66.

Wood, R., T. Hawkins, E. Hertwich et al. (2014), 'Harmonizing national input–output tables for consumption accounting – experiences in EXIOPOL', *Economic Systems Research*, **26** (4), 387–409.

Wood, Richard, Konstantin Stadler, Tatyana Bulavskaya et al. (2015), 'Global sustainability accounting – developing EXIOBASE for multi-regional footprint analysis', *Sustainability*, **7** (1), 138–63.

World Bank (2017), *Global Consumption Database*, accessed 11 February 2019 at http://datatopics.worldbank.org/consumption/detail.

5 Evaluating the sustainability impacts of the sharing economy using input–output analysis

Andrius Plepys and Jagdeep Singh

1. Introduction

Although sharing has been practised for millennia in different societies, today, the emerging notion of the sharing economy (SE) is regarded as a new social phenomenon. It refers to various forms of transactions between strangers enabling access to goods without ownership, utilizing the capacity of privately owned assets not currently in use and exploiting the benefits of information technologies to reduce transaction costs.

Recent studies define SE as peer-to-peer (P2P) sharing of underutilized assets among strangers without a change in ownership (Botsman and Rogers, 2011; Owyang et al., 2014; Codagnone and Martens, 2016). Such a definition excludes many business-to-consumer (B2C) business models that purposefully acquire assets for sharing (Belk, 2014). Umbrella terms, such as access-based (Bardhi and Eckhardt, 2012), collaborative consumption (Botsman and Rogers, 2011) or the SE (Schor, 2016) are often used to refer to a variety of consumption forms. Frenken (2017), for example, distinguishes four models of collaborative consumption: sharing, on-demand access, second-hand markets and product-service systems. In this chapter, SE is defined as P2P transactions granting access to physical goods and services and facilitated by digital platforms (Frenken and Schor, 2017).

SE is often associated with positive socio-economic and environmental benefits. SE could, for example, provide a step towards cost-effective and resource-efficient livelihoods in less affluent societies. SE can enable access to goods or services to people who currently could not afford to buy or access them. Some of the frequently advertised benefits of SE include resource savings, participatory democracy, better quality of life, access to more goods and services at lower cost, flexible working hours and new earning opportunities.

However, the overall effects of SE on economic growth, employment or the environment are still underexplored and a better understanding of these impacts is needed to support policies that could steer the more sustainable evolution of SE.

Comprehending the complexity of these effects requires the analysis of cross-sectoral interactions and behavioural responses to SE activities. This chapter discusses the methodological and data challenges of analysing the effects of SE using static macroeconomic modelling frameworks, such as environmentally extended economic input–output (EE–I/O) analyses. A hypothetical case of car sharing (CS) will be used as an illustration in this chapter.

2.   The multi-faceted effects of sharing economy

The discourse on the sustainability potential of the is SE generally positive and the environmental benefits are often taken for granted and directly associated with resource efficiency. However, much of the existing research lacks insights into consumers' behavioural responses and the complexities of cross-economic consequences for production value chains (Codagnone et al., 2016a; Goudin, 2016; Frenken and Schor, 2017). A lot of research is largely qualitative and the empirical evidence of the costs and benefits of SE is inconclusive and patchy (Codagnone and Martens, 2016).

Some of the negative impacts of SE highlighted in different studies include the exploitative nature of the labour force (Schor, 2016). Commercial sharing platforms primarily follow an economic rationale and are not always necessarily 'green' or 'fair'. Schor (2017) argues that 'gig economy' platforms reduce employment opportunities for less-skilled people since better-educated service providers now take supplementary jobs, such as driving, cleaning and other household errands. There has been increased media coverage about different controversies and legal disputes regarding the impacts of large platforms such as Uber and Airbnb, including labour rights, social protection, wages, property prices and rents and job losses in the incumbent businesses. In SE, participants face poorly defined liability rules and consumer protection. Governments anticipate a potential loss of tax revenues and difficulties in formalizing and enforcing their fiscal policies, and the incumbent formal business actors expect more competition and erosion of their revenues (Miller, 2016). The economic and competitive advantages offered by SE can partly be viewed as due to the non-compliance of current social norms in some countries, as highlighted in several studies on social impacts of SE (for example, Stokes et al., 2014; Katz, 2015; Martin, 2016). This has indeed prompted a regulatory debate which has polarized into a 'liberal' side advocating less regulation and a 'moderate' side proposing innovative and smart forms of regulation (Codagnone and Martens, 2016). Owing to these concerns, some reviews of different media sources conclude that public rhetoric on the promises of SE is probably changing from generally positive and praising to less optimistic (Codagnone et al., 2016b).

Other SE externalities include the negative environmental and social implications of induced additional consumption (Denegri-Knott, 2011) and their rebound effects (Demailly and Novel, 2014; Verboven and Vanherck, 2016; Frenken, 2017; Frenken and Schor, 2017). The direct rebound effects refer to increased demand when technological or organizational improvements lead to lower prices of goods and services.[1] Indirect effects are secondary increases in consumption of other goods and services when the residual savings from the consumption of primary goods and services are made available. Readjustments to final demand can cause further ripple effects throughout the entire economy by adjusting prices and total outputs in many sectors. These effects can also move across national borders with consequences for employment, economic growth and the environment as the footprints of the additional consumption might be higher than those reduced by sharing.

Various potential impacts of sharing assets mentioned so far can be illustrated by a simplified causal loop diagram (CLD) as shown in Figure 5.1. CLDs facilitate qualitative understanding of interrelationships between different variables in a system via feedback loops, which can reinforce (R) and balance (B). CLDs connect variables in a system by representing causal relationships between variables and indicate how

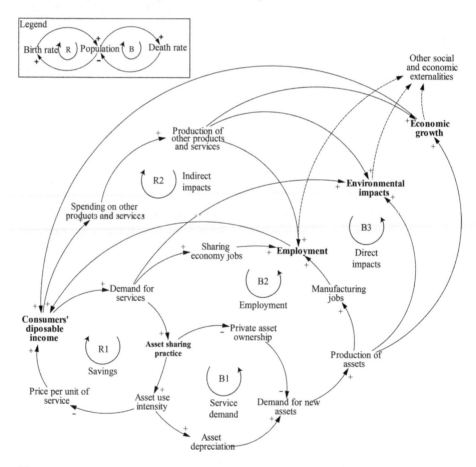

Figure 5.1 CLD representing various reported and potential impacts of a generic sharing system

a causal relationship reacts to a change by using positive or negative polarity. In the case of positive polarity, the variables move in the same direction (increase or decrease) towards a change in the variables and vice-versa (Lane, 2008).

SE has been growing rapidly across many sectors, but the sustainability implications and the rebound effects of SE are still largely unknown. The inconclusiveness of the overall impacts of sharing and the recent controversies surrounding the unintended negative impacts of SE call for systematic evaluations that could guide a more sustainable evolution of SE (Goudin, 2016). A systematic assessment is essential in order to assist possible regulatory interventions to steer a more sustainable development of SE.

Some of the key social, economic and environmental implications of SE can be summarized as in Table 5.1. These implications have varied impacts across stakeholders, value chains and nations, depending on the current structure of regulations and institutions in the society. This implies that some stakeholders or parts of society are more vulnerable (than others) to the negative implications of SE. The following sections provide an overview of different modelling approaches and their strengths and weaknesses for evaluating the impacts of SE.

3. Limitations in sustainability evaluations of sharing economy

Although SE exists in several economic sectors, research on its environmental implications has focused mainly on CS and accommodation sharing using case studies of large international sharing platforms like car2go, Lyft, Uber and Airbnb. Many of the existing environmental evaluations of SE are made or facilitated by commercial platforms and they sometimes lack methodological transparency. Moreover, many environmental evaluations have limited scope focusing largely on the direct implications of reduced consumption induced by sharing within a particular product group. Airbnb, for example, has reported environmental gains in energy (78%), water (48%), waste (32%) and greenhouse gas emissions (89%) by comparing a typical occurrence of home sharing with staying in a hotel (Airbnb, 2018). At the same time, studies are often not transparent about methods and system boundaries used or the assumptions made (Codagnone et al., 2016a). Studies conducted by the sharing platforms may overestimate environmental benefits by including only the impacts of sharing and excluding the rebound effects.

Many studies have compared CS to car ownership and explored its environmental impacts (Martin and Shaheen, 2011a; Zhou and Kockelman, 2011; Fagnant and Kockelman, 2014; Santi et al., 2014; Chen and Kockelman, 2016a; Nijland and van Meerkerk, 2017). In many cases CS exhibited environmental gains due to reductions in driving distance, vehicle ownership rates and parking space used. For example, a shared car in the UK removed 3.5 to 8.6 new and second-hand private vehicles from the road (Steer Davies Gleave, 2016), while in the USA, this replacement was

Table 5.1   Sustainability implications of SE

Impacts	Social	Economic	Environmental
Direct	• inclusive participatory service democratization using fair rating systems (+) • flexible working hours (+) • social cohesion (+) • access to services to broader societal groups (+) • increase of jobs in sharing sectors (+) • potential exploitation of work force (−) • risks with non-compliance of social norms (−)	• new economic opportunities for providers (+) • lower cost of per unit service for users (+) • revenue generation through taxes for local governments (+) • growth of new sectors (+) • rapid economic depreciation (−)	• dematerialization of per unit service (+) • utilization of idle resources (+) • additional consumption due to lower per unit prices (−) • accelerated asset depreciation (shortened lifetime) (−)
Indirect	• reallocation of employment opportunities (−) • could make some workforce more vulnerable (−) • decrease in jobs negatively impacted incumbent sectors (−)	• additional economic growth due to increase in public spending (+) • negative economic impacts on incumbent businesses (−) • revenue losses by competing businesses (−) • may cause unintended negative cross-sectoral impacts (−)	• additional consumption of other products or services due to income effects (−)

estimated as 9 to 13 cars with a reduction of household driving distance of 27 to 43 per cent (Shaheen et al., 2015; Martin and Shaheen, 2016).

However, overall environmental gains can be different if changes in other systems and the rebound effects caused by sharing are included. As discussed, SE may not necessarily lead to less consumption since access-based consumption models could contribute to significant changes in disposable income and the reallocation of spending (Verboven and Vanherck, 2016). Zipcar, for example, estimates up to USD 5000 in annual savings for car owners who have moved to CS (Zipcar, 2018). Providers of shared assets, for example Uber, Lyft and Airbnb, can attain additional income between USD 2000 and USD 5000 per year (Earnest, 2018). Environmental evaluations also point to data uncertainties that are often based on self-reported surveys, which are subject to inaccuracies, exaggerated travel behaviour, misestimates of travel distances, induced changes in car ownership and assumptions regarding the use of other travel modes induced by sharing activities.

More accurate estimates require collaboration with CS platforms and companies; however, businesses are often reluctant to disclose this information due to matters of individual privacy and the proprietary nature of the information (Shaheen and Cohen, 2018). Table 5.2 presents some studies that have evaluated the sustainability impacts of SE in the CS sector and which employ different modelling approaches ranging from life cycle assessment (LCA) to EE–I/O analysis as well as hybrid methods.

The main difference between LCA and EE–I/O analyses is the type of data they rely on, that is, bottom-up and top-down data. LCA represents a bottom-up approach that uses environmental assessment based on the life cycle perspective. It requires the collection of data on input materials, energy carriers, land resources and the associated emissions and wastes for each small process unit. As unit process data are usually derived from direct measurements and surveys of companies and facilities manufacturing products of interest, LCAs can potentially be quite accurate and product- and process-specific, if high-quality data is used. However, LCAs are data intensive and time-consuming and require high technological, time and geographical representativeness of data. The lack of process-specific data can often result in the use of data from generic processes based on averages or unrepresentative sampling. Furthermore, the ambition of mapping the details of the entire life cycle system can result in highly complex systems of interlinked unit processes, especially in the upstream sections of the production chain. This often requires introducing upstream system boundary cut-offs, which result in truncation errors (Pomponi and Lenzen, 2018).

EE-I/O is a classic representative of a top-down assessment approach based on economic input–output (I/O) analysis. It uses aggregated sectoral data derived from national statistical accounts describing economic inter-industry relationships, factor inputs and total outputs for final consumption. The I/O framework allows modelling of the way changes in final demand will be reflected in the outputs of regional economic structure in the directly affected sectors and also the indirect changes in other sectors (a very detailed methodological description of I/O is provided by Miller and Blair, 2009). The I/O framework was developed in 1930s by the Nobel Prize winner Wassily Leontief; today, most industrialized countries use it in macroeconomic assessments. In the 1970s, the I/O framework began to be applied to environmental assessments and was formalized as environmentally extended I/O (EE-I/O) models. Here, the economic or physical transactions reflected in I/O tables are combined with satellite environmental accounts (for example, emissions, energy, waste, land use) using Leontief's premise that any industrial output needs not only the intermediate inputs from other sectors but also 'requires' the emissions and other environmental loadings that accompany

Table 5.2 Examples of approaches for studying different impacts of CS

Modelling approach	Impacts analysed	Method employed	Type of data used	System boundaries
Bottom-up-based model	GHG savings due to: car mileage and car ownership rates (Martin and Shaheen, 2011a)	Different models of car fleet systems, LCA	Online user survey on type of vehicle and vehicle kilometres travelled	Only environmental impacts from driving considered; social and economic rebound impacts excluded. Vehicle depreciation not included
	Car ownership rates and extent of private car use (Nijland and van Meerkerk, 2017)		User survey on changes in mobility pattern	Rebound effects not considered. Vehicle depreciation not included
	Changes in mobility patterns, user behaviour, costs, parking and newer vehicles (Baptista et al., 2014)		User survey of consumer behaviour and life cycle inventory data of the vehicles	
	Changes in overall mobility pattern (Lane, 2005)		User survey of changes in modal split due to car sharing	Systemic impacts such as supply chain impacts and rebound effects not included
Top-down-based model	Material efficiency and employment impacts (Cooper et al., 2016)	Multi-regional input–output (MRIO) model	Material flow inventory and economic data for material efficiency improvements in mobility and construction sectors	
Hybrid models	Changes in passenger mileage, transport mixes (Briceno et al., 2005)	LCA and EE-I/O	Consumer expenditure on transport sector	Direct rebound effect from household spending. Indirect rebound impacts from the consumption of other products excluded

these inputs (Leontief, 1970). The environmental data are normalized per unit of total output from a particular sector and are treated the same way as other production factors, such as capital and labour, in the I/O framework. As EE-I/O analysis is based on I/O data, it avoids the truncation errors characteristic of LCAs. On the other hand, the I/O-based analyses suffer from high data aggregation, poor capture of post-consumer life cycle stages and the inherent assumptions regarding price homogeneity and uniformity of outputs from each industrial sector. The inherent strengths and weaknesses of LCAs and EE-I/O approaches are summarized in Table 5.3.

A promising way forward is the exploitation of the strengths of LCA and I/O in hybrid-LCA approaches, which are viewed today, at least in academia, as the state of the art in product life cycle assessments (Wiedmann, 2009). Information from the I/O framework allows a more informed selection of system boundaries and the capture of the impacts of upstream processes, whereas LCA-based data allows a more process/product-specific analysis and the capture of the impacts of post-consumer life cycle phases. *The International Journal of Life Cycle Assessment* has been providing extensive research coverage of LCA, I/O and hybrid approaches since 2003 (Suh, 2003).

Employing LCA, I/O-based and hybrid approach methods to evaluate a relatively new consumption model such as SE presents numerous challenges and creates new research needs. In this chapter, we highlight some of these challenges and new research needs while employing the EE-I/O framework to evaluate the sustainability implications of SE. We will discuss how, in view of the multi-faceted impacts of SE that span value chains and territories, top-down modelling approaches and hybrid models employing input–output analysis can be employed. To illustrate this, we will use the hypothetical example of generic CS without distinguishing between B2C or P2P types of sharing.

4. An example of I/O-based sustainability assessment: The case of car sharing

4.1 Causalities in car sharing

A wealth of studies exist that explore the environmental implications of CS in different countries (Martin and Shaheen, 2011a; Sioui et al., 2012; Clewlow, 2016; Feigon et al., 2016; Martin and Shaheen, 2016; Stapleton et al., 2016; Becker et al., 2017; Livingston and Storer, 2017; Shaheen and Cohen, 2018). These studies indicate that the emergence of CS practice usually leads to direct changes in households' disposable income, consumption patterns for transport services and of other goods and services, as well as indirect changes in employment and economic outputs of other sectors. The main variables determining the direct environmental implications of CS are changes in the modal split of transport, disposable income, demand for personal vehicles and emission factors of the vehicles used. Figure 5.2 describes different consumption causalities using CLD as well as

Table 5.3 Strengths and weaknesses of different modelling approaches

Modelling approaches	Examples	Strengths	Weaknesses
Bottom-up-based models or life cycle-based	Life cycle assessment	• Allows high level of data specificity • Better for consequential simulations with marginal data (in case consequential approach is taken for allocation and marginal changes) • Better for evaluating direct impacts	• Introduces truncation errors due to system boundary cut-offs • Not suitable for evaluating cross-sectoral economic implications • Demands large amount of data • Prone to random errors due to varying data quality
Top-down-based models	Input–output analysis, general economic equilibrium models	• Addresses truncation errors of life cycle-based approaches for upstream processes • Suitable for evaluating cross-sectoral implications • Availability of databases at various regional and international aggregations of economy	• Unrealistic assumptions regarding sectoral/commodity homogeneity and price proportionality relative to scale of activities • Does not reflect well on product end-of-life phase • High level of data aggregation
Hybrid methods	Hybrid I/O analysis	• Addresses truncation errors of life cycle-based approaches • Allows reducing the potential errors due to sectoral aggregation	• Requires data specificity, can be data-intensive

showing the various driving mechanisms of the changes induced by household participation in CS.

One of the main factors influencing changes in original consumption for households participating in CS is the different cost structure compared to car ownership. In the latter, households have to pay for the initial investment, operation, service and maintenance costs, insurance and road taxes. For CS users, all these costs are internalized in the pricing of CS schemes and some of these costs are shared with other users. Although the marginal costs of using CS mobility services are relatively higher than those of private cars, these are much lower than the total ownership costs of private cars. Until a certain threshold of distance driven is reached, the annual costs of CS are lower than those of a private car. Indeed, many studies point to cost savings as the prime reason for participation in CS. Therefore, CS can generate significant economic savings in mobility expenditure (reinforcing the feedback loop: R1 Savings in Figure 5.2). These savings may induce changes in overall transport demand, leading to direct rebound effects (B2, Figure 5.2) due to, for example, longer driving distances or an increased use of public transport and other

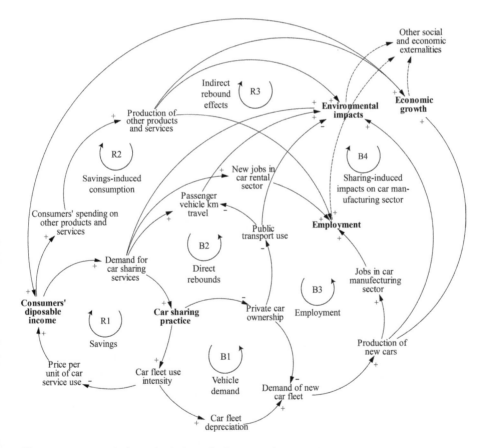

Figure 5.2 CLD of a hypothetical car sharing example

means of transport, as identified in several studies (Martin and Shaheen, 2011b; 2016; Shaheen and Cohen, 2018). In addition, the economic savings could also influence overall consumption patterns, thus resulting in changes in final demand for some of the industrial sectors depending on how and where the savings are spent (indirect rebound effects R2, Figure 5.2).

From the *consumer* perspective, changes in the personal mobility bundle described by the amount of transport demanded from different transport modes (cars, bus, train, cycling or walking) lead to direct impacts (balancing feedback loop B2: Direct rebounds, Figure 5.2). The reallocation of household expenditure on other products and services can lead to the indirect impacts (reinforcing feedback loop R2: Savings-induced consumption, Figure 5.2). The additional income of CS providers also belongs to this category. However, it is also possible that less money would be available for expenditure on other commodities. Therefore, an evaluation of the sustainability profile of CS also requires information on any changes in demand for new products and services enabled by extra savings/income. This demand can be assumed to be either an elastic function of the savings/income (for instance, the new demand will increase or decrease proportionally for *all* products and services) or a combination of elastic and inelastic functions (for instance, an increased propensity for demand of certain type of products and services). Furthermore, the broader intersectoral impacts of the changing consumption patterns can include changes in employment (balancing feedback loop B3: Employment, Figure 5.2).

From the *producers'* perspective, changes in final demand for private vehicles can result in direct and indirect effects due to the accompanying changes in other supplying sectors (balancing feedback loop B4 and reinforcing feedback loop R3, Figure 5.2). A sustainability evaluation could also include broader systemic ripple effects generated due to overall changes in employment, environmental impacts and economic growth.

4.2   Implications for modelling impacts from changes in consumption patterns

This section describes some implications for modelling changes in consumption patterns and the subsequent impacts on producing sectors.

4.2.1   Profiling users of car sharing

Modelling consumer behaviour in CS schemes requires greater understanding of users. Cervero et al. (2007), for example, suggest that potential users of CS are people who use their cars less frequently, live in higher density areas and have better access to alternative mobility services. With typical car ownership costs and prevailing CS prices, CS is an economically feasible option when compared to car ownership if annual personal car use is less than 12 000 to 15 000 km (Loose, 2010). Understanding users is therefore essential for analysing impacts caused by changes in overall mobility profile, financial savings and expenditure patterns.

4.2.2 Changes in mobility bundle

The shift to CS implies changes in the mobility bundle with regard to modal split and distances travelled. The overall vehicle kilometres of travel (VKT) could be reduced since CS often leads to 10–20 per cent more walking and biking (Lane, 2005; Martin and Shaheen, 2011b). Since the marginal costs of CS use are much higher than those for private cars, CS can significantly decrease their vehicle mileage (10 to 20 times less) and also increase walking/cycling and the use of public transport (up to 10% more) (Lane, 2005). Meanwhile, users who did not own a car could now increase VKT and decrease the use of public transport. The overall effect will be highly contextual and location-specific; however, the majority of studies agree that CS generally facilitates more use of public transport and reduces overall VKT (for example, Chen and Kockelman, 2016b).

4.2.3 Emission factors of vehicles in car sharing

Generally, vehicles used in B2C CS schemes have a better emissions profile than the average national fleet since their vehicles are usually smaller, newer and have a higher share of hybrid or fully electric cars. The difference in average CO_2 emissions between private and CS vehicle fleets is estimated in the range of 15–35 per cent (Loose, 2010; Steer Davies Gleave, 2017). Thus, when evaluating the direct environmental impacts of CS, it is important to differentiate between B2C and P2P CS segments. It is likely that vehicles provided by P2P schemes have an emissions profile closer to the national average. P2P providers, on the other hand, largely exploit the underutilized potential of their existing vehicles and want to make extra income from unused resources. Indeed, very few P2P providers share new vehicles so they can recuperate high initial investment. B2C providers, on the other hand, often cooperate with car manufacturers utilizing their premium leasing schemes to facilitate user access to the latest car models with the latest engine technologies and highest emissions standards. Vehicle occupancy rate is another important parameter that must be included when evaluating the emissions factor as this could significantly differ between shared and private cars.

4.2.4 Car ownership effects

It is estimated that CS can lead to car shedding effects of 10–20 per cent (Cervero et al., 2007; Zhou and Kockelman, 2011). However, there is no consensus regarding these estimates. Although CS has been praised for its potential for reducing private car ownership and freeing up parking spaces, this does not necessarily mean that the number of cars in traffic will be reduced. There could also be unintended impacts due to significant numbers of users opting for CS and diverting some users away from public transport. CS can influence overall demand for new cars and therefore the automobile manufacturing industry. Market research suggests this affect could range from mild/positive to neutral in the worst-case scenario (Cornet et al., 2012).

4.2.5   *Final consumption bundle*

Evaluation of the impacts of CS on final household demand implies the analysis of any changes in final consumption expenditure after a household has begun to engage in sharing activities. In the case of CS, this involves the analysis of new expenditure on CS services, reduced private car ownership expenses and more expenditure allocated to public transport as well as potential savings that are real-located to the consumption of other products and services (as described in Figure 5.2).

The sustainability implications of the above-mentioned consumption patterns using I/O analysis require an examination of any changes in final (largely house-hold) demand. New final demand requires information about annual savings from removing car ownership costs, annual depreciation, fuel costs, insurance and taxes, and service and maintenance costs. Savings can be counted as extra income avail-able for new mobility demands and/or other products and services. New mobility demand, that is, the modal split between CS, public transport, taxis, walking or biking, could be estimated from household travel surveys, consumer expenditure surveys or complimentary case-based empirical observations. Empirical observa-tions could assist in providing scenarios for disposable income being spent on other products and services.

4.3   Implications for modelling impacts from changes in production sectors

4.3.1   *Disaggregating an sharing economy sector*

Current input–output tables (IOT) lack detailed information on intersectoral impacts (for instance, the production recipes) of SE sectors. Thus, some sectors may require disaggregation in order to include these impacts. In disaggregation, additional sectors are created by adding rows and columns into the existing IOT. Creating a new hypothetical sector in EE-I/O framework requires data on the inter-sectoral production inputs required to produce the product or service in question and the environmental burdens of their production process. The economy-wide environmental burdens of one unit output of the sector can then be estimated. Joshi (1999) provides methodological recommendations in the examples of Models II–IV. Existing IOTs may contain the transactions of formal businesses engaged in SE transactions, which, under Standard Industrial Classification (SIC) categoriza-tion are likely to be included with the traditional industrial sectors such as 'taxi services' or 'car rental services'. This could present challenges for an estimation of the share of the total output of the CS sector and of the share of different types of business models such as B2C and P2P sharing.

The production recipe for CS (the intermediary industry requirements matrix column, Figure 5.3) can be assumed to be representative of the sectors from which they are drawn (for instance, the original technical coefficient matrix is unaffected by the introduction of the new sector). It can be assumed that CS requires similar

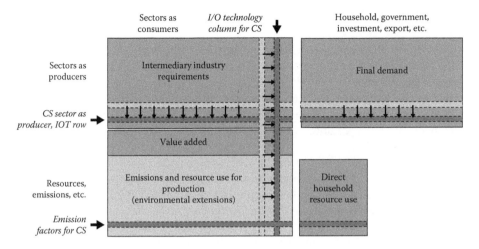

Figure 5.3   Sectoral disaggregation and activity-specific satellite account in an EE-I/O table

amount of inputs from the same industrial sectors as the rental sector. CS can require different inputs from other sectors such as administrative services, insurances and repair or vehicle capital depreciation due to significant differences in the type of vehicles in the sharing fleet and their depreciation rates. This would require empirical information on sharing business models (design, revenues, pricing and cost structure), factor inputs (capital, labour and taxes), asset characteristics (utilization/replacement rate, energy/material intensity) and environmental data (energy, emissions, materials). Similarly, the new CS sector as a producer (a new row representing a disaggregated new sharing sector in the I/O table in Figure 5.3), requires estimates regarding the outputs of this sector to others. The output to some sectors can be assumed to be proportional to the existing rental sector. However, in the case of a large share of mobility services used by private individuals, the output coefficients must be adjusted using expert estimates and available statistics. Depending on the scale of the disaggregated sector, IOT may require rebalancing. Indeed, this could be the case for some SE sectors, such as shared mobility or accommodation sharing, which can have a significant impact on the incumbent sectors and the entire regional economy. Methodological advancements and alternative methods for matrix balancing are provided, for example, by Lenzen et al. (2009) and Junius and Oosterhaven (2003) with their KRAS and GRAS methods for matrix rebalancing, respectively.

5.   Reflections

This section presents some of the key challenges and future research needs in the context of evaluating the sustainability impacts of SE.

5.1   Challenges

The main challenges to evaluating the sustainability implications of SE are not due to lack of methods or assessment frameworks but to lack of data. The challenges include the diversity of SE business models, poor information about sharing activities between individuals and difficulties in measuring potential non-monetary transactions (Office for National Statistics, 2016). Data on the size of various market segments of the SE are unreliable due to the lack of a shared definition for SE.

Existing national economic accounts have been assembled for the SIC where companies in traditional manufacturing and service sectors are clustered by commonly established characteristics of their outputs. SE does not fit within this classification system; indeed, SE is often classified under standard sectoral codes along with other traditional business activities. The fact that SE is not a separate sector, but rather a cluster of transaction models, complicates the collection of statistical information. A shared understanding of SE and its characteristic business models could facilitate the standardization of statistics.

Another issue is that not only companies (for instance, formal economic entities), but also private individuals engage in sharing activities. Estimating the value of SE transactions using current official statistics is difficult because economic exchanges between individuals are not included in gross domestic product or the consumer price index (CPI). At best, in theory, only the formalized part of exchanges could be measured. For example, statistics authorities could track B2B and B2C production, expenditure and income. However, individual revenues from sharing are not accounted for in national statistics due to underreporting or being under the taxable threshold.

It would be feasible for businesses facilitating for-profit platform services to account for sharing revenues. However, many SE platforms offer flat-rate membership fees, not-for-profit services run on donations or free labour input from participants, or there are non-monetary exchanges (for example, reciprocal services).

Assumptions regarding homogeneity and proportionality in the I/O framework could pose challenges. For example, using the existing satellite accounts in environmental evaluations may significantly differ for sharing. Indeed, CS belongs to the 'taxi, car rental and leasing of personal vehicles' sector, but the emission factors of vehicles in CS can differ significantly from the average emissions in this sector, due to large share of relatively new and electrical vehicles in the fleet.

Other models, such as econometric or computable general equilibrium (CGE) models, could be suitable for modelling dynamic price–volume relationships in economies of scale. However, these demand much more information about the economic system and rely on assumptions with regard to current and future behavioural responses, which introduces a high level of uncertainty into the results. CGE models would be more suitable for modelling old established economic sectors with ample historical data and relatively less dynamics when compared to emerging markets, such as the SE.

6. Need for future research

In order to employ the I/O approach in sustainability evaluations of SE, existing national accounting frameworks would need to accommodate the specifics of emerging SE, including its diverse business models. This would require detailed information on the various inputs and outputs of sharing businesses, for example: total turnover, employment costs, total purchases, profit margins, duties, levies and taxes, the value of acquisitions of a capital asset, shares of imports and exports, and spending on capital assets. Furthermore, data is needed on specific environmental intensities of SE business models, especially in the dominant SE segments such as accommodation, space, mobility and household goods.

Better measurements of labour inputs and annual income in SE are needed (for example, employment status, hours worked, earnings and type of work). Behavioural studies could be devised to better understand consumer responses to the income/savings from sharing activities. Time surveys could be employed to analyse the behavioural changes of households since time can be a limiting factor for emerging consumption patterns and, therefore, the environmental footprint of consumption (ESRC, 2018).

SE is a global phenomenon and analysing it through I/O framework requires a multi-regional perspective. Today significant advancements have been made in the development of multi-regional I/O tables (MRIOTs), including EXIOBASE, GTAP, EORA, WIOD and AIIOT (see Tukker and Dietzenbacher, 2013; Wood et al., 2014; Lenzen et al., 2017). These MRIOTs have varying resolutions and diverse geographical and sectoral coverage. Further work is needed to adapt these datasets to the needs of SE analysis, including the satellite environmental accounts in different databases, such as UNFCC, CDIAC and EDGAR.

NOTE
1 Research on the rebound effect has been extensively covered in journals such as *Energy Policy*, *The Energy Journal*, *Energy Economics* and *Journal of Industrial Ecology*.

References

Airbnb (2018), 'The environmental impacts of home sharing', accessed 21 January 2018 at https://blog. atairbnb.com/environmental-impacts-of-home-sharing.
Baptista, P., S. Melo and C. Rolim (2014), 'Energy, environmental and mobility impacts of car-sharing systems: Empirical results from Lisbon, Portugal', *Procedia – Social and Behavioral Sciences*, **111**, 28–37.
Bardhi, F. and G.M. Eckhardt (2012), 'Access-based consumption: The case of car sharing', *Journal of Consumer Research*, **39** (4), 881–98.

Becker, H., F. Ciari and K. W. Axhausen (2017), 'Comparing car-sharing schemes in Switzerland: User groups and usage patterns', *Transportation Research Part A: Policy and Practice*, **97**, 17–29.

Belk, R. (2014), 'You are what you can access: Sharing and collaborative consumption online', *Journal of Business Research*, **67** (8), 1595–600.

Botsman, R. and R. Rogers (2011), *What's Mine Is Yours: How Collaborative Consumption is Changing the Way We Live*, London: Harper Collins.

Briceno, T., G. Peters, C. Solli et al. (2005), 'Using life cycle approaches to evaluate sustainable consumption programs: Car-sharing', Working Paper 2, Norwegian University of Science and Technology, Faculty of Engineering and Technology, Programme for industrial ecology.

Cervero, R., A. Golub and B. Nee (2007), 'City CarShare: longer-term travel demand and car ownership impacts', *Transportation Research Record: Journal of the Transportation Research Board*, **1992** (1), 70–80.

Chen, D. and K. Kockelman (2016a), 'Carsharing's life-cycle impacts on energy use and greenhouse gas emissions', *Transportation Research Part D: Transport and Environment*, **47**, 276–84.

Chen, D. and K. Kockelman (2016b), 'Management of a shared, autonomous, electric vehicle fleet: Implications of pricing schemes', *Transportation Research Record Journal of the Transportation Research Board*, **2572**, 37–46.

Clewlow, R.R. (2016), 'Carsharing and sustainable travel behavior: Results from the San Francisco Bay Area', *Transport Policy*, **51**, 158–64.

Codagnone, C. and B. Martens (2016), 'Scoping the sharing economy: Origins, definitions, impact and regulatory issues' (Digital Economy Working Paper), Institute for Prospective Technological Studies.

Codagnone, C., F. Abadie and F. Biagi (2016a), 'The future of work in the "Sharing Economy": Market efficiency and equitable opportunities or unfair precarisation?', JRC Science for Policy report EUR 27913 EN, Institute for Prospective Technological Studies.

Codagnone, C., F. Biagi and F. Abadie (2016b), 'The passions and the interests: Unpacking the "sharing economy"', JRC Science for Policy report, EUR 27914 EN, Institute for Prospective Technological Studies.

Cooper, S., A.C.H. Skelton, A. Owen et al. (2016), 'A multi-method approach for analysing the potential employment impacts of material efficiency', *Resources, Conservation and Recycling*, **109**, 54–66.

Cornet, A., D. Mohr, F. Weig et al. (2012), 'Mobility of the future: Opportunities for automotive OEMs', accessed 21 January 2019 at http://worldmobilityleadershipforum.com/mobility-of-the-future-opportunities-for-automotive-oems.

Demailly, D. and A.-S. Novel (2014), 'The sharing economy: Make it sustainable' (study), Institut du développement durable et des relations internationales (IDDRI), Paris, France.

Denegri-Knott, J. (2011), 'Have it now: Ebay and the acceleration of consumer desire', *European Advances in Consumer Research*, **9**, 373–9.

Earnest (2018), 'How much are people making from the sharing economy?', accessed 21 January 2018 at https://www.earnest.com/blog/sharing-economy-income-data.

ESRC (2018), 'United Kingdom time use survey 2014–2015', UK Data Service, Economic and Social Research Council, UK, accessed 21 January 2018 at https://discover.ukdataservice.ac.uk/series/?sn=2000054.

Fagnant, D. and K. Kockelman (2014), 'The travel and environmental implications of shared autonomous vehicles, using agent-based model scenarios', *Transportation Research Part C: Emerging Technologies*, **40**, 1–13.

Feigon, S., C. Murphy and Shared-Use Mobility Center (2016), 'Shared mobility and the transformation of public transit', TCRP Report 188, Transit Cooperative Research Program, Washington DC, USA: Transportation Research Board.

Frenken, K. (2017), 'Political economies and environmental futures for the sharing economy', *Philosophical Transactions of the Royal Society A*, **375** (2095).

Frenken, K. and J. Schor (2017), 'Putting the sharing economy into perspective', *Environmental Innovation and Societal Transitions*, **23**, 3–10.

Goudin, P. (2016), 'The cost of non-Europe in the sharing economy: Economic, social and legal challenges and opportunities', Brussels: European Parliamentary Research Service.

Joshi, S. (1999), 'Product environmental life-cycle assessment using input–output techniques', *Journal of Industrial Ecology*, **3** (2–3), 95–120.

Junius, T. and J. Oosterhaven (2003), 'The solution of updating or regionalizing a matrix with both positive and negative entries', *Economic Systems Research*, **15** (1), 87–96.

Katz, V. (2015), 'Regulating the sharing economy', *Berkeley Technology Law Journal*, **30** (4), 1067.

Lane, C. (2005), 'PhillyCarShare: First-year social and mobility impacts of carsharing in Philadelphia, Pennsylvania', *Transportation Research Record: Journal of the Transportation Research Board*, **1927** (1), 158–66.

Lane, D.C. (2008), 'The emergence and use of diagramming in system dynamics: A critical account', *Systems Research and Behavioral Science*, **25** (1), 3–23.

Lenzen, M., B. Gallego and R. Wood (2009), 'Matrix balancing under conflicting information', *Economic Systems Research*, **21** (1), 23–44.

Lenzen, M., A. Geschke, M.D. Abd Rahman et al. (2017), 'The Global MRIO Lab – charting the world economy', *Economic Systems Research*, **29** (2), 158–86.

Leontief, W. (1970), 'Environmental repercussions and the economic structure: An input–output approach', *The Review of Economics and Statistics*, **52** (3), 262–71.

Livingston, D. and T. Storer (2017), 'Uber-ization for decarbonization? The carbon consequences of new mobility', *MEDIUM*, 26 May, accessed 21 January 2019 at https://medium.com/@WolfLivingston/ uber-ization-for-decarbonization-the-carbon-consequences-of-new-mobility-22cef2cd8387.

Loose, W. (2010), 'The state of European car-sharing', Project Momo Final Report D, 2, Momo car-sharing.

Martin, C.J. (2016), 'The sharing economy: A pathway to sustainability or a nightmarish form of neoliberal capitalism?', *Ecological Economics*, **121**, 149–59.

Martin, E. and S. Shaheen (2011a), 'Greenhouse gas emission impacts of carsharing in North America', *IEEE Transactions on Intelligent Transportation Systems*, **12** (4), 1074–86.

Martin, E. and S. Shaheen (2011b), 'The impact of carsharing on public transit and non-motorized travel: An exploration of North American carsharing survey data', *Energies*, **4** (11), 2094–114.

Martin, E. and S. Shaheen (2016), 'Impacts of car2go on vehicle ownership, modal shift, vehicle miles traveled, and greenhouse gas emissions: An analysis of five North American cities', Working Paper, Transportation Sustainability Research Center (TSRC), Berkeley: University of California, Institute of Transportation Studies.

Miller, R.E. and P.D. Blair (2009), *Input-output Analysis: Foundations and Extensions*, Cambridge: Cambridge University Press.

Miller, S.R. (2016), 'First principles for regulating the sharing economy', *Harvard Journal on Legislation*, **53** (147), 147–202.

Nijland, H. and J. van Meerkerk (2017), 'Mobility and environmental impacts of car sharing in the Netherlands', *Environmental Innovation and Societal Transitions*, **23**, 84–91.

Office for National Statistics (2016), 'The feasibility of measuring the sharing economy', UK: Office for National Statistics,.

Owyang, J., A. Samuel and A. Grenville (2014), '"Sharing is the new buying": How to win in the collaborative economy' (report), Vision Critical and Crowd Companies.

Pomponi, F. and M. Lenzen (2018), 'Hybrid life cycle assessment (LCA) will likely yield more accurate results than process-based LCA', *Journal of Cleaner Production*, **176**, 210–15.

Santi, P., G. Resta, M. Szell et al. (2014), 'Quantifying the benefits of vehicle pooling with shareability networks', Proceedings of the National Academy of Sciences, **111** (37), 13290–4.

Schor, J. (2016), 'Debating the sharing economy', *Journal of Self-Governance and Management Economics*, **4** (3), 7–22.

Schor, J. (2017), 'Does the sharing economy increase inequality within the eighty percent?: Findings from a qualitative study of platform providers', *Cambridge Journal of Regions, Economy and Society*, **10** (2), 263–79.

Shaheen, S. and A. Cohen (2018), 'Impacts of shared mobility', *ITS Berkeley Policy Briefs*, **02**.

Shaheen, S.A., N.D. Chan and H. Micheaux (2015), 'One-way carsharing's evolution and operator perspectives from the Americas', *Transportation*, **42** (3), 519–36.

Sioui, L., C. Morency and M. Trépanier (2012), 'How carsharing affects the travel behavior of households: A case study of Montreal, Canada', *International Journal of Sustainable Transportation*, **7** (1), 52–69.

Stapleton, L., S. Sorrell and T. Schwanen (2016), 'Estimating direct rebound effects for personal automotive travel in Great Britain', *Energy Economics*, **54**, 313–25.

Steer Davies Gleave (2016), *Carplus Annual Survey of Car Clubs 2014/2015 (London, Scotland, England and Wales)*, London: Steer Davies Gleave.

Steer Davies Gleave (2017), *Carplus Annual Survey of Car Clubs 2016/2017*, London: Steer Davies Gleave.

Stokes, K., E. Clarence, L. Anderson et al. (2014), 'Making sense of the UK Collaborative Economy', NESTA, available at https://www.nesta.org.uk/report/making-sense-of-the-uk-collaborative-economy/.

Suh, S. (2003), 'Input–output and hybrid life cycle assessment', *The International Journal of Life Cycle Assessment*, **8** (5), 257.

Tukker, A. and E. Dietzenbacher (2013), 'Global multiregional input–output frameworks: An introduction and outlook introduction', *Economic Systems Research*, **25** (1), 1–19.

Verboven, H. and L. Vanherck (2016), 'The sustainability paradox of the sharing economy', *uwf UmweltWirtschaftsForum*, **24** (4), 303–14.

Wiedmann, T. (2009), *Carbon Footprint and Input–Output Analysis – an Introduction*, Abingdon, UK: Taylor and Francis.

Wood, R., T.R. Hawkins, E.G. Hertwich et al. (2014), 'Harmonising national input–output tables for consumption-based accounting. Experiences from EXIOPOL', *Economic Systems Research*, **26** (4), 387–409.

Zhou, B. and K. Kockelman (2011), 'Opportunities for and impacts of carsharing: A survey of the Austin, Texas market', *International Journal of Sustainable Transportation*, **5** (3), 135–52.

Zipcar (2018), 'Consumers drive down costs by car-sharing', accessed 21 January 2018 at https://www.zipcar.com/press/releases/cost-savings-data-released.

PART II

Alternative Systems of Provisioning and Consuming

6 The role of business models for sustainable consumption: A pattern approach

Florian Lüdeke-Freund, Tobias Froese and Stefan Schaltegger

1. Introduction

1.1 Navigating the sustainable consumption corridor

In October 2018, the International Panel on Climate Change (IPCC) published a special report on the impacts of greenhouse gas (GHG) emissions and related global warming. The researchers are highly confident that: '1.5°C pathways that include low energy demand . . . low material consumption, and low GHG-intensive food consumption have the most pronounced synergies and the lowest number of trade-offs with respect to sustainable development and the SDGs [Sustainable Development Goals] . . .' (International Panel on Climate Change, 2018: 21).

This indicates how closely consumption and climate change – but also other forms of ecological and social collapse – are related. Remaining below 1.5°C warming requires strong sustainable consumption (SSC), that is, staying within absolute ecological limits of resource use and resultant GHG emissions (Spangenberg, 2014). In addition, striving for sustainable consumption also entails eliminating socially unsustainable levels of consumption due to poverty and other barriers such as unequal educational opportunities (Spangenberg, 2014). The socially acceptable minimum of consumption possibilities is defined by social values such as human dignity and justice, taking into account the conditions for active participation in society (for example, political engagement, education, culture) (Spangenberg, 2014).

The conventional idea is to achieve such minimum standards by means of economic growth. However, proponents of degrowth, among others, criticize this approach because they estimate the risk of ever increasing impacts on the biosphere as being too high to pursue economic growth on a global level, particularly with respect to already affluent world regions (Weiss and Cattaneo, 2017). Accordingly, the debate on degrowth revolves around a liberation from the growth ideology as well as 'a radical call for a voluntary and equitable downscaling of the economy towards a sustainable, just, and participatory steady-state society' (Weiss and Cattaneo, 2017: 220). Contributions in this realm refer to insights indicating that sustainable levels of consumption also have an upper limit from a social point of view.

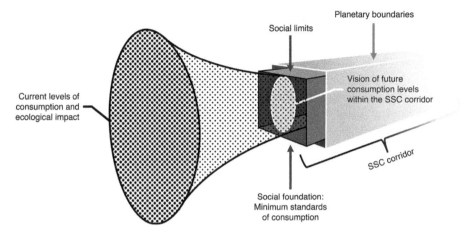

Figure 6.1   The strongly sustainable consumption (SSC) corridor

For example, Kallis (2015), referring to Hirsch (1976), points out that people in affluent societies spend their income increasingly on positional consumption. Yet, if consumption is progressively based on a competitive comparison with others, then, ultimately, it jeopardizes leisure time, sociability and social relations. It takes up time that could be spent on political and other societal engagement. This calls for individuals to consider maximum consumption levels (Di Giulio and Fuchs, 2014).

Considered together, SSC represents a 'corridor' which, as illustrated in Figure 6.1, has both a floor and a ceiling. The floor represents the social foundations for a decent life for all people around the globe, that is, minimum access to the natural and social resources required for human dignity and active participation in society (Spangenberg, 2014). Certainly, towards and within the SSC corridor, different pathways are conceivable and the option for differences in individual consumption remains. To a certain extent, technological and organizational innovations may lift the ceiling for sustainable consumption of products and services. Still, even technological and other innovations have limitations with regard to resource availability and thus leave resource consumption in a range with clear – that is, absolute – limits. As a consequence, the space left between the corridor's floor and ceiling is the space left for collectively achieving SSC. Hence, the corridor's ceiling can be defined by 'maximum standards for every individual's use of resources guaranteeing access to sufficient resources (in terms of quantity and quality) for others, both in the present and the future' (Di Giulio and Fuchs, 2014: 184). But as indicated above, these are not just planetary boundaries of a 'safe operating space for humanity' (Steffen et al., 2015) but also of social and societal limits to sustainable consumption.

Consequently, we must ask: how can social and individual well-being be secured by supporting degrowth and restructuring consumption patterns to stay within the

SSC corridor? How can life be improved for those suffering from malnutrition, for example, without us collectively 'bumping our heads' against the ceiling? Defining and achieving SSC is closely linked to the quest for a good life, which refers to a broad and well-balanced spectrum of human needs (see Chapter 2 by Lorek and Fuchs in this volume). It is not just about the consumption of commodities and services but also about non-material factors such as safety, feelings of belonging and equity (Lorek and Fuchs, 2013). This implies that SSC is not merely an economic challenge, but also one involving many societal actors (for example, businesses, non-governmental organizations (NGOs) and governments) who care about values and cultural aspects of production and consumption beyond business success and individual distinction.

Indeed, SSC requires a socio-cultural and economic transition away from a social paradigm that emphasizes ever more production and consumption, to one that promotes sustainable levels of consumption (Lorek and Fuchs, 2013). Thus, approaches to improve consistency, efficiency, and sufficiency (including degrowth) are called for in the industrially and economically developed regions of the world – particularly with regard to the reduction and replacement of the most energy- and resource-intensive fields of consumption (for example, replacing energy from lignite with renewables, or avoiding air travels) (Stengel, 2011). At the same time, growth and access to consumption opportunities is required in those regions, respectively for those social groups that do not benefit from increases in global wealth (Spangenberg, 2014). In addition, transition countries may face both challenges simultaneously.

This then implies questioning which human needs are addressed by certain modes of production and consumption, and to what extent (Lorek and Fuchs, 2013). It raises questions such as how to move from owning to sharing goods (Mont, 2002; Mont and Tukker, 2006), or how to make use of marketing techniques that favour more responsible consumption styles (Belz and Peattie, 2013). From a business perspective, this leads to challenges at the very heart of the core businesses of companies: how can companies, as the key designers of production–consumption systems, help society to navigate safely through the SSC corridor? What are the sustainability strategies and business models that support SSC? What is the role of business models, and which options to develop alternative business models are available today?

1.2   Outlook on the chapter

The next section will discuss major strategies for sustainable production and consumption and introduce sustainable business model (SBM) patterns as a way of supporting these strategies within the framework of SSC. Building on our prior work in this domain (Froese, 2017; Lüdeke-Freund et al., 2018a; 2018b; 2019a; 2019b; Schaltegger et al., 2012; 2016), the authors of this chapter will discuss the link between business models and SSC and introduce a framework focusing on sustainability strategies and SBM patterns. Finally, we will introduce some new ideas on how SBM patterns could be used by business model designers to tackle SSC challenges.

2. The link: Sustainable consumption and business models

Business models are used to describe, analyse, communicate and design the value creation logic of companies and other types of organization, which includes their value propositions as well as value creation, delivery and capture mechanisms (Massa et al., 2017). Within this domain, business model research and practice that deal with sustainability challenges are rather new (Lüdeke-Freund and Dembek, 2017). According to the core assumptions of this new field, well-designed and successfully implemented business models are expected to create value not only for the company, its customers and business partners but also for other stakeholders, such as groups concerned about the natural environment, local communities or otherwise neglected social groups. In line with this, the notion of a *business model for sustainability* has recently been defined as 'describing, analyzing, managing, and communicating (i) a company's sustainable value proposition to its customers and all other stakeholders, (ii) how it creates and delivers this value, and (iii) how it captures economic value while maintaining or regenerating natural, social, and economic capital beyond its organisational boundaries' (Schaltegger et al., 2016: 6).

But how do business models and SSC interrelate? Many ways of conceptualizing this relationship exist since business models are multidimensional constructs that offer various options, for example, in terms of value proposition design, alternative production processes or managing customer relationships. These business model design options can be used to address certain challenges of SSC, such as the repeatedly observed attitude–behaviour gap: most consumers state that they would prefer more sustainable forms of consumption (for example, healthy and organic food), but only a minority behaves accordingly (see for example, Belz and Peattie, 2013). This observation points to some fundamental barriers that inhibit SSC from the consumer side, such as the lack of information about better offers, the lack of convenience when using alternative products or services or the lack of additional services that help reduce consumption footprints (for example, take-back systems). Figure 6.2 displays exemplary barriers in the different phases of the consumption process.

Business models can be seen as market devices that connect sustainability innovations like ecologically and socially benign products to existing or new markets and thus connect supply and demand (Boons and Lüdeke-Freund, 2013; Doganova and Eyquem-Renault, 2009). Modifications to existing business models and the development of new ones may help to overcome SSC barriers, for example, by offering dematerialized services instead of physical products to increase consumer convenience (Tukker, 2015), or improving the accessibility of health care or education in less developed regions through alternative financing models (Seelos and Mair,

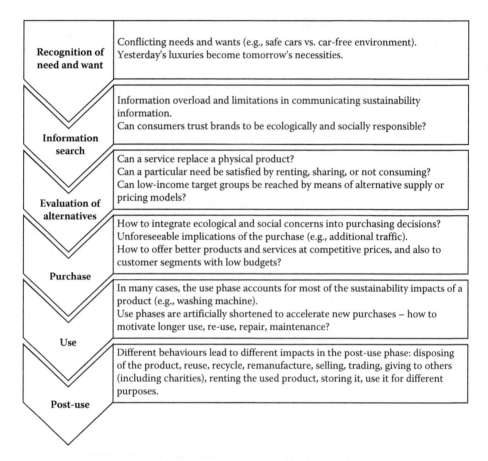

| **Recognition of need and want** | Conflicting needs and wants (e.g., safe cars vs. car-free environment). Yesterday's luxuries become tomorrow's necessities. |

| **Information search** | Information overload and limitations in communicating sustainability information. Can consumers trust brands to be ecologically and socially responsible? |

| **Evaluation of alternatives** | Can a service replace a physical product? Can a particular need be satisfied by renting, sharing, or not consuming? Can low-income target groups be reached by means of alternative supply or pricing models? |

| **Purchase** | How to integrate ecological and social concerns into purchasing decisions? Unforeseeable implications of the purchase (e.g., additional traffic). How to offer better products and services at competitive prices, and also to customer segments with low budgets? |

| **Use** | In many cases, the use phase accounts for most of the sustainability impacts of a product (e.g., washing machine). Use phases are artificially shortened to accelerate new purchases – how to motivate longer use, re-use, repair, maintenance? |

| **Post-use** | Different behaviours lead to different impacts in the post-use phase: disposing of the product, reuse, recycle, remanufacture, selling, trading, giving to others (including charities), renting the used product, storing it, use it for different purposes. |

Source: Based on Belz and Peattie, 2013.

Figure 6.2   Barriers to SSC in the consumption process

2007). It can be concluded that business models bear the potential to support SSC: first, because they function as market devices that bring sustainable consumption alternatives to the market, which can complement or replace conventional offers (for example, Schaltegger et al. 2016), and, second, because they are multidimensional 'tools' that offer a broad range of design options.

The former point (market device) can be illustrated with the impressive case of Aravind Eye Care Systems, an Indian eye care hospital chain offering high-quality medical treatments for free to half of its patients (Seelos, 2014). This is possible because Aravind uses a social freemium business model. The latter point (multitude of design options) is illustrated by a study on circular economy business models, which concludes that (theoretically) millions of options to design business models for the circular economy are possible (Lüdeke-Freund et al., 2018b).

3.   Business models for sustainable consumption: Strategies, cases and criticism

3.1   The framework

Using business models as market devices that offer a broad range of design options allows for a systematic and, to a certain degree, replicable development of operational activities that contribute to more sustainable production–consumption systems. But how can business models for SSC be developed, and how can they become effective? We propose that this can be achieved by using business model patterns that guide the adaptation, innovation or even the complete redesign of business models in line with sustainability strategies (Schaltegger et al., 2012), as illustrated in Figure 6.3.

As every business model follows an implicit or explicit strategy, conventionally with the goal of improving a company's competitive positioning and financial performance (Casadesus-Masanell and Ricart, 2010), we contend that sustainability strategies can also guide business model design to include criteria of ecological and social effectiveness and efficiency, as well as the SSC corridor, in strategic planning, business modelling and implementing operational activities. The next section elaborates on major sustainability strategies which could serve this purpose.

These strategies can help in selecting and developing SBM patterns (Lüdeke-Freund et al., 2018a; 2018b; 2019a) as a source of inspiration and a tool to develop business models for sustainability supporting SSC. The notion of 'pattern' comes from domains such as design or architecture. Alexander et al. (1977: 17) define that a pattern 'describes a problem which occurs over and over again in our environment and then describes the core of the solution to that problem in such a way that you can use this solution a million times over without ever doing it the same way twice'. Patterns are problem–solution combinations that can be repeatedly applied in different contexts. This allows learning from past experiences and increases the efficiency of design processes. Patterns have always been part of business model research and practice, whereas their relationship to sustainability considerations has only recently been defined (Lüdeke-Freund et al., 2018a: 148):

> A sustainable business model pattern describes an ecological, social, and/or economic problem that arises when an organisation aims to create value, and it describes the core of a solution to this problem that can be repeatedly applied in a multitude of ways, situations, contexts, and domains. A sustainable business model pattern also describes the design principles, value-creating activities, and their arrangements that are required to provide a useful problem-solution combination.

Finally, the framework proposes that business model patterns can be used to define the operational activities of companies (Gassmann et al., 2014), that is, their value-creating activity systems (Zott et al., 2011). Designing business models in support of sustainable production–consumption systems is thus about creating operational

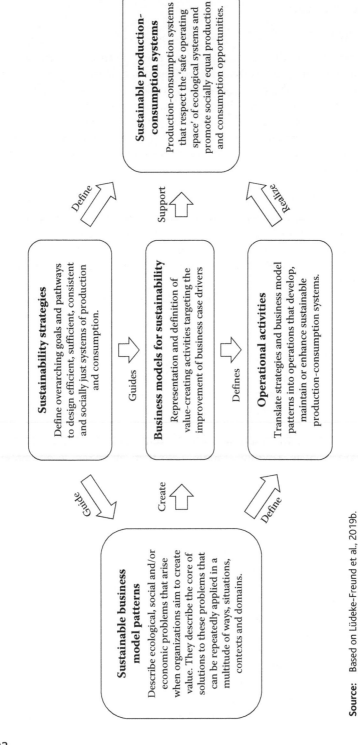

Source: Based on Lüdeke-Freund et al., 2019b.

Figure 6.3 The interplay of sustainability strategies, business models and production–consumption systems

activity systems that help companies and consumers to navigate through the SSC corridor.

3.2   Strategies for sustainable production and consumption

The question that follows on from the previous considerations is how business model design can support companies and consumers in achieving their personal values and ideals of a good life. Any proposed answers to this question must fit in with the SSC corridor as discussed in this chapter's introduction. Considered together, this leads to the following question: how can companies, in an economically feasible manner, support consumers in not, or no longer, collectively overshooting ecological boundaries while achieving a socially balanced level of, and access to, meaningful consumption opportunities?

To approach this essential question, we propose taking a look at a set of strategies presented by Huber (2000) in the early days of the global sustainable development debate: efficiency, consistency and sufficiency. In addition, this strategy triad must be accompanied by socially oriented considerations about fair inclusion, due to important social and cultural aspects. It is important to consider the interplay between these four types of strategy and their mutual influence on each other. Thus far, they have mostly been used in isolation, which should be avoided in system design, such as value-creating activity systems (for instance, business models) and production–consumption systems. Even well-intended strategies such as efficiency or sufficiency can have unintended consequences (for example, rebound effects or decreasing consumer convenience), which can backfire and create higher barriers to future action on SSC. Considering the interplay of these strategies is one way of avoiding such negative side effects.

3.2.1   Efficiency strategies

To begin with, efficiency strategies aim at improving the ecological input–output relations of existing production–consumption systems (Huber, 2000). Typical examples are energy-efficient light bulbs and lean production processes. At best, efficiency decouples increases in consumption and profit-making from resource use (Bartelmus et al., 2004). Correspondingly, '[t]he efficiency strategy is the most applicable and appealing in the prevailing economic system' (Huber, 2000: 280).

The latter, however, may also be its greatest shortcoming. Striving for eco-efficiency is tempting, but it does not always guarantee eco-effectiveness, that is, achieving the absolute goals of SSC. To take one example: once a type of product – be it cars or drilling machines – is open to sharing, less production of the same is required. Consumers might even be able to afford access to higher quality products that last longer or can share repair costs. All these aspects increase use efficiency. Indeed, certain sharing business models such as car sharing are clearly gaining in acceptance and are rapidly scaling up. Consumers who were not able to afford a car, and thus relied on their bike or public transportation, could now choose to use a car more often. Thus, while some might no longer own a car, others will use less public transport. Moreover, with regard to former car owners, sharing potentially sets free financial resources that can be used for additional consumption in other areas leading to indirect rebound effects (Chitnis et al., 2013).

Considered together, efficiency can help reduce environmental impacts and resource use and thereby support competitiveness. Yet, instead of supporting alternative production and consumption practices, improvements in eco-efficiency may also be used to legitimize traditional technologies and structures (for example, individual car traffic). Hence, it may also lead to lock-in and path-dependencies and even stimulate demand through reduced costs ('Jevons paradox', also known as the rebound effect (see Polimeni et al., 2008)). Whether the overall effect of applying an efficiency strategy is positive, large or small thus depends on many interrelated aspects and may often not be clear.

3.2.2   Consistency strategies

Against the background of such shortcomings, Huber (2000) considers consistency as the means for opening up a truly sustainable development path. Following Huber (2000: 280, italics in original), consistency is 'a strategy of *qualitative* change of the industrial metabolism . . .'. The idea of consistency is to create material and energy flows in technological or biological cycles that are either completely separated from, or perfectly compatible with, natural material flows of the biosphere (Braungart et al., 2007). Examples are eco-farming, which contributes to soil quality and biodiversity, or products such as bio-based detergents, designed and produced according to cradle to cradle (C2C) principles.

While some problems of the efficiency strategy are not inherent in the consistency strategy, this approach also faces limitations. Producing biodegradable packaging, for example, could require biomass production in monocultures and cause related problems of biodiversity loss, erosion, and so on. Furthermore, closing technical loops can reduce production costs and consumption after some loops and thus also cause the income effect described above, leading to additional production and consumption.

Furthermore, when Huber discussed this strategy nearly 20 years ago, he stated that asking for practical examples or corresponding predictions is tempting but 'difficult and risky, if not impossible' (Huber, 2000: 281). Yet even today, truly convincing examples are still rare. Consistency goes beyond improved product and production design and requires consonant solutions along the entire life cycle of a product and the corresponding consumption processes (see Figure 6.2), including customer education and take-back services (Belz and Peattie, 2013; Lüdeke-Freund et al., 2018b). In fact, taking the idea of consistency seriously implies thinking about future generations of products and services, too. Thus, consistency strategies imply systemic innovations that conflict with existing dominant designs and interests of incumbents. This becomes even more relevant if we consider that mobilizing the necessary innovative and economic capacities actually requires multi-level efforts and support from industry, finance, research and political leadership, as well as social acceptance on an international level (Huber, 2000).

All things considered, while consistency and efficiency bear the potential to extend the height of the SSC corridor's ecological ceiling, they have (so far) fallen short of aligning it with humanity's actual impact on the biosphere (see Steffen et al., 2015). This then demands sufficiency, that is, renunciation, modesty and being satisfied with less – particularly from affluent consumers (Stengel, 2011).

3.2.3   Sufficiency strategies

Based on considerations of the earth's carrying capacity and resource scarcity, in combination with ethical claims for distributive justice and solidarity, sufficiency strategies aim for shifts in cultural values, institutions and practices of production and consumption. This approach is typically expressed in phrases such as 'sufficiency means doing without' (Huber, 2000). Accordingly, sufficiency includes reduction of resource use and impacts on the natural environment, substitution of non-sustainable practices and stimulation of altered consumer habits. Still, transferring the sufficiency principle to the dominating, growth-driven business world (and private domains of consumers) is challenging.

To briefly discuss an exemplary case, Bocken and Short (2016) refer to Patagonia, an icon in the area of sustainable clothing, as an example of a sufficiency-driven business model. Patagonia is said to produce useful, lasting products, to offer repair and recycling services and even to attempt having their customers reflect on whether they truly need new clothing. Altogether, this suggests that Patagonia's management aims at supporting their customers in adopting more sufficient lifestyles. Yet here, too, objections can be made (Hepburn, 2013; Khmara and Kronenberg, 2018). Patagonia's marketing activities include statements as radical as *Don't Buy This Jacket*, which, in effect, create a highly attractive brand. Thus, Khmara and Kronenberg (2018: 729) conclude that, for the vision of people living happily with less, '. . . Patagonia is not a good example (although neither is hardly any other company)'. Ultimately, Patagonia sells high-priced status symbols to a growing community of 'involved' consumers (Hepburn, 2013).

Nevertheless, acknowledging that ecological (and social) boundaries must be respected, sufficiency-oriented business strategies and business models are called for. To be effective these must overcome several critical barriers, ranging from psychological and behavioural barriers on the individual level, to a culture of consumerism and a growth paradigm dominating business and political economics (Huber, 2000; Lorek and Fuchs, 2013). What is more, even if sufficiency sets free ecological capacities (for example, unused natural resources or forests' capacity to absorb CO_2), which are then safe to be used, this does not directly address the issue of fairly distributing these free capacities.

In conclusion, the introduced strategies must be accompanied by a fourth type of strategy that specifically contributes to an inclusive and fair distribution of available production and consumption opportunities within the SSC corridor.

3.2.4   Inclusion strategies

Based on the considerations above, we add a fourth sustainability strategy under the umbrella of 'social inclusion strategies'. Approaches that can be attributed to this socially focused strategy type are, for instance, forms of social or inclusive business (Yunus et al., 2010).

On the one hand, business models can focus on including fringe groups in value creation and delivery activities to ultimately have them participate in SSC. For example, business models can make use of homeless people's local knowledge or the tactile sense of blind people. Yet, to avoid crossing the thin line between inclusiveness and exploitation, measures such as flat governance structures, balanced salaries, cooperation with NGOs or external supervision are called for (Lüdeke-Freund et al., 2016). On the other hand, inclusion can be focused on the fair redistribution of access to production and consumption opportunities. Here, we see some potential, for example, in freemium business model patterns. These are based on the idea of having affluent consumers pay a premium price, which is then used to subsidize poorer people's access to a product or service (for example, the aforementioned example of Aravind Eye Care Systems; see also Seelos, 2014).

Yet, focusing solely on inclusion strategies bears the risk of being ecologically adverse. For example, eradicating poverty by merely increasing the poor's access to consumption is hardly in line with achieving ecologically feasible levels of resource consumption or GHG emissions. Staying within the confines of the SSC corridor thus requires combining different ecologically and socially oriented strategies.

3.3   From trade-offs to complementary strategies and business model design

Building on the above considerations, we argue that entrepreneurs and managers must find ways to translate the notion of living a *good life* within the SSC corridor into actionable blueprints for their value creation activities. When doing so, they will face absolute ecological, social and economic goals associated with SSC, which must be considered in relation to one another: What trade-offs might occur? (see for example, Hahn et al., 2010) However, taking a different perspective, we argue that the designers of business models for SSC need support in their search for complementary and mutually reinforcing strategies and design options, for example, in order to commercialize products that are healthier, more efficient and effective, and to allow producers to compete in the market (such as Seventh Generation's carcinogen-free detergents, which are not only healthier but also more effective than competing cleaning products (Environmental Defense Fund, n.d.). Aiming for such complementarities, instead of focusing on trade-offs, might sound illusionary

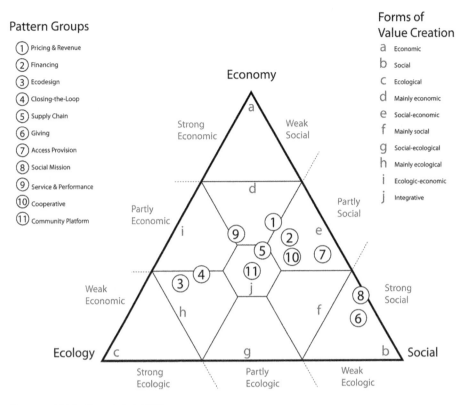

Source: Lüdeke-Freund et al., 2018a.

Figure 6.4   Triangle view on SBM patterns

or maybe even naive. Still, we assume that this perspective bears the potential to motivate a successful search for new and creative solutions.

The available solution space in the search for complementarities and balance between the different sustainability strategies and associated goals of SSC can be illustrated with a 'sustainability triangle' (Schaltegger and Burritt, 2005). The triangle view starts with putting one sustainability dimension at each corner of an isosceles triangle (Figure 6.4). Contributions to the individual dimensions can be measured in absolute terms (for example, tons of CO_2 avoided or number of people having access to healthy nutrition). This means that achieving social, ecological and economic goals is considered separately as a matter of effectiveness. However, as discussed above, the sustainability strategies should also be examined in relative terms, that is, in relation to each other. The same holds for sustainability contributions resulting from these strategies. For example, the economic effectiveness of increased sales volumes could contribute to reaching social objectives but could also conflict with protecting natural resources. In other words, increasing sales volumes may reveal social-economic efficiency, yet also a negative correlation of economic and ecological measures. The integration of all sustainability dimensions can therefore be defined as the overarching goal of designing business models for SSC, that is, to achieve positive contributions, or at least no step backwards, in all dimensions.

4.   Business model patterns for sustainable production–consumption systems

An example of applying a sustainability triangle to explore the design options for business models supporting SSC is demonstrated in Figure 6.4. This builds on the 'integrative sustainability triangle' by Kleine and von Hauff (2009), which is used to structure SBM patterns according to their expected value creation potential. Eleven SBM pattern groups are mapped against different forms of value creation (Lüdeke-Freund et al., 2018a).

The closer a pattern group (respectively the individual patterns in this group) is to one of the corners of the triangle, the more it is associated with value creation in the respective sustainability dimension. Partial associations imply that a pattern is expected to contribute to multiple forms of value creation and, accordingly, is arranged more centrally between the corresponding dimensions. Thus, the centre represents the special case of patterns integrating ecological, social and economic demands. The arrangement of patterns relative to their assumed value creation potential results from an expert consensus, that is, it reflects the expectations of researchers and practitioners and thus builds on theoretical as well as practical knowledge (Lüdeke-Freund et al., 2018a). Patterns codify and pass on this knowledge in a very efficient way, which allows designers to use this knowledge directly without any further 'translation'. Patterns addressing similar or related sustainability challenges, such as closing material or energy flows (pattern group 4 in Figure 6.4), form a group. In total, the eleven groups comprise 45 individual SBM patterns, one of which is shown in Table 6.1. The description of each pattern is standardized and follows a template including information about the problem it addresses and the solution it offers, the context in which it can be applied as well as related patterns and examples.[1]

The 'Differential Pricing' pattern shown in Table 6.1 belongs to the Pricing and Revenue pattern group shown in Figure 6.4. It exemplifies how multiple barriers to SSC can be addressed by applying SBM patterns, and, even more so, by combining different patterns. While the notion of 'Differential Pricing' – offering different prices for the same product or service to different target groups – is not new and has been used across diverse industries, the idea of combining this pattern with other patterns (such as 'Access Provision' or 'Closing-the-Loop' patterns) opens up new ways of designing SBMs in general and business models for SSC in particular. The 'Differential Pricing' pattern could thus serve as one approach for companies to achieve inclusion strategies while navigating through the SSC corridor.

Table 6.1 Exemplary pattern: Differential Pricing

Pattern name	Differential Pricing
Problem statement	Customers need a similar product but have different payment thresholds. Some customers are unable to pay as much as others for the same product.
Solution statement	Charging groups with higher payment thresholds higher prices to subsidize those groups who cannot afford to pay as much.
Context description and related patterns	Due to price barriers, low-income groups and customers at the 'base of the pyramid' are often excluded from consuming certain products and services. To address this, companies can increase their availability through Micro Distribution and Retail, make donations based on a Buy One, Give One pattern or involve low-income customers by Building a Marketplace. Typically, companies use Differential Pricing patterns to widen the spectrum of involved customer segments, that is, to grow their customer base, revenues and profits. From a sustainability perspective, the notion of growing a company's customer base is about including neglected customer groups, for example, by offering basic services such as food and health care at lower prices.
Further explanations and examples	The majority of consumers in developed and developing countries spend a significant share of their income to satisfy essential needs, such as health and mobility. By adjusting the price of an offering with regard to what target groups can afford, Differential Pricing creates benefits for those who might otherwise be excluded from consumption. In developing countries, high costs of medicine and treatment are a barrier to accessing health care for low-income groups. Novo Nordisk has addressed this challenge by selling insulin in developing countries at prices that are up to 20% below the mean prices charged in Europe and elsewhere.
Further related patterns	Differential Pricing can be combined with Closing-the-Loop Patterns (e.g. Repair, Reuse or Take-Back Management) to offer discounts to customers who return used goods.

Source: Based on Lüdeke-Freund et al., 2018a; 2019a.

Using SBM patterns in combination leads to an SBM pattern 'language' (Lüdeke-Freund et al., 2019a). Figure 6.5 illustrates the idea of such a language by combining different patterns (words) to create more comprehensive business model designs (sentences or stories). Different patterns can embellish, integrate and support each other, which allows for the development of much richer business model designs. The 'Differential Pricing' example indicates how pattern combinations can lead to more complete and versatile business models that are better suited for implementing the above-discussed sustainability strategies and considering their complementarities, but also their downsides and potential trade-offs. For example, improving the accessibility of medical treatments in developing countries may increase medical waste and create new risks to people and the environment. This downside, in turn, could be mitigated through take-back mechanisms. An SBM pattern language

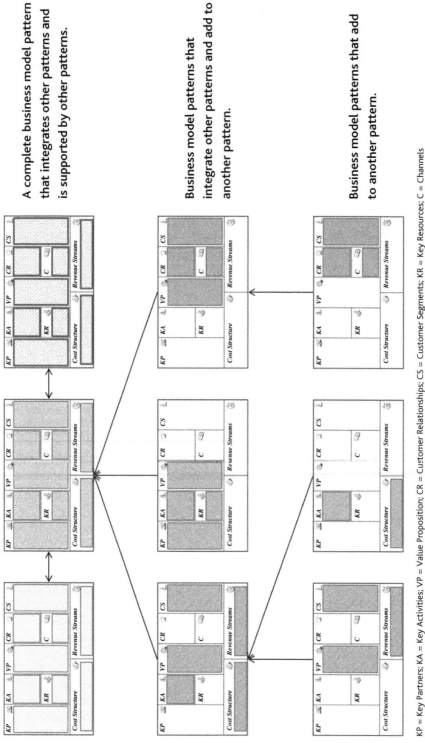

A complete business model pattern that integrates other patterns and is supported by other patterns.

Business model patterns that integrate other patterns and add to another pattern.

Business model patterns that add to another pattern.

KP = Key Partners; KA = Key Activities; VP = Value Proposition; CR = Customer Relationships; CS = Customer Segments; KR = Key Resources; C = Channels

Source: Lüdeke-Freund et al., 2019a; Business Model Canvas based on Osterwalder and Pigneur, 2009.

Figure 6.5 Illustration of connections between business model patterns

could thus be an effective approach to design more integrative and balanced business models for SSC.

5.   Final remarks and outlook

The main ideas discussed in this chapter relate to the role of business models in supporting SSC, the consideration of major sustainability strategies and finally how SBM patterns can be a way of designing better business models for SSC. These ideas are meant to serve as a starting point for more comprehensive debates about how business models can support SSC, going beyond the often-heard calls for efficiency, consistency and sufficiency, which too often do not acknowledge that neither sustainability strategies nor business models unfold in a vacuum. Therefore, it is important to consider multiple sustainability strategies and business model design options at the same time – a complex but, as we think, worthwhile effort to create business models for a *good life* within the corridor of SSC. To support business model designers, an increasing number of tools is already available (see the review in Breuer et al., 2018). The aforementioned 45 SBM patterns can already be used online, together with an additional set of 25 patterns for circular economy business models (Lüdeke-Freund et al., 2018a; 2018b; Smart Business Modeler, 2019).

Coming back to the issues laid out in the introduction and the promises of using sustainability strategies and SBM patterns, some final remarks are necessary. All in all, each strategy and pattern has the (theoretical) potential of contributing to SSC, yet in different ways and, moreover, each approach is in itself limited and may even be a trigger for negative consequences in other places of our global, networked and highly complex production–consumption systems.

Efficiency gains may be overcompensated by increasing demand and economic growth (which does not mean that efficiency gains are unimportant, but that they are often not enough to achieve the required improvement). Consistency goes beyond incremental improvements and aims for 'compatibility between the industrial and natural metabolism' (Huber, 2000: 275), but as described above, faces problems, too. Together, these two strategies strive for a radical systems change, but merely from a technological perspective on resource use (McDonough and Braungart, 2013). Thus, to be sufficiently effective, also considering minimum standards of living as well as social limits to consumption, these strategies must be combined with approaches aiming for sufficiency and inclusion that will not concurrently reach the floor and crush the ceiling of the SSC corridor. Sufficiency strategies build upon values such as distributional justice and solidarity as well as the idea of a *good life*. Its full achievement, however, appears difficult in face of our economic and cultural realities and does not fully address questions of distributive justice. This blind spot is addressed by strategies for inclusion. As Huber remarked in 2000, to reveal their full strength, the introduced sustainability strategies must be discussed and applied as a set of interrelated, mutually reinforcing strategies, and the same holds for the different SBM patterns that are available today. Only if applied in conjunction ('smart design') do they have the potential to contribute to a re-design of production and consumption practices for strong sustainability.

Yet, while there is potential for business to contribute to more inclusive access to consumption, for example, by designing SBMs that integrate multiple and well-balanced patterns, it is first and foremost a political issue at both the intra- and international level. Sustainability politics has not been considered in this chapter but is addressed in other chapters of this book (see Chapters 2 and 9). Moreover, achieving 'eco-justice' (Schaltegger and Burritt, 2005), that is, achieving social objectives while remaining within ecological limits, requires free and distributable ecological capacities in the first place. The ongoing negotiations about national commitments to combat climate change reveal how difficult this is.

NOTE

1 For more details on the SBM patterns and groups, see Lüdeke-Freund et al. (2018a; 2019b).

References

Alexander, C., S. Ishikawa, M. Silverstein et al. (1977), *A Pattern Language: Towns, Buildings, Construction*, New York: Oxford University Press.

Bartelmus, P., S. Moll, S., Bringezu et al. (2004), 'Translating sustainable development into practice: A "patchwork" of some new concepts and an introduction to material flows analysis', in R. Bleischwitz and P. Hennicke (eds), *Eco-Efficiency, Regulation and Sustainable Business*, Cheltenham, UK and Northampton, MA, USA: Edward Elgar Publishing, pp. 1–38.

Belz, F.-M. and K. Peattie (2013), *Sustainability Marketing: A Global Perspective*, 2nd edn, Chichester: Wiley.

Bocken, N.M.P. and S.W. Short (2016), 'Towards a sufficiency-driven business model: Experiences and opportunities', *Environmental Innovation and Societal Transitions*, **18**, 41–61.

Boons, F. and F. Lüdeke-Freund (2013), 'Business models for sustainable innovation. State-of-the-art and steps towards a research agenda', *Journal of Cleaner Production*, **45**, 9–19.

Braungart, M., W. McDonough and A. Bollinger (2007), 'Cradle-to-cradle design: creating healthy emissions – a strategy for eco-effective product and system design', *Journal of Cleaner Production*, **15** (13–14), 1337–48.

Breuer, H., K. Fichter, F. Lüdeke-Freund et al. (2018), 'Sustainability-oriented business model development: Principles, criteria and tools', *International Journal of Entrepreneurial Venturing*, **10** (2), 256–86.

Casadesus-Masanell, R. and J. Ricart (2010), 'From strategy to business models and onto tactics', *Long Range Planning*, **43** (2–3), 195–215.

Chitnis, M., S. Sorrell, A. Druckman et al. (2013), 'Turning lights into flights: Estimating direct and indirect rebound effects for UK households', *Energy Policy*, **55**, 234–50.

Di Giulio, A. and D. Fuchs (2014), 'Sustainable consumption corridors: Concept, objections and responses, *GAIA*, **23** (1), 184–92.

Doganova, L. and M. Eyquem-Renault (2009), 'What do business models do? Innovation devices in technology entrepreneurship', *Research Policy*, **38** (10), 1559–70.

Environmental Defense Fund (n.d.), 'Seventh generation LLC case study summary', accessed 30 January 2017 at http://business.edf.org/projects/7th-generation-case-study.

Froese, T. (2017), 'Time for new relationships: Stakeholder relationship patterns of post-growth businesses', Master's thesis, University of Hamburg.

Gassmann, O., K. Frankenberger and M. Csik (2014), *The Business Model Navigator: 55 Models that will Revolutionise your Business*, London: Pearson Education Limited.

Hahn, T., F. Figge, J. Pinkse et al. (2010), 'Trade-offs in corporate sustainability: You can't have your cake and eat it', *Business Strategy and the Environment*, **19** (4), 217–29.

Hepburn, S.J. (2013), 'In Patagonia (clothing): A complicated greenness', *Fashion Theory*, **17** (5), 623–45.

Hirsch, F. (1976), *Social Limits to Growth*, Cambridge, MA: Harvard University Press.

Huber, J. (2000), 'Towards industrial ecology: Sustainable development as a concept of ecological modernization', *Journal of Environmental Policy Planning*, **2** (4), 269–85.

International Panel on Climate Change (2018), 'Summary for policymakers', in V. Masson-Delmotte, P. Zhai, H.-O. Pörtner et al. (eds), *Global warming of 1.5°C. An IPCC special report on the impacts of global warming of 1.5°C above pre-industrial levels and related global greenhouse gas emission pathways, in the context of strengthening the global response to the threat of climate change, sustainable development, and efforts to eradicate poverty*, Geneva: World Meteorological Organization.

Kallis, G. (2015), 'Social limits of growth', in Giacomo D'Alisa, Federico Demaria and Giorgos Kallis (eds), *Degrowth: A Vocabulary for a New Era*, New York, Abingdon, UK: Routledge, pp. 137–40.

Khmara, Y. and J. Kronenberg (2018), 'Degrowth in business: An oxymoron or a viable business model for sustainability?', *Journal of Cleaner Production*, **177**, 721–31.

Kleine, A. and M. von Hauff (2009), 'Sustainability-driven implementation of corporate social responsibility: Application of the integrative sustainability triangle', *Journal of Business Ethics*, **85**, 517–33.

Lorek, S. and D. Fuchs (2013), 'Strong sustainable consumption governance – precondition for a degrowth path?', *Journal of Cleaner Production*, **38**, 36–43.

Lüdeke-Freund, F. and K. Dembek (2017), 'Sustainable business model research and practice: Emerging field or passing fancy?', *Journal of Cleaner Production*, **168**, 1668–78.

Lüdeke-Freund, F., L. Massa, N.M.P. Bocken et al. (2016), 'Business models for shared value, main report', accessed 21 January 2019 at http://www.nbs.net.

Lüdeke-Freund, F., S. Carroux, A. Joyce et al. (2018a), 'The sustainable business model pattern taxonomy – 45 patterns to support sustainability-oriented business model innovation', *Sustainable Production and Consumption*, **15**, 145–62.

Lüdeke-Freund, F., S. Gold and N.M.P. Bocken (2018b), 'A review and typology of circular economy business model patterns', *Journal of Industrial Ecology*, **23** (1), 36–61.

Lüdeke-Freund, F., R. Bohnsack, H. Breuer et al. (2019a), 'Research on sustainable business model patterns – status quo, methodological issues and a research agenda', in A. Aagaard (ed.), *Sustainable Business Models*, London: Palgrave, pp. 25–60.

Lüdeke-Freund, F., S. Schaltegger and K. Dembek (2019b), 'Strategies and drivers of sustainable business model innovation', in F. Boons et al. (eds), *Handbook of Sustainability Innovation*, Cheltenham, UK and Northampton, MA, USA: Edward Elgar Publishing.

Massa, L., C. Tucci and A. Afuah (2017), 'A critical assessment of business model research', *Academy of Management Annals*, **11** (1), 73–104.

McDonough, W. and M. Braungart (2013), *The Upcycle*, New York: North Point Press.

Mont, O. (2002), 'Clarifying the concept of product–service system', *Journal of Cleaner Production*, **10**, 237–45.

Mont, O. and A. Tukker (2006), 'Product-service systems: Reviewing achievements and refining the research agenda', *Journal of Cleaner Production*, **14**, 1451–4.

Osterwalder, A. and Y. Pigneur (2009), *Business Model Generation: A Handbook for Visionaries, Game Changers and Challengers*, Amsterdam: self-published.

Polimeni, J., K. Mayumi, M. Giampietro et al. (2008), *Jevons Paradox and the Myth of Resource Efficiency Improvements*, London: Earthscan.

Schaltegger, S. and R. Burritt (2005), 'Corporate sustainability', in H. Folmer and T. Tietenberg (eds), *International Yearbook of Environmental and Resource Economics 2005/2006*, Cheltenham, UK and Northampton, MA, USA: Edward Elgar Publishing, pp. 185–222.

Schaltegger, S., F. Lüdeke-Freund and E. Hansen (2012), 'Business cases for sustainability: The role of business model innovation for corporate sustainability', *International Journal of Innovation and Sustainable Development*, **6** (2), 95–119.

Schaltegger, S., E. Hansen and F. Lüdeke-Freund (2016), 'Business models for sustainability: Origins, present research, and future avenues', *Organization and Environment*, **29** (1), 3–10.

Seelos, C. (2014), 'Theorising and strategising with models: Generative models of social enterprises', *International Journal of Entrepreneurial Venturing*, **6** (1), 6–21.

Seelos, C. and J. Mair (2007), 'Profitable business models and market creation in the context of deep poverty: A strategic view', *Academy of Management Perspectives*, **21** (4), 49–63.

Smart Business Modeler (2019), 'Sustainable business model pattern pack', accessed 12 February 2019 at https://smartbusinessmodeler.com/business_model_database/sustainable-business-models/.

Spangenberg, J.H. (2014), 'Institutional change for strong sustainable consumption: Sustainable consumption and the degrowth economy', *Sustainability: Science, Practice and Policy*, **10** (1), 62–77.

Steffen, W., K. Richardson, J. Rockström et al. (2015), 'Planetary boundaries: Guiding human development on a changing planet', *Science* **347** (6223).

Stengel, O. (2011), *Suffizienz. Die Konsumgesellschaft in der ökologischen Krise*, [*Sufficiency: Consumer society in ecological crisis*], Munich: Oekom Verlag.

Tukker, A. (2015), 'Product services for a resource-efficient and circular economy – a review', *Journal of Cleaner Production*, **97**, 76–91.

Weiss, M. and C. Cattaneo (2017), 'Degrowth – taking stock and reviewing an emerging academic paradigm', *Ecological Economics*, **137**, 220–30.

Yunus, M., B. Moingeon and L. Lehmann-Ortega (2010), 'Building social business models: Lessons from the Grameen experience', *Long Range Planning*, **43** (2–3), 308–25.

Zott, C., R. Amit and L. Massa (2011), 'The business model: Recent developments and future research', *Journal of Management*, **37**, 1019–42.

7 Prosumption for sustainable consumption and its implications for sustainable consumption governance

Matthias Lehner

1. Introduction: The triumph of the linear input-use-disposal economy

The market economy has turned individuals in Western societies from self-sufficient, low-throughput producers of goods to highly interdependent, high-throughput consumers of goods. It has also turned our societies into massive resource-consuming and waste-creating operations. Dramatically improved production methods offer access to new goods at lower prices. This has shifted the economic logic of maintaining and repairing goods to replacing them frequently instead. However, this development has also turned once resource-efficient sufficiency economies into industrialized overconsumption societies with high environmental impacts. There are two main reasons for the replacement of sufficiency with overconsumption; (1) productivity gains in industrial production processes resulting in increased purchasing power, and (2) sophisticated marketing and sales tactics.

First, since the Industrial Revolution, production in factories capitalizing on technological innovation and specialization have greatly outperformed the largely self-reliant production system that preceded it. It became cheaper for individuals to consume that which other people produced rather than producing themselves. Highly productive factories lowered per unit production costs and increased economies of scale, making their products even cheaper. Furthermore, increased productivity resulted in great increases in gross domestic profit (GDP) per capita and purchasing power (Lucas, 1988). The world population grew from 3 billion in 1960 to 5.2 billion in 1990 (Lucas 1998), while world production grew from USD 6.7 trillion to USD 22.3 trillion. Production per person in real income (purchasing power parity) grew at 2.2 per cent per year, and thus more than doubled for the average world citizen. More productive individuals needed to work less to attain more purchasing power, and thus a large global consumer class with extra income at its disposal was created. Productivity expressed as GDP per hour worked increased from USD 22.30 in 1970 to USD 59.80 in 2016 for Germany (a 168% rise in 46 years), or from USD 31.10 per hour in 1970 to USD 63.30 in 2016 for the USA (a 104% rise in 46 years) (Organisation for Economic Co-operation and Development, n.d.). This led to almost complete abandonment of self-sufficiency in industrialized economies as it simply did not make economic sense to grow your own vegetables, sew your own clothes, or make your own furniture, compared to purchasing them on the market. Likewise, repairing items became increasingly uneconomical compared to the production of new consumption goods. In industrialized societies, most individuals are specialists, not generalists, dependent on others to produce most of the goods they need in their lives (Toffler, 1980).

Second, increased purchasing power in industrialized economies made it possible for individuals to purchase new goods for pleasure and not out of necessity. This spurred the marketing industry to develop strategies to increase sales of new goods in order to attract this disposable income. Critics go so far as to claim that marketing has changed Westerners' lives from 'consuming to live' into 'living to consume' (Shaw and Newholm, 2002). Marketing, it is argued, has perpetuated the commodification of life in which the market economy absorbs non-market areas of life, equating growing consumption levels with increased quality of life (Kilbourne et al., 1997). Marketing, seen through this lens, thereby perpetuates the ideology of consumerism, with all its negative environmental and social consequences. It is argued that marketing has even co-opted the sustainability debate and turned it into products and profit (Moisander et al., 2010), thereby perpetuating the linear production–consumption model of the market economy (Arvidsson, 2005).

Together, productivity gains, increased purchasing power and a sophisticated marketing industry have created environmentally harmful levels of overconsumption in industrialized countries. Productivity gains have made mass production cheaper than sufficiency production and have simultaneously resulted in more disposable income. Sophisticated marketing and sales strategies have successfully encouraged individuals to spend any extra income on seeking pleasure and meaning through ever more consumption. Unfortunately, individuals with higher incomes also have higher ecological footprints (Aşıcı and Acar, 2016).

Overconsumption is thus a problem of the global consumer class. This chapter discusses the idea of the prosumer as a remedy for overconsumption and its environmental consequences. I argue that there are two types of prosumption – for pleasure and out of economic necessity. I also argue that these two types of prosumption must be discussed in different ways within sustainable consumption governance in order for prosumption to become a force for achieving more sustainable levels of consumption.

2.   The age of prosumption

The term 'prosumer' originally coined by Alvin Toffler (1980) refers to the development of the individual's participation in markets from being a passive consumer to an active participant in production, maintenance and repair of consumer goods (Ritzer et al., 2012). This participatory role of consumers in production is enabled by modern technology: for example, DIY tutorials on the Internet; peer-to-peer platforms (Ritzer et al., 2012); better access to tools and raw materials; makerspaces with professional equipment; lower costs for equipment; cheaper access to parts and materials from across the globe (Bradley, 2016); shifting public preferences towards service- and experience-based consumption (Ritzer et al., 2012); and a (cautious) effort by authorities to counteract a linear production–consumption system. Due to these factors numerous makerspaces, tool libraries, and open workshops have been established by grassroots movements and public actors to encourage and support this development (Bradley, 2016). In its broadest sense, prosumption embraces the co-creation of value proposition, product and service innovation, production, advertising, and extension of use (renting out) (Bardhi and Eckhardt, 2017). It can happen in a commercial setting (for example, Build-a-Bear workshop) or in a less commercial environment (for example, bike kitchens).

Indeed, value creation has moved from the workbench to the marketing depart-ment and, most recently, into the consumption practices of the individual (Prahalad and Ramaswamy, 2004a; 2004b; Vargo and Lusch, 2004; 2008). Toffler (1980) argued that the post-industrial age would lead to an increase in prosumer-ism; individuals who actively participated in the production of the goods they consume. He describes this development in three waves: (1) sufficiency (or pro-duction for use), (2) consumption (production for sale) and (3) prosumption (the co-creation of products). For Toffler, the main distinction between the traditional production process and prosumers was that goods are produced in the first case for someone else, while prosumers produce for themselves. This has implications for product value, which, in the case of prosumption, is measured not only in monetary terms, but also in the time invested in production and in the added value that participation in production adds to the product. This means that the same production process may allow for vastly different levels of value creation, depending on the amount of effort the prosumer puts into the production process. This, for Toffler, will lead to a demarketization and demassification of produc-tion. Toffler attributes this development to societal long-term developments like reduced working hours, higher educational levels, increased labour costs for skilled labour, and a desire among individuals to be physically active, as well as a belief among some people that they can produce an individually more suitable product for themselves than the market.

Toffler's idea was being viewed with some scepticism as early as 1986 (Kotler, 1986), and it must be acknowledged that the changes Toffler anticipated have not yet materialized. Despite some examples from the last 30 years that offer anecdotal evidence for the changes that Toffler believed would emerge, it is hard to ignore the overall trend of increasingly faster linear production and consumption, with more goods being bought for less money and disposed of without maintenance and repair. Mobile phones, for example, are not only famously short-lived, with an aver-age lifetime of two to three years, but they are also notoriously difficult to repair (see the iFixit 'Smartphone Repairability Scores' (iFixit, n.d.).[1] Unfortunately, many other products also exemplify the short-lived consumer culture of today (Cooper, 2016).

Against this context, prosumerist practices are largely niche; they are also often performed in addition to high-volume 'conventional' consumption rather than instead of it. Kotler (1986) refers to the latter as 'the avid hobbyist': individuals who spend most of their time producing for others and consuming from others and who fill their leisure time with practices (hobbies) that turn them into prosumers during these moments. According to Kotler, this is distinct from what he terms 'the archprosumer'. This second type of prosumer practises a lifestyle of 'voluntary simplicity';[2] they are also highly productive (see also Salvia and Cooper, 2016). Their underlying theme is 'small is beautiful' and 'less is more' (Kotler, 1986).

Despite Kotler's scepticism, Ritzer and Rey (cited in Davis, 2016: 160) claim that we are about to witness 'the age of the prosumer'. No doubt aware of the loaded nature of their statement, they qualify their claim by putting it into historical context. They acknowledge both its beginnings in 1980 with Toffler, and Kotler's more cautious approach in 1986. They further acknowledge that despite the three decades since the claimed mass arrival of prosumerism, it is still marginal. What makes them argue that we might finally have arrived at 'the age of the prosumer' is the revolution in information and communication technology (ICT). The arrival of the Internet and of social and knowledge exchange platforms, such as Facebook, Wikipedia and YouTube, have led to a dramatically changed production of and access to knowledge (Ritzer and Rey, cited in Davis, 2016) making the distinction between producer and consumer ever more blurred. Much like Toffler (1980), Ritzer (2014) argues that the distinction between production and consumption is a consequence of the Industrial Revolution, during which production changed rapidly during its beginnings, while consumption patterns and levels have changed in its later stages. Ritzer and Rey (in Davis, 2016) claim that the US society of today is a consumption and not a production society. Not only is the average American more often a consumer than a producer, but she receives increasing responsibility (or freedom) to take charge of the production process, for example: ordering food at a self-service counter, putting together self-build furniture or preparing food delivered in bags with ingredients and cooking instructions.

Marketing scholars discuss this idea of market-supported self-production of products and services as co-creation or co-production. The idea that has taken hold is that of the consumer as the ultimate value creator. Vargo and Lusch (2004) argue that value creation over the last half century has moved from the production line (as in the post-Second World War thrift economy) to the marketing department (in the recent needs creation and consumption perpetuation overflow economy), now ending with the consumer (in the global, highly competitive and connected economy of today).

The justification for this development can be found both in economic reasoning (fewer employees are necessary in a shop where consumers operate their own scanning and payment machines or where consumers build their own furniture from parts) and emotional reasoning (a child values a bear that she has built herself more than a teddy bear from the shelf that looks the same as any other). Marketing scholars such as Prahalad and Ramaswamy (2004b), or Vargo and Lusch (2004) argue that the lines between producers and consumers are becoming increasingly blurred in postmodern societies and that this offers new opportunities for businesses to create and capture value.

3.   Prosumerism as sustainable consumption?

The individual acting primarily as consumer in society has been heavily criticized in relation to the environmental cost of an (over-)consumption lifestyle. Alternative, less environmentally harmful ways to satisfy individuals' need for goods have had limited success. Low production and transaction costs for purchasing new products, compared with high production and transaction costs for maintenance and repair of older products, combined with the marketing-induced social desirability of new products, have doomed any attempt to reverse the consumption logic towards high-quality, low-throughput consumption.

Prosumption has received attention in recent years due to its perceived potential to achieve the functions that consumption performs for the individual, but with reduced environmental impact (Eden, 2017). The hope expressed is that prosumption will lead to increased demand for products of high quality and an uptake in the maintenance, repair and reuse of goods (Kohtala, 2015). This hope builds on a few recent changes in society, the economy and technology.

3.1   Awareness of environmental problems related to overconsumption

First, collective awareness about the problems associated with high levels of consumption are receiving more attention (see Reser et al., 2011 for a study regarding concern about climate change). While the 1960s, 1970s, 1980s and partly the 1990s were dominated by a lack of awareness and a belief in technological solutions for any potential consumption-related problem, the turn of the millennium has seen increasing scepticism towards humankind's ingenuity in finding technological solutions and a growing awareness about the scale of the problem. This has resulted in a shift in values and attitude with regard to the purchase of new goods compared to the maintenance and repair of quality goods. In fact, the very nature of newness and 'untouchedness' is somewhat losing its allure. Sharing usage and reusing what others have used before is becoming ever more popular. This is evident, not least, in the surge of popularity in second-hand (vintage) clothes and the consequent loss of stigma associated with wearing used clothes (Cassidy and Bennett, 2012; Fischer, 2015; Parsons, 2002; Veenstra and Kuipers, 2013). It has become more socially acceptable to preserve, repair and reuse (Salvia and Cooper, 2016). This is also reflected in cautious political action. While politicians have proven wary of disrupting the market economy in any major way, they have indeed been experimenting with incentives to encourage maintenance and repair/reuse. The Swedish government, for example, lowered VAT on repair services for bicycles, shoes, leather goods, clothes and home textiles from 25 per cent to 12 per cent (Swedish Ministry of Finance, 2016).

This change in what is deemed societally preferable holds the potential for prosumption to change how people think about themselves and who they strive to be, or at least how they appear to others.

3.2   Information and communication technology

Technological innovation has resulted in a dramatic reduction in the transaction costs of prosumption. The revolution in ICT has resulted in a cornucopia of readily available knowledge on how to maintain and repair goods. Fox (2014), for example, lists several ICT-enabled tools for DIY work:

1.   OpenMaterials, a website dedicated to the open source making of materials;
2.   Instructables, a website for users to share DIY tutorials;
3.   Make Magazine, a web- and print magazine for the DIY community.

The same ICT revolution has also allowed for very different interaction between end-consumers and producers (producer-to-consumer) (Vargo and Lusch, 2004) as well as among consumers (peer-to-peer) (Eden, 2017), allowing for much closer interaction between actors. In the case of producer-to-consumer interaction, this development opens up the potential for long-term interaction between producers and consumers that thrives on more than sales (for example, service agreements, skills training and education). This is what Vargo and Lusch (2004) have called service-oriented logic in business, leading to value co-creation. On the level of consumer-to-consumer interaction, it allows the formation of decentralized networks of individuals that blur the lines between producers and consumers (Eden, 2017). Furthermore, the ease with which ICT allows for such peer-to-peer interaction pushes such behaviour from niche to mainstream (Eden, 2017). Indeed, Ritzer (2014) suggests that the Internet is the natural home of prosumers today.

Interestingly, this development not only offers simple, cheap and fast access to knowledge, but also offers a simple, cheap and readily available platform to communicate and self-promote consumption acts. In Eden's (2017) words, the Internet offers a space to harness 'likes' for one's prosumption achievements.

3.3   Cheaper access to production resources

The revolutionary changes in ICT have also made it significantly easier for individuals to access raw materials and tools. Nowadays high-tech components, parts and professional tools can be ordered from across the globe via online retailers such as Alibaba and Amazon at relatively low prices. Furthermore, platforms such as 100kGarages or Shapeways allow creative individuals to connect with manufacturers who will custom manufacture their designs (Fox, 2014). Equipment and tools for DIY maintenance and repair have also become more accessible, even for non-professionals, and access to specialized tools has become much easier (Fox, 2014), not least due to the proliferation of DIY workshops of all sorts that can be accessed for free or a small fee. Makerspaces have emerged in many urban areas.

Here individuals can – for low fees or for free – access advanced equipment, as well as skills or parts.

Together, higher awareness of the environmental and social consequences of over-consumption, easier access to equipment and parts, and the knowledge of how to use them could push prosumption from being a niche activity into the mainstream and thus have the potential to reduce overconsumption.

4.   Two ways in which prosumption can result in more sustainable consumption

As stated by Kotler (1986), there are two types of prosumers – (1) the 'avid hobby-ist' and (2) the 'archprosumer' – to which the above forces apply in different ways. Increased consciousness about the negative consequences of overconsumption and a resulting shift in desirable behaviour towards quality and maintenance, as well as significantly easier access to the necessary knowledge and skills, increase the experience value gained from prosumption for the avid hobbyist. In order for these individuals to become prosumers, an act of prosumption must be attractive enough to invest time that would otherwise be spent on other (consumption) behaviour. Time, not products, is the primary factor that differentiates this from other consumption behaviour. For this to happen, individuals must find more value in spending time on prosumption than on consumption. The archprosumer, on the other hand, is more often limited by money and engages in prosumption for primarily economic reasons. For the archprosumer, any prosumption activity will directly reduce the need to consume the product since the primary motivating force is the ability to gain access to goods more cheaply than through consumption.

I have modified Kolter's terminology and adopted different terms for these two distinctly different types of prosumption in order to capture this main distinction in the motivational force to engage in prosumption: (1) 'emotional prosumption' (primarily connected to the avid hobbyist) and (2) 'economic prosumption' (primarily connected to the archprosumer).

This distinction is important as prosumption only has an impact on overconsumption patterns if an act of prosumption replaces an act of consumption. Indeed, where prosumption is an add-on to unchanged consumption behaviour, no positive impact on consumption levels can be expected. This distinction becomes more relevant due to the continuously widening wealth gap in industrialized economies of recent decades. Wealth and income in industrialized economies are becoming more unequal, with some individuals having a great deal of money, but little time, while others have a great deal of time but little money at their disposal.[3] For the latter group, the maintenance and repair of old goods has become a more attractive option as DIY has become more financially attractive due to the above-mentioned reasons. These consumers are money-poor, but time-rich, and it is most likely that prosumption will replace the need to purchase goods (Figure 7.1).

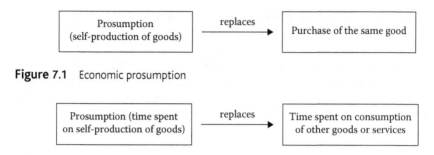

Figure 7.1   Economic prosumption

Figure 7.2   Emotional prosumption

Any act of economic prosumption will therefore primarily be an add-on to the consumption these individuals can afford, while they use their time to free up their limited disposable income for other acts of consumption. This has further implications for the nature of prosumption engaged in by these individuals, as only money-saving prosumption is of interest to this type of prosumer.

However, this type of prosumption is of limited relevance for the problem of overconsumption, as overconsumption is not caused by economically restrained individuals. The wealthy consumer class – those individuals with excess income to spend on consumption not essential to their existence – is the main cause of global overconsumption. Their prosumption activity is an expression of emotional preference for prosumption compared to other activities they could do in their limited time (Figure 7.2).

These consumers are rich in money but have little (or no) excess time and self-production replaces another leisure activity. An act of emotional prosumption thus results in less time to spend on other activities.

To illustrate this distinction, I would like to refer to the example of *Cykelköket* (bike kitchen) in Malmö, Sweden. This is a DIY repair workshop for bicycles that offers free access to tools and used spare parts, as well as a community of people interested in bicycles, and provides the possibility for them to learn from each other (Bradley, 2016). As a regular visitor, the author of this chapter has observed that there are two types of users: those that come to the bike kitchen to practise their hobby and whose primary motivation is to enjoy themselves, and those that come in order to gain access to a bicycle as cheaply as possible. While the observable actions of both groups are identical – they both build, repair and maintain bicycles – the impact of their actions on their consumption patterns will be very different. For the economically constrained individual, time spent in the bike kitchen will most likely replace the purchase of a bicycle. The bike kitchen primarily enables this individual to put a cheap resource (time) to work to get access to a needed product (bicycle). For the emotionally motivated individual, however, the same act will most likely replace other activities. This is because the individual has adequate economic resources, but not enough time on their hands. Putting time into prosumption results in less time to spend on other activities, including consumption. Furthermore, consumption replaced by an act of prosumerism must by no means be directly linked to this act of prosumption. The wealthy consumer spending time at the bike kitchen in Malmö might already own a bicycle, and even buy a new one at the same time that she repairs a bicycle at the bike kitchen. What appears counterintuitive at first makes perfect sense if one reflects upon the reasons why an individual chooses to spend time at the bike kitchen. If pleasure is the primary reason, then pleasure is associated with bicycles for this individual. It is therefore likely that the individual derives pleasure from bicycles even outside of the context of the bike kitchen and, since money is not the limiting factor for her consumption patterns, it is likely that she spends money on cycling even beyond the act of prosumerism. An emotional prosumer's activity at the bike kitchen is unlikely to reduce consumption in the field of cycling; in fact, the opposite is the case. The consumption replaced could be anything from a beer with friends, a day trip to the beach, an afternoon spent in front of the TV or fashion shopping on the high street. In essence, what is happening is that self-identity is derived through emotional prosumption and that this derived self-identity has the potential to replace acts of gaining self-identity that are more environmentally harmful (for example, through fashion shopping). Here, the opportunity cost of prosumption is not so much measured in monetary terms as it is measured in the pleasure (and self-identity) derived from these activities. Prosumption therefore has a meaningful impact on overconsumption only when the time spent on prosumption replaces another less sustainable activity. In practice, this means that emotional prosumption is sustainable if the time spent on repairing a bicycle replaces a shopping spree at the mall or a road trip with a gas-guzzling SUV. In short, the sustainability of prosumerism depends on the *crowding out* of less sustainable behaviour.

5. Discussion

The following discusses what this distinction between economic and emotional prosumption entails for business as well as policymakers.

5.1 A market economy for prosumption

Sustainable consumption is usually conceptualized as meaning that some people need to consume significantly less (the global consumer class), while other people need to consume more (those living in poverty). Ideally, increased prosumption can have a positive effect on the lives of both groups and do so in a way that is compatible with the market economy. For those consumers with low purchasing power and thus a small environmental footprint, increased opportunities for prosumption can provide cheap access to necessary products with low additional environmental impact. For those consumers with high purchasing power and thus a high environmental footprint, increased interest in prosumption has the potential to crowd out more resource-intense consumption behaviour.

A significant difference between economic prosumption and emotional prosumption is that only the latter lends itself to swift integration into the mainstream market economy. While prosumption conducted in the pursuit of saving money will more likely thrive on community action or on public subsidies of this behaviour, emotional prosumption lends itself well to monetization. Indeed, marketers have long argued that successful businesses can emerge from the appetite of wealthy individuals for experience rather than ownership. There are two reasons why such a profit-oriented, market-based approach to prosumption as a tool to reduce overconsumption is desirable: (1) the greater likelihood that prosumption will crowd out consumption due to superior experiences and (2) the reduced purchasing power of prosumers for spending on 'traditional consumption'.

5.1.1   Crowding out consumption

The increased involvement of for-profit businesses in the development of prosumption would lead to intensified focus on improving the positive experience of prosumption activities. In particular, when the prosumer is a wealthy individual who can put extra spending power into prosumption, if this is deemed a desirable experience, businesses should prove capable of improving prosumption experiences. This, in turn, should result in prosumption becoming an increasingly attractive activity compared to 'simple' consumption.

5.2.2   Reduced purchasing power

Available income significantly influences overall consumption of individuals. Indeed, standard economic theory argues that consumption levels are fundamentally a function of income (Campbell and Mankiw, 1989). The ability of for-profit businesses to create additional value in prosumption and to extract higher prices in exchange reduces the remaining purchasing power of emotional prosumers, thus limiting their ability to increase their ecological footprint from consumption. While counterintuitive at first, from this perspective, a more expensive prosumption experience is in fact better. Time is the limiting factor in prosumption for the wealthy, overconsuming individual, but disposable income is the primary factor for determining total consumption levels. To clarify, even an intensive prosumer who embraces self-production in various aspects of her life can still cause much damage with her disposable income during the rest of the time. As long as prosumption does not influence overall disposable income, even a person who spends many hours a week gardening at home and fixing their own bicycles can spend remaining disposable income on several long-distance flights. However, when increased prosumption also means a diversion of part of the disposable income of a person to prosumption, increased prosumption then means that the person has less disposable income available for other consumption (Figure 7.3).

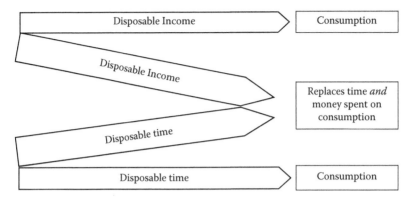

Figure 7.3 Marketization of prosumption

5.2 Sustainable consumption governance and prosumption

My distinction between economic and emotional prosumption in conceptualizing the potential of prosumption has relevance for sustainable consumption governance in two ways. First, it implies that policymakers should not focus their attention on the actual *products* replaced by prosumption. Instead their focus should be on the *time* prosumers engage in productive or non-productive self-production. Indeed, the productivity of prosumption is secondary. In a way, the more non-productive time a prosumer spends on the act of self-production, the more time is channelled away from other types of consumption (or from other aspects of the individual's life). Thus, while focusing on replaced goods means that inefficiency in prosumption is problematic (Salvia, 2015; Smith et al., 2013), it is not time that is the decisive factor. To take one example, we could compare a prosumer repairing her own bicycle with her bringing it to a bicycle repair shop. The bicycle repair shop is most certainly more efficient in using the resources needed to repair bicycles. If we only compare the outcome – a working bicycle – then it is likely that prosumption is less sustainable than a professional repair service. However, a repair done at the bicycle repair shop does not mean any time sacrifice for the owner of the bicycle, while prosumption, on the other hand, does entail this.

For sustainable consumption governance, this means that not only monetary incentives have to be changed (such as Sweden's decision to reduce VAT on repairs), but that incentives to use time differently, for example, by working less and spending more time on prosumption, are also needed.

Second, my discussion counters the argument raised by activists and some scholars (for example, Bradley, 2016; Hult and Bradley, 2017; Seravalli, 2014, cited in Salvia and Cooper, 2016) that prosumption and the DIY movement are most sustainable when they are non-profit. Instead, the argument detailed in this chapter provides a more nuanced understanding of prosumption and sustainability. While not-for-profit community-driven prosumption might be more beneficial for economic prosumption (and thus for social sustainability in that it provides a new low-cost option for financially constrained citizens to access the products they need), from an environmental sustainability point of view, I argue that for-profit prosumption can have a greater positive impact on consumption levels. For-profit organizations are particularly good at creating additional value for consumers, while also extracting disposable income for this added value. In a prosumption future, where many for-profit organizations compete to provide the best prosumption experience, the total amount of time and money spent on emotional prosumption would be much greater than if not-for-profit organizations were to drive development towards more prosumption. The potential to divert consumption time and spending power towards prosumption is therefore greater.

6. Conclusions

This chapter has focused on the distinction between economic and emotional prosumption in conceptualizing the significance of the idea of prosumption for overconsumption. It discussed the two main motivations for individuals engaging in acts of prosumption, and their respective impact on consumption behaviour. The bike kitchen in Malmö was taken as an example.

This chapter argues that economic and emotional prosumption are two distinct behaviours with different implications for sustainable consumption. Economic prosumption, while having potential to result in more social sustainability, provides little potential to mitigate the environmental consequences of overconsumption. This latter potential is only inherent in emotional prosumption.

The latter implies the necessity of emotional prosumption becoming more of a market-led development, moving away from not-for-profit, voluntary-run projects supported by public funding. This argument weighs even heavier when considering that emotional prosumption often caters to a group that is well-funded and is not dependent on public financing for activities that provide pleasure. My argument thus raises the question of whether municipalities such as Malmö should focus their resources on places such as *Cykelköket*. Municipal and national policymakers could instead focus on prosumption as a more general behaviour, expressed in any form, be it at home, in a community workshop or a commercial space. The broader the push towards prosumption, the more successful the value shift will be towards valuing uniqueness, skill and maintenance instead of mass production, convenience and innovation. Public funding should be reserved for economic prosumption, while emotional prosumption should be encouraged by other means (such as regulations, taxes or business development). In line with the argument of this chapter, not only would such an approach save limited public funds, but it would also increase the success and societal dissemination of prosumption. As argued, the emotional prosumer derives satisfaction from the continuous engagement with one consumption object as opposed to the consumer who derives satisfaction from the engagement with new consumption objects. The emotional prosumer pays for this satisfaction not only with money but partly also with time. A successful push for market-led prosumption could very well lead to the refocusing of consumption from the rapid consumption of mass products to the extended consumption of high-quality products. This is the main contribution of prosumption to more sustainable consumption. Ultimately, it can contribute to a development from a goods-centred approach to consumption (focused on ownership) to an experience-centred approach, and ultimately an accomplishment-centred approach (in which *how* consumption is achieved becomes equally important as what is consumed).

7.   Concluding remarks

With this chapter I hope to encourage three things: first, a willingness by policy-makers and others to engage with the idea of prosumption as a tool to achieve more sustainable consumption patterns in order to critically evaluate real world examples of the trend (for example, makerspaces, bike kitchens, community gardens or experience-centred businesses) and to distinguish between initiatives that have the potential to change consumption patterns and those that have no measurable impact on overall consumption levels. For example, despite a noticeable increase in popularity of prosumption (Salvia, 2015; Salvia and Cooper, 2016), the absolute volume of saved resources and prevented waste for initiatives such as the bike kitchen in Malmö are questionable. According to Bradley (2016) the bike kitchen in Malmö prevented 1000 bikes from going to landfill during its first three years. This compares to an annual market for new bicycles in Sweden of 600 000 sold units in 2015 alone (Svensk Cykling, 2015).

Second, I hope to expand debate on the scalability of prosumption niches, which would most likely involve their integration into the market economy or increased support for them from the public sector. Both options are possible, but both come with consequences.

Third, I hope that a change in the debate about prosumption can be encouraged, away from a focus on the products that prosumers prevent from going to landfill towards a focus on the lifestyle changes that greater prosumption would imply. Ultimately, prosumption should be interpreted as a development from consumption focusing on ownership towards consumption focusing on experience and expertise (for instance, knowledge and skills). The latter has the potential to change consumption from a fast throughput model to a high-quality and high-maintenance model.

8.   Future research

For future research, several questions arise from this chapter, which all need to be answered to understand the actual impact of prosumption on overall consumption levels. A case-specific understanding needs to be developed of the actual environmental footprint of an hour spent as prosumer in comparison to an hour spent on whatever else the prosumer would have done during this hour. Further research on the actual environmental costs of prosumption is thus necessary. It is easy to argue that an hour spent at the bike kitchen in Malmö does not result in a large environmental footprint, even though we should not forget that the existence of the bike kitchen itself results in a certain environmental footprint. However, if we were to imagine a makerspace that provided heavy duty or specialized equipment resulting in high resource use, the question arises whether an hour spent using this equipment is preferable to an hour spent in front of the TV or sitting in a café drinking coffee with friends.

This leads us to the second relevant question: the type of behaviour that is crowded out by increased prosumerism. As argued in this chapter, prosumption has its largest impact on behaviour by crowding out other types of behaviour. It is therefore important to understand which types of behaviour the prosumer is reducing as a result of more hours spent on prosumption.

A third research direction emerges from this chapter's suggestion that commercial prosumption could make a significant contribution to the reduction of consumption levels. It is far from clear how willing individuals are to pay for the experience of prosumption. Studies should therefore look into this issue with regard to 'emotional prosumers'.

Finally, it is relevant to study the indirect effects of prosumption. This chapter has been mostly concerned with the immediate outcome of time and money spent on prosumption. It has not discussed any potential change in values, attitudes and preferences that prosumption could bring about. It is conceivable that an individual engaged in bicycle prosumption could also develop a positive attitude towards used but well-maintained clothes, household goods and electronics. Potentially, prosumption could even lead to a change in personal values, in which newness and ownership lose their appeal and could result in a general rejection of overconsumption as a way of seeking pleasure and defining identity. It is thus conceivable that a prosumer would not only prefer the activity of repairing a bicycle over a road trip in an SUV but that the individual loses interest in owning an SUV completely.

NOTES

1 According to the website Statista, the average replacement cycle length of a mobile phone in 2016 was only 22.7 months in the USA, 21.6 months in Western Europe and 20.2 months in urban China (Statista, n.d.).

2 Shaw and Newholm (2002) define voluntary simplicity as a generic term for a variety of behaviours that have in common the fact that individuals voluntarily forgo maximum possible consumption, and maximum possible achievable income.

3 For a study analysing increasing wealth inequality and disparity in working hours in the USA between 1967 and 2006, see Heathcote et al. (2010).

References

Arvidsson, A. (2005), 'Brands: A critical perspective', *Journal of Consumer Culture*, **5** (2), 235–58.

Aşıcı, A.A. and S. Acar (2016), 'Does income growth relocate ecological footprint?', *Ecological Indicators*, **61** (2), 707–14.

Bardhi, F. and G.M. Eckhardt (2017), 'Liquid consumption', *Journal of Consumer Research*, **44** (3), 582–97.

Bradley, K. (2016), 'Bike kitchens – spaces for convivial tools', *Journal of Cleaner Production*, **197** (2), 16–83.

Campbell, J.Y. and G. Mankiw (1989), 'Consumption, income and interest rates: Reinterpreting the time series evidence', *NBER Macroeconomics Annual*, **4**, 185–216.

Cassidy, T.D. and H.R. Bennett (2012), 'The rise of vintage fashion and the vintage consumer', *Fashion Practice*, **4** (2), 239–61.

Cooper, T. (2016), *Longer Lasting Products: Alternatives to the Throwaway Society*, Boca Raton, FL, CRC Press.

Davis, M. (2016), *Liquid Sociology: Metaphor in Zygmunt Bauman's Analysis of Modernity*, Abingdon, UK: Routledge.

Eden, S. (2017), 'Blurring the boundaries: Prosumption, circularity and online sustainable consumption through Freecycle', *Journal of Consumer Culture*, **17** (2), 265–85.

Fischer, N.L. (2015), 'Vintage, the first 40 Years: The emergence and persistence of vintage style in the United States', *Culture Unbound: Journal of Current Cultural Research*, **7** (1), 45–66.

Fox, S., (2014), 'Third wave Do-It-Yourself (DIY): Potential for prosumption, innovation, and entrepreneurship by local populations in regions without industrial manufacturing infrastructure', *Technology in Society*, **39**, 18–30.

Heathcote, J., F. Perri and G.L. Violante (2010), 'Unequal we stand: An empirical analysis of economic inequality in the United States, 1967–2006', *Revue of Economic Dynamics*, **13** (1), 15–51.

Hult, A. and K. Bradley (2017), 'Planning for sharing – providing infrastructure for citizens to be makers and sharers', *Planning Theory and Practice*, **18** (4), 597–615.

iFixit (n.d), 'Smartphone Repairability Scores – Fixit', accessed 24 January 2018 at https://www.ifixit.com/smartphone-repairability.

Kilbourne, W., P. McDonagh and A. Prothero (1997), 'Sustainable consumption and the quality of life: A macromarketing challenge to the dominant social paradigm', *Journal of Macromarketing*, **17** (1), 4–24.

Kohtala, C. (2015), 'Addressing sustainability in research on distributed production: An integrated literature review', *Journal of Cleaner Production*, **106**, 654–68.

Kotler, P. (1986), 'The prosumer movement: "A new challenge for marketers"', *Advances in Consumer Research*, **13**, 510 –13.

Lucas, R.E. (1988), 'On the mechanics of economic development', *Journal of Monetary Economics*, **22** (1), 3–42.

Lucas, R.E., (1998), 'The Industrial Revolution: Past and future', University of Chicago, mimeograph.

Moisander, J., A. Markkula and K.K. Eräranta (2010), 'Construction of consumer choice in the market: Challenges for environmental policy', *International Journal of Consumer Studies*, **34** (1), 73–9.

Organisation for Economic Co-operation and Development (n.d.), 'Level of GDP per capita and productivity', accessed 24 January 2018 at http://stats.oecd.org/index.aspx?DataSetCode=PDB_LV.

Parsons, E. (2002), 'Charity retail: Past, present and future', *International Journal of Retail Distribution Management*, **30** (12), 586–94.

Prahalad, C.K. and V. Ramaswamy (2004a), 'Co-creating unique value with customers', *Strategy and Leadership*, **32** (39), 4–9.

Prahalad, C.K. and V. Ramaswamy (2004b), 'Co-creation experiences: The next practice in value creation', *Journal of. Interactive Marketing*, **18** (3), 5–14.

Reser, J.P., S.A. Morrissey and M. Ellul (2011), 'The threat of climate change: Psychological response, adaptation and impacts', in I. Weissbecker (ed.), *Climate Change and Human Well-Being*, New York: Springer, pp. 19–42.

Ritzer, G. (2014), 'Prosumption: Evolution, revolution, or eternal return of the same?', *Journal of Consumer Culture*, **14** (1), 3–24.

Ritzer, G., P. Dean and N. Jurgenson (2012), 'The coming of age of the prosumer', *American Behavioral Scientist*, **56** (4), 379–98.

Salvia, G. (2015), 'Design in the new Do-It-Yourself age: Trialling workshops for repairing', presented at Virtuous Circle, Summer Cumulus Conference, Politecnico di Milano, 3–7 June 2015, Milan, Italy.

Salvia, G. and T. Cooper (2016), 'The role of design as a catalyst for sustainable DIY', in A. Gensu (ed.), *Sustainable Consumption: Design, Innovation and Practice*, Cham, Switzerland: Springer, pp. 15–34.

Shaw, D. and T. Newholm (2002), 'Voluntary simplicity and the ethics of consumption', *Psychology and Marketing*, **19** (2), 167–85.

Smith, A., S. Hielscher, S. Dickel et al. (2013), 'Grassroots digital fabrication and makerspaces: Reconfiguring, relocating and recalibrating innovation?', SPRU Working Paper Series 2013–02, SPRU – Science Policy Research Unit, University of Sussex Business School.

Statista (n.d), 'Infographic: Smartphone life cycles are changing', accessed 24 January 2018 at https://www.statista.com/chart/8348/smartphone-life-cycles-are-changing.

Svensk Cykling (2015), 'Cykelförsäljning fortsätter öka – elcyklar och motionscyklar rekordökar' ['Sales of bicycles continue to rise – with record sales of e-bicycles and exercise bicycles'], accessed 24 January 2018 at http://svenskcykling.se/2015/10/05/cykelforsaljning-fortsatter-oka-elcyklar-och-motionscyklar-rekordokar.

Swedish Ministry of Finance (2016), 'Sänkt mervärdesskatt på mindre reparationer', March 2016. Accessed 12 February 2019 at http://www.regeringen.se/495ab5/contentassets/82bebd0a54644d729f d2fac79819fc1b/sankt-mervardesskatt-pa-mindre-reparationer.

Toffler, A. (1980), *The Third Wave*, New York: Bantam.

Vargo, S.L. and R.F. Lusch (2004), 'Evolving to a new dominant logic for marketing', *Journal of Marketing*, **68** (1), 1–17.

Vargo, S.L. and R.F. Lusch (2008), 'Service-dominant logic: Continuing the evolution', *Journal of Academic Marketing Science*, **36** (1), 1–10.

Veenstra, A. and G. Kuipers (2013), 'It is not old-fashioned, it is vintage: vintage fashion and the complexities of 21st century consumption practices', *Sociology Compass*, **7** (5), 355–65.

8 Putting the sharing economy into perspective*

Koen Frenken and Juliet Schor

1. Introduction

In the spring of 2014, the sharing economy held an unusual gathering in San Francisco, a sort of "coming out" party. Entitled "SHARE," the conference included not only founders, funders and fans of the sharing economy, but also harsh critics. Politically progressive insiders and outsiders raised questions about access, exclusion and the distribution of value in the sector. They discussed their vision of a fairer, lower-carbon, more transparent, participatory and socially connected economy, and whether those goals are consistent with the actions of the large, moneyed players— the successful platforms and the venture capitalists who are backing them with vast sums of finance. More recently, a key figure from the French sharing economy think tank OuiShare stated at their annual conference in Paris that "the sharing economy is over" as it did not live up its initial promises (De Grave 2016).

It is clear that the sharing economy is creating enormous amounts of wealth, and that it has been using a socially progressive feel-good rhetoric to do so. But will the platforms share that wealth with users—on both the provider and user sides of the market? Will the platforms ensure widespread access—by expanding their user base beyond the mostly white, highly educated, able-bodied urbanites who have comprised the bulk of users in the first stage? Will they make good on their promises to provide decent livelihoods for providers, opportunities for so-called "micro-entrepreneurs" and will they continue to provide real value to customers? Or is the rhetoric merely a thin veneer to hide a predatory business model that will ultimately appropriate value to investors and founders, once the market develops and users are locked into the platforms? Will the platforms behave like the monopolies that some seem poised to become? While it's too early for definitive answers to answer these questions, we believe it is crucial we start asking them in a more analytical, empirical and critical manner.

Our aim with this paper is to put the sharing economy into perspective by providing a conceptual framework that allows us to *define* the sharing economy and its close

* Reprint of paper Frenken, Koen and Schor, Juliet (2017). 'Putting the sharing economy into perspective', *Environmental Innovation and Societal Transitions*, **23**, 3–10. https://doi.org/10.1016/j.eist.2017.01.003; https://creativecommons.org/licenses/by/4.0/ [with updated references]

cousins and to *understand* its sudden rise from an economic-historic perspective (Section 2), to *assess* sharing economy platforms in terms of the economic, social and environmental impacts (Section 3), and to *reflect* on current regulations and possible alternative platform architectures (Section 4). We end with some research questions for future research (Section 5).

2.   Definitional issues

There has been widespread ambiguity and even confusion about the term "sharing economy" among academics and the public alike. One reason is due to a common misconception about the sharing economy: its novelty. Participants in the sharing economy employ a discourse of trendiness, technological sophistication, progress and innovation. However, this characterization betrays both class and race myopia, as well as what historians call "presentism," or blindness to the past. Humans have always shared. Sharing reproduces social relations and solidifies cultural practices (Belk 2009). Furthermore, sharing is not just a relic of pre-modern societies. Carol Stack's classic ethnography of the dense relations of reciprocity and interdependence among poor black urbanites in the U.S.A. showed how important sharing was to survival even a few decades ago (Stack 1974). By contrast, Hochschild's (2012) recent work on the growth of outsourced services among middle-class whites suggests lower and declining levels of sharing. Thus, the claim that sharing is new ignores the higher levels of sharing that the working class, poor and communities of colour have historically practiced and have partially maintained in the face of the growth of markets.

However, there *is* something new about the sharing economy, which one of us has called "stranger sharing" (Schor 2014). Historically, although there are some exceptions, people tended not to share with strangers or those outside their social networks. Sharing was confined to trusted individuals such as family, friends and neighbours. Today's sharing platforms facilitate sharing among people who do not know each other, and who lack friends or connections in common. Stranger sharing consequently entails a higher degree of risk, and for many of these platforms the situations are quite intimate—sharing one's home or car, or eating food prepared by unknown cooks. The digital platforms are able to make stranger sharing less risky and more appealing because they source information on users via the use of ratings and reputations. Although there is a growing body of evidence that ratings are generally inflated and not very accurate (Overgoor et al. 2012, Zervas et al. 2015), rating systems have nevertheless been sufficient to entice large numbers of people to enter into novel, unknown situations.

It is also important to note the historical links between the sharing platforms and activity such as the collaborative software movement that harnesses the unpaid work of software engineers to write code and solve problems collectively (Benkler 2004). The success of the open source movement paved the way for other kinds of peer-produced content such as Wikipedia and citizen science (which is produced by massive numbers of volunteers) as well as shared online content such as file-sharing, video posting and music sharing. There is a strong historical and global connection between the emergence of peer-to-peer platforms and a widespread feeling that the new technology-enabled practices these platforms allow for, empower people (Benkler 2006). This explains why file sharing, open source software, distributed computing, crowdfunding, peer-to-peer (p2p) lending, bitcoin, and sometimes even social media, are quite often put under the umbrella term of the sharing economy.

To add to the confusion, some critics have argued that sharing by definition does not include financial remuneration (Belk 2007). Indeed, this is a popular response to the use of the word sharing, when a more accurate term is "renting." But a moment's reflection suggests that the word is used in many cases where money is part of the arrangement, including cases such as sharing an apartment, or sharing the cost of a meal, or even the commonly used term "sharing expenses." We talk about sharing in many contexts, such as sharing on social media, or sharing secrets, sharing experiences, or sharing friends. As such, there's plausibility to using the term to denote a person renting out an asset such as a room, a car or a durable good. But it is certainly stretching the term beyond reasonable usage to say that paying a person $8 to make a pizza delivery (as on Postmates) or a bit more to clean one's house or put together Ikea furniture (as on Task Rabbit) has anything to do with "sharing."

It should be obvious from the foregoing that the sharing economy tent has become quite capacious. Platforms want to be under the big tent of the "sharing economy," because of the positive symbolic value of sharing. Put differently, the confusion about the definition of the sharing economy is self-propelling due to the performativity of the term itself. From an academic point of view, there are two relatively easy routes to deal with the definitional issue. First, one chooses not to define and delineate the sharing economy but rather tries to understand why different actors attribute different meanings, and why such rhetoric tactics may or may not suit them. This is an interesting research question in itself that can be linked to the broader question of how innovations are shaped and framed by discursive practices, roles and positions. A second stance is to abandon the term altogether. This seems logical from an analytical point of view, but obstructs communication outside academia where the term may last for a long time and may even continue to gain in importance. Hence, in our opinion, the current confusion is an untenable state of affairs and the easy ways out do not solve the fundamental problem. If we are to ask questions about the entity called the sharing economy, we will be unable to come up with coherent answers if the object itself is incoherent.

Here we do not wish to disregard alternative definitions as these have been reviewed and discussed elsewhere (Puschmann and Alt 2016). Rather, we want to put forward one particular definition that not only helps to define the sharing economy, but can also be used as an analytical tool to define closely related forms of economy which are often associated with sharing. We follow Frenken et al. (2015) and define the sharing economy as: *consumers granting each other temporary access to under-utilized physical assets ("idle capacity"), possibly for money.* Typical goods that are currently being shared are cars and homes. These are examples of what Benkler (2004) called "shareable goods." In essence, shareable goods are goods that by nature provide owners with excess capacity, providing the consumer with an opportunity to lend out or rent out their goods to other consumers. Excess capacity of a consumer good is present when the owner does not consume the product all the time. A majority of consumer goods can be understood as having excess capacity, including houses, cars, boats, houses, clothing, books, toys, appliances, tools, furniture, computers, and so on. The few exceptions would include, for example, eyeglasses and mobile phones. Another dimension of excess capacity is the lumpiness of some goods. Many items can only be purchased with excess capacity such as the unused memory capacity of computers or the unused car seats for daily commuters.

The notion of sharing of idle capacity is central to the definition of sharing economy, because it distinguishes the practice of sharing of goods from the practice of on-demand personal services. There is a fundamental difference between ordering a taxi through Uber, Lyft or Didi and sharing a ride through BlaBlaCar or another hitchhiking or carpooling platform (Meelen and Frenken 2015). In the case of a taxi service, the consumer creates new capacity by ordering a taxi on demand to drive the passenger from A to B. Without the order, the trip would not have been made in the first place. In this case, the term now coming into common use is the on-demand economy. By contrast, in the case of hitchhiking/carpooling, the consumer occupies a seat that would otherwise not have been used as the driver had planned to go from A to B anyway. Hitchhiking and carpooling are examples of ride-sharing and part of the sharing economy (Benkler 2004). Indeed, in the context of transportation, this distinction between on-demand economy and sharing economy has become clearer over time as most commentators now call Uber, Lyft and Didi ride-hailing companies instead of ride-sharing.[1]

The notion of under-utilization is also key to the current discussion about home sharing platforms such as Airbnb. When a house owner is away for holidays or a business trip, or has a spare bedroom, the asset is not utilized. That is, the unoccupied house can be considered as temporary idle capacity. If, however, a person were to buy a second home and rent it out to tourists permanently, that constitutes running a commercial lodging site, such as a B&B or hotel.

Based on this definition, the sharing economy can be distinguished from three other types of platforms that are sharing economy examples pre-dating the Internet. In Figure 8.1, the sharing economy is placed in the centre as it adheres to the three defining characteristics: consumer-to-consumer interaction (c2c), temporary access and physical goods.

Consumers selling goods to each other is called the *second-hand economy*. This does not fall under the sharing economy as consumers grant each other permanent access, rather than temporary access to their goods. Large platforms

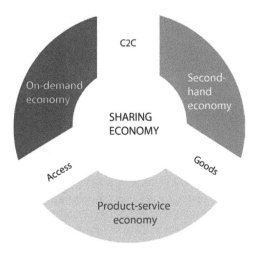

Figure 8.1 Sharing economy and related forms of platform economy

intermediating such transactions are Ebay and Taobao. There are also platforms where people give away goods to each other, without payment (including Facebook groups). This would also fall under the category of consumers who grant another permanent access. Renting goods from a company rather than from another consumer we call the *product-service economy*. The service provided by the company consists of giving the consumer access to a product while the company retains ownership of it. Once the product has been used and returned, it becomes available again for another renter. An example is a car rental service such as Hertz. Finally, if we are dealing with p2p service delivery instead of p2p good sharing, the term *on-demand economy* is used. More recently, commentators in this context also tend to speak of the "gig economy." The on-demand or gig economy includes purchasing personal services such as a ride, a handyman or a cooked meal.

The definition that we use for sharing economy platforms, and the three other types of platforms that can be distinguished from it, accommodates the notion of sharing as a historical practice. Before the arrival of Internet platforms, people were already lending or renting out goods to others. They shared with family and friends because they were known and trusted social contacts. What is new is that users now also lend goods to strangers, because the Internet has enormously decreased transaction costs between unknown others. By transaction costs, economists mean all the costs and trouble incurred in making an economic transaction (Williamson 1981). This refers especially to the costs related to search and arranging a contract. Among strangers, these were high before the advent of the Internet, as there was little information available about supply, reliability and contract forms (Benkler 2004). This is one reason why sharing was generally limited to a circle of friends and family. As a result of Internet platforms, the costs of the search and the contract have become much lower. Consumers now find it much easier to locate goods and services they want, and transactions are regularized via standard contracts and online payment systems. In addition, on most sharing-economy platforms information on the past behaviour and therefore trustworthiness of users is elicited as a regular feature of transactions. This further lowers transaction costs and lowers risk.

3.   Assessing the sharing economy

Early enthusiasm about the sharing economy, as reflected in the influential book by Botsman and Rogers (2010), was to a considerable extent driven by its expected sustainability impacts. Not only would consumers get cheap access to goods by renting or borrowing them from others, by doing so they would become less dependent on ownership. As a result, the total number of new goods produced was hypothesized to decline. This feeling was largely fuelled by the perceived environmental benefits of car sharing. As cars stand idle 95 percent of the time,[2] any type of sharing scheme that made cars accessible to non-owners would reduce the number of cars required for a given mileage level.

In addition to the environmental benefits, social benefits have also been claimed for the sharing economy. As we noted above, the advent of Internet platforms makes stranger sharing more desirable, thereby extending an existing practice to a larger social scale. On some platforms strangers meet face-to-face after a matching process, and from such face-to-face meetings new social ties are thought to emerge. Furthermore, sharing economy practices do not necessarily lead to stratification, since owners may be expected to differ in socio-demographic background from renters and borrowers. Possibly, with more expensive goods like cars and houses, providers may be richer and older than the renters on average. To the extent that sharing peers also create meaningful contacts, sharing practices increase social mixing.

The alleged sustainability benefits of the sharing economy are, however, much more complex than initially assumed. Following the people, planet, prosperity triple of sustainability impacts, we review them here in reverse order.

The direct economic effects of the sharing economy are indisputably positive. People who voluntarily enter into a transaction in the sharing economy only do so if it is beneficial to both parties. Even in the case of goods lending there is a benefit: there are few costs for the lender because the person did not need the product during the lending period, whereas the borrower gains access to the product without charge. The rise in income or consumer welfare can be understood as a direct consequence of lower transaction costs. Millions of transactions now take place that did not happen in the past, because the transaction costs involved in stranger sharing were simply too high (Benkler 2004).

Yet, the full economic effects are far more complex. First, the rise of p2p sharing markets will have indirect effects on other markets. For example, legacy businesses and their workers in related markets are likely to experience lower earnings. One study found that hotel earnings in Texas declined significantly in places where Airbnb grew (Zervas et al. 2017). Further analysis also showed that the impacts were uneven across the industry, with lower-end hotels and hotels not catering to business travellers being the most affected. This indicates that Airbnb is a partial substitute for hotel nights, especially in the cheaper segments of the hotel market. The same effect may be expected in the market for car rentals which now face increased competition due to the rise of p2p car-sharing platforms. There are also potentially effects on the supply and price of housing, if home sharing becomes more widespread. This would mean that residents would see their rents go up in neighbourhoods where home sharing is popular.

Second, there are externalities as third parties may experience losses as the two parties transact. This is especially a problem with house sharing with neighbours experiencing nuisance and feelings of danger from strangers. Increasingly, neighbourhoods have attempted to stop the further growth of home sharing in tourist cities like Amsterdam, Barcelona, Berlin, New York and Paris. In response, municipalities are tightening their regulations toward home sharing platforms (Woolf 2016).

Third, the distribution of increased income and welfare are likely to be uneven. Sharing economy websites are two-sided platforms characterized by strong network externalities, creating the tendency toward natural monopoly and allowing for high margins to be charged by the platform. Note here that ratings account for a significant part of the value of the platform. Even though the ratings are the products of platform users, the value generated is appropriated by the platform itself. The second group of people profiting most are owners of valuable assets. As consumers can more easily turn their consumer goods into capital assets to earn rents, and such valuable consumer goods are typically concentrated in a small group of well-off people, one can speak here of the Piketty-effect of the sharing economy (Piketty 2013; Frenken 2017). This is most evident in home sharing, but also applies to renting out parking spaces, cars and boats in times and places where such goods are scarce. Finally, as Schor (2017) has argued, sharing platforms seem to be leading to increased inequality within the bottom 80 percent of the income distribution, as highly educated providers capture market opportunities like driving, cleaning and household tasks that were once the province of lower-educated blue- and pink-collar workers. Overall, while it is safe to say that participants in the sharing economy are experiencing increases in consumer welfare from lower prices and more variety, economic inequality driven by provider side dynamics is likely to increase as well.

The environmental effects associated with the sector are also complex. Many platforms advertise themselves as green, and particularly as carbon-footprint reducing. It is also a common belief among participants that sharing is less resource intensive (Schor and Wengronowitz 2017). Sharing is thought to be eco-friendly because it is assumed to reduce the demand for new goods or the construction of new facilities (in the case of hotels or shared spaces). Despite these widespread beliefs, there is not yet empirical evidence on these claims, apart from car sharing where substantial reductions in CO_2-emissions are realized (Chen and Kockelman 2015; Nijland and Van Meerkerk 2017). For ride-sourcing services (for example, Uber), however, there is evidence that it often substitutes for public transport and does not decrease congestion (Jin et al. 2018). The standard argument on eco-impacts addresses substitutions among types of goods or services that have different technologies. This type of reasoning is what economists call partial-equilibrium analysis, which only looks at first-round effects. To determine full carbon and eco-impacts it is also necessary to analyze all the changes that are set in motion in the system as a result of a new sharing practice (Schor 2014; Frenken 2017). For example, if the sale of a household's used items creates earnings that are then used to buy new goods ("rebound effect"), the original sale may not reduce carbon emissions or other environmental impacts. Another second-round impact can occur if sharing practices shift income across classes, because eco-impact per dollar of expenditure varies by income class.

There is the additional question of macro-economic impacts. Many of the platforms are creating new markets that expand the volume of commerce and inject additional purchasing power into the economy. For carbon, there is a close association between gross domestic profit (GDP) and emissions/footprint. Among high-income Organisation for Economic Co-operation and Development (OECD) countries, a 1 percent increase in GDP raises carbon emissions by between 0.64 percent and 1 percent depending on the carbon metric and the type of estimation technique (Knight and Schor 2014). In the post-2009 period of shortfall in aggregate demand in the global North, new activities are more likely to expand demand, rather than substitute one kind of demand for another. Indeed, advocates of the sharing economy believe that it is creating economic opportunities in the wake of the 2009 downturn. The foregoing should make clear that the relation between the new sharing economy and carbon emissions and other ecological impacts is a complex one that can only be assessed with careful studies of particular effects. These studies are now long overdue.

Regarding the social benefits, there is a widespread "common good" claim by a number of platforms, as well as participants on both sides of the market which is the benefit of meeting people, making friends and getting to know others (Fitzmaurice et al. 2018). Schor (2015a) finds that the site that has been most successful at creating new social ties is Airbnb. Findings from one small interview study are that for half the Airbnb hosts social interaction was central to their motivation and practice on the site. These hosts socialized with their guests, ate with them, took them out, and in some cases became friends with them. A small group reported that they would host even if they had all the money they needed, and a few offered their homes on both Airbnb and Couchsurfing, for which they received no money. This finding is in line with Böcker and Meelen (2017) who find that people who state that they are willing to share their home often have social motivations next to economic ones. Ladegaard (2016), using a Boston area sample, further qualifies these results showing that socially oriented hosts are eager to interact with foreign guests who are "comfortably exotic," that is, different enough to be interesting, but similar enough to be comfortable.

Participants on other sites also note the importance of social ties. Schor (2015a) and Fitzmaurice et al. (2018) found that TaskRabbits say the platform helped them build new social networks they can rely on and afforded the opportunity to meet people they would have never met. They report satisfaction with the relations they developed with the people they do tasks for. This result is also in line with Parigi et al. (2013) who found, in a large-scale study of the lodging site Couchsurfing, that participation resulted in new friendships. However, they found that the ability of the platform to create these connections, especially close ones, has declined since its inception in 2003 (Parigi and State 2014). Users became "disenchanted" as the relationships they formed had become more casual and less durable. This study raises the question of whether the social benefits of sharing sites will continue as they become a less novel and more normative part of daily life. It seems that earlier adopters are more open to social connection and that as more people participate in the platforms for economic reasons, social interaction will decline.

The quality of ratings may also contribute to the declining importance of social contacts on sharing platforms. As participants acquire more ratings over time, trust is codified and there is less need for face-to-face interaction. This trend is reinforced by technological and business developments such as "smart locks" where the owner provides digital access to the rentier by a temporary pin code, and businesses that provide additional supporting services including check-in and key handover.

It is also possible that sharing platforms may be harmful to social cohesion as reflected in existing social ties. Platforms economize private things in the sense that at any time these stand idle, an opportunity cost arises. This in itself does not affect social relations. However, while idle capacity was generally available to family and friends for free in the past, researchers and commentators have expressed concern about the viability of non-monetized sharing within networks as people prefer earning money (Belk 2014; Schor 2015b). Standard economic analysis suggests this will happen, although it does not offer a prediction on how large this effect will be. There is only anecdotal evidence on this issue at the moment. For example, one Airbnb host said he will now require his friends and relatives to transact with him via the platform, to insure against damage to his apartment and possessions (Ravenelle 2016). Another host reported being unhappy about having her in-laws stay for an extended period because of the money she lost (Schor 2015b). In these studies, however, the prevalence of crowding out of altruistic sharing thus far appears to be low.

Furthermore, the peer-to-peer nature of sharing economy transactions may also increase peer-to-peer discrimination. One analysis of Airbnb in the United States found that male African American Airbnb hosts earn 12 percent less rent than other hosts for the same type of house in the same type of location (Edelman and

Luca 2014). A follow-up field experiment found that African American guests are more frequently turned down by hosts (Edelman et al. 2017), prompting widespread reporting on social media of discriminatory experiences (#Airbnbwhileblack), the establishment of a black-oriented platform (Noirbnb) and policy changes by Airbnb. A more recent analysis of more than 200,000 Airbnb listings across the U.S.A. found evidence of significant racial disadvantage in ratings, reviews and prices charged (Cansoy and Schor 2017). Furthermore, recent experiments suggest that Uber and Lyft chauffeurs discriminate against African Americans in terms of longer average waiting times and more frequent cancellations (Ge et al. 2016). More generally, there are indications that people engage in a variety of exclusionary behaviours in their choice of trading partners or collaborators in the sharing economy (Schor et al. 2016).

In all, the economic, social and environmental effects of sharing economy platforms are largely unknown. While the direct economic benefits are obvious from the large volume of monetary transactions taking place, the distributional effects may be quite skewed. Since the bulk of revenue in the sharing economy (as defined) accrues via home sharing, already well-off home owners will profit most. Environmental benefits mostly lie in car and ride-sharing, and the overall effects of sharing economy platforms are likely to be small due to rebound effects. Finally, social effects are complex and not necessarily inclusive.

4. Alternatives

Despite the call for scientific assessments of the sustainability impacts of sharing economy platforms, we should acknowledge that the precise impacts are likely to remain unclear for a long time to come. The reason for the lasting gap in our knowledge is not only theoretical, but empirical. For a proper assessment of the impacts, access to the user data currently held by platforms is key. However, the platforms have been restrictive and selective in granting researchers access to their user data, citing privacy and competition concerns. Instead, platforms release their own research results (for example, Airbnb 2014), which tend to emphasize the direct benefits without much consideration of the more complex and indirect effects just discussed.

In this context, it has been noted that the social process of assessing the desirability of sharing platforms follows a reverse logic. Frenken (2016) speaks of "reverse technology assessment" in this context. In many countries, established sectors like food, drugs, transportation, construction and children's toys are subject to detailed scientific analysis and normative deliberation before new products are allowed to enter the market. Sharing economy platforms, by contrast, are introduced onto the market without consultation, and due to their fast growth they prompt ad hoc government action without much evidentiary basis. This reverse process has advantages, as users "vote with their feet" and provide individual platforms with practical legitimacy. However, these users are likely to be less affected by externalities and

second- and third-round effects. Given the recent backlash and opposition to particular platforms from various social groups, more systematic evidence is needed to
resolve the current debate, with more room for nuanced opinions by independent
actors (for example, academics, journalists, consumer organizations).

Restricted access to user data also hampers the enforcement of regulations and,
consequently, policy evaluation. Though the advent of sharing economy platforms
is recent, the volume of activity on some of these platforms is already sizeable and
still growing exponentially. Understandably, calls for regulations are getting louder
given the negative externalities caused by home sharing and unfair competition
between platform and traditional operators in sectors like tourism, restaurants,
short-stay, transport and appliances. What is more, there is reason to assume that
many avoid paying taxes or are not even aware that taxes should be paid for some
activities (especially home sharing).

The typical response of regulators has been to create institutional boundaries
between the sharing economy and the regular economy by putting a cap on a
sharing activity. For example, an increasing number of cities allow home sharing
for a fixed number of days (for example, 30, 60 or 90 days). This "cap" logic can be
applied to operators of home restaurants and owners of boats, campers and parking
spaces. The principle of a cap is consistent with our definition of sharing economy
as consumers who grant each other temporary access to their under-utilized goods,
as it avoids cases where people purchase goods or houses for the purpose of renting them out on a permanent basis. With caps, governments solve two problems
at once because they meet the incumbent businesses halfway by creating clear
boundaries between professional providers and incidental providers, and they
"solve" the tax avoidance practice by users pragmatically as the sums gained by
incidental providers are small enough that they can be ignored or otherwise fall
under existing tax exemption levels (except for home sharing where revenues are
quite skewed and the foregone tax revenues are sizeable). This logic of containment
is sustainable as long as the caps can be effectively monitored. Currently, however,
governments struggle to enforce such rules, since the platforms do not give them
access to user data as they are protected under current privacy laws, while alternative ways of monitoring do not outweigh the costs involved. The government, thus,
follows a cap logic which may turn out to be hard to enforce in practice. In all, current governmental institutions have not yet come up with an adequate and credible
response to the concerns of incumbent business interests and the unions.

Against this background, it is not surprising to see various alternative platforms
being founded. Serious experiments are emerging ranging from cooperative-based
and crowdfunded platforms to platforms that make use of alternative currencies
or more novel block-chain technology (Scholz 2014; Scholz and Schneider 2016).
At the same time, some of the existing commercial platforms are now changing
the ways in which they engage with users and governments, and are looking for
workarounds to help with enforcement of their regulations.

From an economic-historical point of view, the possibilities for a fully socialized sharing sector, with platforms owned and governed by their users is an intriguing option. If users are able to construct and use their own platforms on a large-scale basis, they may benefit equally from network externalities without having to pay the 10–20 percent margins typically charged by commercial platforms. Furthermore, users would retain control of their user data. Whether users, other than current commercial platforms, would be willing to share (some of) the data with governments for enforcement purposes and with scientists and the wider public for research purposes, remains an open question.

More generally, the initial fear that platforms may naturally grow into monopolies as has happened with search engine and social media platforms may turn out to be ill-founded. Sharing markets are local markets given the transport cost involved in sharing one's goods (the exceptions being the markets for home sharing and long-distance carpooling). Hence, the critical mass that is needed to successfully launch a new platform is much smaller in local markets than in global markets. This means that with limited network externalities there is scope for alternative platforms. Furthermore, the key assets of platforms lose their value over time as platform software has become ubiquitous, and risk management is integrated into standard insurance policies. Users may also become increasingly aware of the limited information value of specific platform ratings as they become more experienced practitioners themselves. This does not mean that attracting a critical mass of users to alternative platforms is easy. However, switching costs may go down as ratings become more easily transferable legally (as with mobile telephone numbers) or technologically (by centralizing one's ratings across platforms on a single site). Furthermore, given the low levels of effort required to become active on any platform, users may become active on competing platforms at the same time. Another challenge for alternative platforms will be alignment to interests and ideologies of its founders, volunteers and users. Indeed, as previous research suggests (Schor et al. 2016), when economic motives are largely absent, participants may seek social status at the expense of others, making collective action and professionalization of the platform more difficult.

5.   A research agenda

From our discussion of the delineation of the sharing economy from other platform economies, and our assessment of its impacts and alternatives, we distill a number of research questions. These questions focus on the varieties of platforms in terms of their governance, scalability and impacts.[3]

1.   What types of sharing economies have historically existed across cultures and epochs, and what can we learn from the economics, governance and impacts of such initiatives and practices in the light of current day sharing economy platforms?
2.   What is the relative importance of trust-generating mechanisms on sharing

economy platforms, including past ratings, personal identification, online communication and extra-platform reputational capital?

3. How can we analytically conceptualize and empirically assess the various impacts of the current sharing economy platforms in terms of people, planet and prosperity? To what extent can we carry out such assessment without access to user data?

4. How can we explain and evaluate the variety of regulatory responses of governments at local, national and supra-national levels as well as the modes of self-governance employed by platforms?

5. What alternative governance schemes for operating a platform are currently being employed? How can we explain their emergence, growth and relative success across sectors, territories and social groups?

Finding answers to these questions will be a challenging endeavour. It will require a range of disciplinary perspectives and methodological approaches and a close eye for historical contexts and geographical specificities. Despite the strong rhetoric of proponents and criticasters alike, the future of the sharing economy is fundamentally open and contingent. In this, clearly, academics have their role to play.

NOTES

1 Our distinction is also consonant with the Associated Press Stylebook, which started to describe the services of Uber and Lyft as ride-hailing from January 2015 onwards: "Ride-hailing services such as Uber and Lyft let people use smartphone apps to book and pay for a private car service or in some cases, a taxi. They may also be called ride-booking services. Do not use ride-sharing." (Warzel 2015). See also http://www.yourdictionary.com/ride-hailing-service. Also note that the distinction between ride-hailing and ride-sharing is not just academic, but also carries legal implications. A judge in the Netherlands argued that Uber should be seen as a taxi service and refuted the claim by Uber that its UberPoP service (which is provided by unlicensed drivers) is to be viewed as carpooling (De Rechtspraak 2014). Judges in Denmark, Finland and France came to the same conclusion (Skydsgaard 2016).

2 Bates and Leibling (2012). For a further discussion on the available evidence, see Barter (2013).

3 There are, of course, many other important questions, for example, related to motivations to participate on platforms, the matching process on platforms and the substitutability of sharing economy services vis-à-vis traditional service operations. These fall outside the scope of the current paper.

References

Airbnb (2014), 'Environmental impacts of home sharing', July 31, accessed January 6, 2017 at http://blog.airbnb.com/environmental-impacts-of-home-sharing.

Barter, P. (2013), '"Cars are parked 95% of the time." Let's check', accessed January 6, 2017 at http://www.reinventingparking.org/2013/02/cars-are-parked-95-of-time-lets-check.html.

Bates, J. and J. Leibling (2012), *Spaced Out: Perspectives on Parking Policy*, London: RAC Foundation.

Belk, R. (2007), 'Why not share rather than own?', *Annals of the American Academy of Political and Social Science*, **611**, 126–40.

Belk, R. (2009), 'Sharing', *Journal of Consumer Research*, **36**, 715–34.

Belk, R. (2014), 'Sharing versus pseudo-sharing in Web 2.0', *Anthropologist*, **18** (1), 7–23.

Benkler, Y. (2004), '"Sharing Nicely": On shareable goods and the emergence of sharing as a modality of economic production', *The Yale Law Journal*, **114**, 273–358.

Benkler, Y. (2006), *The Wealth of Networks: How Social Production Transforms Markets and Freedom* (1st edn), New Haven, CT: Yale University Press.

Böcker, L. and T. Meelen (2017), 'Sharing for people, planet or profit? Analysing motivations for intended sharing economy participation', *Environmental Innovation and Societal Transitions*, **23**, 28–39.

Botsman, R. and R. Rogers (2010), *What's Mine is Yours: How Collaborative Consumption is Changing the Way We Live*, London: Collins.

Cansoy, M. and J.B. Schor (2017), 'Who gets to share in the sharing economy: Racial discrimination on Airbnb', working paper, Boston College.

Chen, T.D. and K.M. Kockelman (2015), 'Carsharing's life-cycle impacts on energy use and greenhouse gas emissions', *Transport Research Part D: Transport and Environment*, **47**, 276–84.

De Grave, A. (2016), 'So long, collaborative economy!', *Ouishare Magazine*, June 22, accessed January 6, 2017 at http://magazine.ouishare.net/2016/06/so-long-collaborative-economy.

De Rechtspraak (2014), 'ECLI:NL:CBB:2014:450', accessed October 23, 2016 at http://uitspraken.recht spraak.nl/inziendocument?id=ECLI:NL:CBB:2014:450.

Edelman, B.G. and M. Luca (2014), 'Digital discrimination: The case of Airbnb.com', Harvard Business School Working Paper, No. 14-054.

Edelman, B.G., M. Luca and D. Svirsky (2017), 'Racial discrimination in the sharing economy: Evidence from a field experiment', *American Economic Journal: Applied Economics*, **9** (2), 1–22.

Fitzmaurice, C., I. Ladegaard, W. Attwood-Charles et al. (2018), 'Domesticating the market: Moral exchange and the sharing economy', *Socio-Economic Review*, **23**, 3–10.

Frenken, K. (2016), 'Deeleconomie onder één noemer' ['The sharing economy under one heading'], lecture, Utrecht University, February 12, 2016, accessed October 23, 2016 at http://www.uu.nl/sites/ default/files/20160211-uu_oratie-frenken.pdf.

Frenken, K. (2017), 'Political economies and environmental futures of the sharing economy', *Philosophical Transactions of the Royal Society A: Mathematical, Physical and Engineering Sciences*, **375** (2095).

Frenken, K., T. Meelen, M. Arets et al. (2015), 'Smarter regulation for the sharing economy', *The Guardian*, May 20, accessed October 23, 2016 at https://www.theguardian.com/science/political-science/2015/may/20/smarter-regulation-for-the-sharing-economy.

Ge, Y., G.R. Knittel, D. MacKenzie et al. (2016), 'Racial and gender discrimination in transportation network companies', *National Bureau of Economic Research*, NBER Working Paper No. 22776, October 2016.

Hochschild, A.R. (2012), *The Outsourced Self: Intimate Life in Market Times*, New York: Metropolitan Books.

Jin, S.T., H. Kong, R., Wu et al. (2018), 'Ridesourcing, the sharing economy, and the future of cities', *Cities*, **76**, 96–104.

Knight, K. and J. Schor (2014), 'Economic growth and climate change: A cross-national analysis of territorial and consumption-based carbon emissions in high-income countries', *Sustainability*, **6** (6), 3722–31.

Ladegaard, I. (2016), 'Hosting the comfortably exotic: Cosmopolitan aspirations in the sharing economy', unpublished paper, Boston College.

Meelen, T. and K. Frenken (2015), 'Stop saying Uber is part of the sharing economy', *Fast Company*, January 14, accessed October 23 2016 at http://www.fastcoexist.com/3040863/stop-saying-uber-is-partof-the-sharing-economy.

Nijland, H. and J. Van Meerkerk (2017), 'Mobility and environmental impacts of carsharing in the Netherlands', *Environmental Innovation and Societal Transitions*, **23**, 1–114.

Overgoor, J., E. Wulczyn and C. Potts (2012), 'Trust propagation with mixed-effects models', in J.G. Breslin, N.B. Ellison, J.G. Shanahan and Z. Tufekci (eds), *Proceedings of the Sixth International AAAI Conference on Weblogs and Social Media*, The AAAI Press.

Parigi, P. and B. State (2014), 'Disenchanting the world: The impact of technology on relationships', *Social Informatics*, **8851**, 166–82.

Parigi, P., B. State, D. Dakhlallah et al. (2013), 'A community of strangers: The dis-embedding of social ties', *PLoS ONE*, **8** (7), e67388.

Piketty, T. (2013), *Capital in the Twenty-First Century*, Cambridge, MA/London: Belknap Press.

Puschmann, T. and R. Alt (2016), 'Sharing economy', *Business and Information Systems Engineering*, **58**, 93–9.

Ravenelle, A. (2016), 'Our community: Airbnb, circuits of commerce and the distinction-reducing paradox of money', working paper, New York: City University of New York.

Scholz, T. (2014), 'Platform cooperativism vs. the sharing economy', *Medium*, December 5, 2014, accessed October 23, 2016 at https://medium.com/@trebors/platform-cooperativism-vs-the-sharing-economy-2ea737f1b5ad.

Scholz, T. and N. Schneider (eds) (2016), *Ours to Hack and to Own: The Rise of Platform Cooperativism, A New Vision for the Future of Work and a Fairer Internet*, New York: OR Books.

Schor, J. (2014), 'Debating the sharing economy', October, accessed October 23, 2016 at https://www.greattransition.org/publication/debating-the-sharing-economy.

Schor, J. (2015a), 'Homo Varians: Diverse economic behaviours in new sharing markets', unpublished paper, Boston College.

Schor, J. (2015b), 'The sharing economy: Reports from stage one', unpublished paper, Lincolnshire: Boston College.

Schor, J. (2017), 'Does the sharing economy increase inequality within the eighty percent? Findings from a qualitative study of platform providers', *Cambridge Journal of Regions, Economy and Society*, **10**, 263–327.

Schor, J. and R. Wengronowitz (2017), 'The new sharing economy: Enacting the eco-habitus', in H. Brown, M. Cohen and P. Vergragt (eds), *Sustainable Consumption and Social Change*, Abingdon, UK: Routledge, pp. 25–42.

Schor, J., C. Fitzmaurice, W. Attwood-Charles et al. (2016), 'Paradoxes of openness and distinction in the sharing economy', *Poetics*, **54**, 66–81.

Skydsgaard, N. (2016), 'Danish high court convicts, fines Uber driver for lacking taxi permits', *Reuters*, November 18, accessed January 6, 2017 at https://www.reuters.com/article/us-uber-denmark-idUSK BN13D1CP.

Stack, C.B. (1974), *All our Kin: Strategies for Survival in a Black Community*, New York: Harper and Row.

Warzel, C. (2015), 'Let's all join the AP Stylebook in killing the term "ride-sharing"', *BuzzFeedNews*, January 8, 2015, accessed January 6, 2017 at https://www.buzzfeed.com/charliewarzel/lets-all-join-the-ap-stylebook-in-killing-the-term-ride-shar.

Williamson, O.E. (1981), 'The economics of organization: The transaction cost approach', *American Journal of Sociology*, **87**, 548–77.

Woolf, N. (2016), 'Airbnb regulation deal with London and Amsterdam marks dramatic policy shift', *The Guardian*, December 3, accessed January 6, 2017 at https://www.theguardian.com/technology/2016/dec/03/airbnb-regulation-london-amsterdam-housing.

Zervas, G., D. Proserpio and J. Byers (2015), 'A first look at online reputation on Airbnb, where every stay is above average', *SSRN Electronic Journal*, January 2015, accessed February 11 2015 at http://papers.ssrn.com/sol3/papers.cfm?abstract_id=2554500.

Zervas, G., D. Proserpio and J. Byers (2017), 'The rise of the sharing economy: Estimating the impact of Airbnb on the hotel industry', *Journal of Marketing Research*, **54**, 687–705.

PART III

Policies and Alternative Governors of Sustainable Consumption

9   It is never too late to give up, or is it? Revisiting policies for sustainable consumption

Carl Dalhammar

1.   Introduction

At a recent event that took place on the premises of a mobile phone manufacturer, I had a discussion with a team of designers. They told me that they had the idea of developing something similar to a Fairphone, but the concept was not considered to be commercially viable.[1] One of the designers stated that their industry was 'stuck in an unsustainable loop that could only be broken through strong regulation'. The company's management team wants a constant flow of new models with novel functions to increase sales, and the same goes for the mobile network operators: new models attract new business and the sales of ever-greater bandwidth subscriptions.

These designers felt 'locked-in', left with few options for adopting more sustainable practices. There was a will but not a way. This is also how Sanne (2002) refers to consumers who would be willing to consume more sustainably: they are also 'locked-in by circumstances' and would be unable to practise more sustainable consumption practices even if they wanted to.

If we look at current climate change and resource use trends, we have no choice but to significantly reduce our resource consumption. This leads us to the question of how to proceed. This question has unfortunately no simple answer. Some answers do exist but these have been ignored since they would require us to call our consumption habits and aspirations into question.

Early discourse on sustainable consumption policies stressed the importance of educating consumers about the implications of consumption, and advocated the use of policies like eco-labelling and consumption-related taxes. This agenda focused mainly on 'greener consumption' rather than 'consumption limits' (see Mont and Dalhammar, 2005), perhaps not surprisingly, since the term 'consumption limits' has never been popular among emerging economies desiring economic development. This agenda and its and associated policies can, at best, achieve (very) modest relative decoupling of gross domestic product (GDP), yet there is little evidence of absolute decoupling, not least because of rebound effects (Jackson 2009).[2]

Indeed, recent studies have taken a more realistic approach, and call for more radical approaches. These studies emphasize that governments need to lead the shift to sustainability by creating the societal structures that make sustainable living the default option, and that innovation in technology and infrastructure, regulation, pricing, marketing and new social norms must be used in combination to create a sustainable choice architecture (Mont et al., 2013).

Although sustainable living should be the default option, it is hard to see how we can attain this. If the issue was only that of informing people about the need for change and the development of a 'new sustainability paradigm' this could be feasible. However, as consumption plays a vital role in the construction and maintenance of our social world, many radical sustainable consumption policies would constitute a threat to our personal identities, and our 'structures of meaning' (see Jackson, 2013: 66). Therefore, countering consumption implies '[the] building of meaning structures, communities of meaning, that lie outside the realm of the market' (Jackson, 2013: 66).

Such developments are, however, nowhere to be seen. Initiatives like the 'degrowth' movement (Latouche, 2010) are still fringe phenomena. When reporting from the latest Davos meeting, Joseph Stiglitz observes only a desire for business as usual among attendees, with little attention paid to sustainability and economic inequality (Stiglitz, 2018). As Stiglitz comments: '. . . CEOs were euphoric about the return to growth, about their soaring profits and compensation. Economists reminded them that this growth is not sustainable, and has never been inclusive. But such arguments have little impact in a world where materialism is king' (Stiglitz, 2018).

The fight against consumption is also hindered by other factors. One important aspect is that products have become less durable. For different reasons, many types of products are cheaper and of lower quality than previously. At times, this is due to planned obsolescence, a strategy introduced during the Great Depression in the 1930s as a way of fostering economic recovery (London, 1932). Planned obsolescence is usually the result of decisions made to manufacture products that are only 'good enough'. At other times, consumers often buy new products, not because the existing ones have broken down but because of the novelty value of something new (Maitre-Ekern and Dalhammar, 2016).

2.   Objective and outline

This chapter will review the relevant literature and discuss why it is difficult to make progress in sustainable consumption policy, while also discussing the issue of governmental intervention. It will also discuss the need to rethink the way markets work, our relation to products, and challenge the 'conventional' view – often advocated by neoclassical economics and industries – that governments should not intervene.

Furthermore, the chapter will investigate what could be one of the most promising policy areas to have emerged in recent years, that of European policies promoting longer product life cycles as a key strategy for achieving the vision of a circular economy (see European Commission, 2015). Recently adopted product policies on, inter alia, longer consumer warranties, access to spare parts and repair services, and more durable design (Maitre-Ekern and Dalhammar 2016; Faure and Dalhammar, 2018; Svensson et al. 2018), represent developments that could change some of the 'rules of the game' over time. Indeed, Perez (2016) has identified the regulation of products as a way of incentivizing durability and maintenance, and of making producers responsible for the entire lifespan of their products. This is seen as a key measure for encouraging the circular economy and manufacturing durability, as well as the growth of a rental and maintenance economy (Perez, 2016).

This chapter aims to complement Chapter 2 in this volume by focusing on European product policies and laws, and how they can contribute to sustainable consumption objectives. Section 3 briefly reviews the literature on sustainable consumption policy and issues related to steering and interventions in markets. The key premise is that strong steering and collective action is required for moving forward, yet also that it is necessary to engage in a discussion that questions some of the most 'sacred' ideas related to markets. Section 4 discusses the promises and shortcomings of current policies, as well as regulatory difficulties surrounding the sharing economy and the circular economy. Section 5 analyses European product regulations, and the most recent developments, and why these policies may provide important contributions to sustainable consumption objectives. Section 6 summarizes the main conclusions and points out the need for future research.

3.   Sustainable consumption policy

3.1   A brief literature review

Early consumption policy research emphasized the need for consumer information and the use of 'softer' policies, such as eco-labelling schemes and green taxes. The proposed policies – and the discourse –promoted 'greener consumption' rather than reducing consumption levels (Mont and Dalhammar, 2005). Sustainable consumption has often been presented as an isolated policy field, while in practice integration with other policy areas, such as consumer policy, is required for effective policy (Mont and Dalhammar, 2005). No adopted policies have challenged the status quo, which suggests that the policies actually legitimize unsustainable consumption patterns (Shove, 2003). In summary, economic growth continues to be the main parameter for measuring the success of policy; existing policy instruments for sustainable consumption are few and ineffective, and even when there has been consensus for action – for example, increased use of economic instruments – little progress has been made. The European Union (EU) does not have a policy for sustainable consumption and very few European countries have developed national strategies (Mont and Dalhammar, 2008).

This limited progress is hardly surprising given the need for a systems perspective based upon long-term targets, as well as the need to question prevailing ideology. Sustainable consumption is an issue that does not fit neatly into current political structures. This inherent conflict is evident everywhere: people need to fly less, yet many smaller cities continue to subsidize their airports. Many cities support new shopping malls outside cities, even though these encourage private car use, and have a negative effect on the attractiveness of city centres.

If greener consumption is to be accommodated within the current market paradigm ('continuous economic growth'), the idea of slowing down, or even reducing consumption levels challenges this prevailing world view, and accordingly, any such policies would be resisted by vested interests. Business leaders acknowledge the need for radical change in private, but hesitate to make such views public (Confino, 2010).

The idea that we can educate consumers to make more sustainable choices seems to have little support in research, which observes a difference between attitudes and actions. Citizens express a concern for social and environmental issues but place low priority on these in their actual consumption choices (European Commission, 2009; Jackson, 2009). One potential explanation for this 'gap' is that people live both as citizens and as consumers (Berglund and Matti, 2006; Hamilton, 2010). The values people have as citizens cannot be acted upon in their role of consumers due to lock-in effects (Sanne, 2002). Therefore top-down action is considered imperative to give guidance and support to community initiatives pro-social cooperation (Berglund and Matti, 2006). In the right circumstances, top-down action could then also be supported by consumers themselves (Defila et al., 2018).

Thus, it seems that behavioural change must occur at the collective level (Jackson, 2005). In this case, governments would need to go beyond being mere 'information providers' and instead instigate changes that would encourage learning, initiation and active participation from all stakeholders (Jackson and Michaelis, 2003). Support for community groups and projects, and local multi-stakeholder processes, and the support for contexts/projects assuring well-being not directly connected to consumption activities could be part of such an undertaking.

Another issue is that of rebound effects (Binswanger, 2001; Alcott, 2010; 2018). While not all consumption savings will lead to rebound effects, Alcott (2010) claims that these occur, not only on the individual level, but that, in a world with a growing population, increasing economic growth and international trade, any 'consumption savings' made would be consumed elsewhere.

The above seems to imply that 'sufficiency' strategies are needed, as discussed in Chapter 2 in this volume. This could imply caps at the international and/or national level (Alcott, 2010; 2018), and/or limits such as rationing or individual carbon quotas at the individual level (Brown et al., 2010). In order to increase acceptance for radical policies, these must be preceded by some kind of 'grand dialogue' at the national – and preferably also the international – level. It would need to discuss complex issues like sufficiency and consumption limits, the potential conflict between an 'individual's right to consume' and an equal distribution of the Earth's resources (Brown et al., 2010). This would be no easy task. Democracy is often considered as the best possible system of government, but many features of current democratic countries make democracy an ill-equipped system for dealing with both urgent and long-term sustainability challenges (Rosanvallon, 2009).

There seems to be growing disappointment, not only due to the lack of positive initiatives for involving citizens in environmental policies, but also in the evident scepticism of public authorities with regard to expecting positive outcomes when appealing to citizens' sense of social responsibility (see Sen, 2004). It seems that politicians and policymakers make hardly any effort to address consumerism and prevalent economic structures (Brown et al., 2010), as they are afraid to influence people's values. These concerns are misplaced, since the state has always been in a position to send out signals (Jackson, 2009). It does so by subsidizing norms it considers prudent, or by taxing behaviours it would seem prudent to curtail, for example, alcohol and tobacco use. Governments also shape social context by establishing educational structures and defining the work–leisure balance via wage policy and parental leave and working week regulations. Interviews with policymakers reveal that they are uncertain about how to start the change process, and that they often find existing research is not always useful for guiding policy (Mont et al., 2013).

Recently a lot of hope has been placed on the use of behavioural science to provide ideas on motivating pro-environmental consumer behaviour, based on the widespread acclaim of the book *Nudge* (Thaler and Sunstein, 2009). However, researchers have noted that, while nudging can be cost-effective and useful, it is hard to measure long-term outcomes, and that nudging can hardly be viewed as a 'silver bullet' (Mont et al., 2014). Furthermore, something stronger than a mere 'nudge' is clearly required, given the scale of the challenge.

3.2   Intervention and policy instruments

From the 1960s on, environmental policies have been applied more consistently in most developed nations (Carter, 2007). Table 9.1 outlines some of the changes from the 1960s to the present day.

Policy instruments are specific governmental interventions that can be adopted on several levels (international/European/national/regional/local) and provide incentives for change for different actors. They are classified by most authors into at least three categories (see Mont and Dalhammar, 2005): administrative, economic and informative (Table 9.2). Other public interventions are also of relevance. For instance, infrastructure developments can have great influence on opportunities for living sustainably (for example, cycle safely).

Table 9.1 Examples of environmental governance trends over time

	Policy focus	Type of steering	Outcomes	Units of regulation
1960s	Local, national policies, local pollution	Command and control regulations	Prescribing behaviour and technological solutions	Industrial process, dangerous substances, air and water pollutants
Today	Also international, EU policies focusing on new pollutants and problems, such as CO2 emissions and biodiversity	Also market-based instruments and information (labelling, certification)	More focus on setting objectives, leaving it to the market to figure out how to reach them	Increased focus on the life cycle environmental impacts from products, and the impacts of consumption

Table 9.2 Examples of environmental policy instruments

	Compulsory instruments	Voluntary instruments
Administrative	Bans, licences, requirement on information, producer responsibility, recycling and recovery quotas, material and quality requirements, emission levels, chemicals regulation, ecodesign regulations	Industry voluntary commitments and similar initiatives, application of product standards, product panels, management systems, functionality panels, agreements between government and industry
Economic	Deposit-refund systems, taxes and charges, liability rules	Green public procurement, technology procurement, R&D investment
Informative	Information requirement for conflict minerals and chemicals, emission registers, ecodesign requirements, material and quality requirements, chemicals regulation on information for professional and private users, energy labelling, marketing regulations	Eco-labelling, environmental product declarations, green claims, energy labelling, organic labelling of food, certification schemes for hotels and other industries, consumer advice, consumer campaigns, education

Source: Mont and Dalhammar, 2005

Mont et al. (2013) argue that regulations are more challenging to implement than other policies, but also that they are the most effective policy tool for changing consumption patterns. Current policy discourse also notes the limitations of economic and informative instruments.

Most likely, positive visions and stronger regulations, combined with outright bans, are a necessary way forward. Ideas related to behavioural science and nudging may be useful but will probably only achieve modest outcomes. Even when policies result in behavioural change, it is not yet known how long-lasting these changes would be. Furthermore such policies tend to be resource intensive, and therefore scaling up may be difficult.[3]

Thus a paradigm change is required as well as a rethinking of some of the fundamental assumptions of our economic system (articulated in terms of 'economic growth', 'competition', and 'private ownership'). Although this would be difficult to achieve, nevertheless stronger regulation that could change some of the 'rules of the game' is a necessary objective. Such regulations could – over time and in combination with information, visions, and economic incentives – also lead to paradigm and systemic change.

Laws can have a great effect on consumption patterns, because laws affect the social context in which ideas of human–nature interactions, consumption, well-being, morale and identity are shaped. Regulations concerning advertising, product standards, trade, social policies and education may influence the attitudes of different actors. Our knowledge on how these mechanisms work is, however, limited (Mont and Dalhammar, 2008).

3.3   Working with existing policies while aiming to change the paradigm

Rather than hoping for a major paradigm change, it is perhaps more fruitful to improve existing policies, and to introduce new ones whenever possible, in the hope that these incremental changes will over time also influence behaviour, markets, and ultimately the paradigm itself. However, we do not have the time to wait and therefore we need to push for major action now. This could entail a new discussion about 'rights', the 'good life' and staying within planetary resource limits (see Hardin, 1968). New concepts have also emerged such as consumption corridors (see Chapter 2 of this book for more discussion on this).

Nevertheless we need to go further than merely promoting new ideas and concepts. Most notably, we need to call into question the positive view of innovation and technological change, and whether innovation equals progress in all cases. There seem to be signs that people have started to tire of technological innovations (Sax, 2017). It might be time to call into question the positive aspects of novelty, flexibility and organizational changes, and to revisit older ideas regarding the individual's role in society, moving away from a focus on the individual and individual well-being (see Brinkmann, 2017). However, this is not easy, since it revisits previous criticism of sustainability advocates as being 'anti-development'. Von Wright (1993) stated that he preferred a 'provocative pessimism' to an 'impotent optimism' that assumes that markets can resolve most problems (von Wright, 1993: 150), and that we should perhaps combine the communication of the need for urgency with positive images of the future to move forward.

Researchers in the sustainable consumption field might also need to revisit their own assumptions and beliefs. Relevant issues include:

- *The benefits of resource sharing and the sharing economy.* Recently the negative aspects of sharing economy have been in focus (Rinne, 2018). The potential of peer-to-peer sharing schemes needs to be questioned: it might make sense to share some resources, but more difficult to encourage sharing in other areas. A recent consumer survey indicates that many Swedes are not very interested in sharing resources, and that this number is not growing (Röhne, 2018). An alternative route might be required, for example, like policies that promote long-lasting, high-quality repairable products.
- *Active consumers, repairers, innovators, and prosumers.*[4] Many sustainable development scenarios presuppose active consumers. These roles can take quite different forms, for example, prosumers, bottom-up innovators and repairers. Yet how many people are willing to become 'activated' in these ways? There are signs that people are becoming tired of optimizing their choices, and perhaps more generally tired of being activated.[5] Instead there could be interest in developments that make sustainable living more of a default option.

4.   The circular economy and the sharing economy

Today, the most progressive environmental policies in many policy areas are often found in the EU.[6] This section includes general observations on the effects of EU environmental policy as well as making a preliminary analysis of the potential of the sharing and circular economies.

4.1   General observations on achievements and deficiencies of EU environmental policy

Environmental policies adopted in the last 50 years have brought significant improvements, but also have major shortcomings. Table 9.3 outlines main achievements and shortcomings in certain policy areas.

There have been some successes but overall little progress in some areas (see also European Environment Agency, 2015). Most notably, water and air pollution levels from industrial production have been reduced[7] and waste treatment has improved, but without any resulting reduction in total waste levels and total resource use, and the problems of automobile traffic in cities remain. It seems that it is indeed easier to address problems related to point source pollution from industrial production than those related to increased consumption: the environmental footprints of Europeans are not decreasing as we import more products and resources.

The overall picture for the planet is bleak (Steffen et al., 2015). Resource use and waste generation is increasing, climate efforts are insufficient, and biodiversity is severely threatened.

Table 9.3   Major achievements and shortcomings in EU environmental policy and law

Policy area	Main achievements	Major shortcomings
Energy and climate	• Binding targets for greenhouse gas reductions, energy efficiency, and renewables • Costs of renewables decreasing rapidly	• Targets not stringent enough to stop dangerous global warming • Carbon markets do not perform well • Energy efficiency difficult to achieve in practice • Many countries have reduced territorial CO_2 emissions, but CO_2 in imported products are increasing
Chemicals	• An increasing number of substances are being examined and banned; the burden of proof that a substance is safe is put on manufacturers • National regulations on microplastics	• Major legal trade-offs means that it is difficult and time-consuming to ban and regulate substances • Implementation problems and limited information in supply chains
Waste and recycling	• A combination of banning certain landfills for waste, and compulsory collection and recycling levels has all but eliminated landfills in some European countries	• The developments are very uneven within Europe • Total waste levels have not been reduced, and there is no reduction in resource use
Water and air	• Significant emission reductions, health benefits • Evident improvement, e.g. in water quality in many regions	• Difficulty in tackling some air emissions, e.g. local air pollution from traffic • Difficult to regulate CO_2 effectively • Some waterways very hard to improve due to e.g. farming
Nature conservation	• Protection of habitats and species has led to some successes	• The overall trend is still negative

Note: Table 9.3 is clearly only a personal account of some major noticeable trends, and does not attempt to provide a complete picture. See also Selin and VanDeever (2015).

4.2   The sharing economy and the circular economy

The sharing economy and the circular economy are two concepts that have experienced major policy developments recently that are of great interest to the consumption policy agenda. The sharing economy can be understood as an umbrella term for different economic activities (see Chapter 8 in this volume). The sharing economy is mainly concerned with the organization of economic activity and is a 'market-oriented' policy field rather than a 'sustainability-oriented' one. It is generally considered a macroeconomic development, driven and enabled by other trends such as digitalization.

Obviously, the sharing economy has some potential to achieve resource savings. A 2017 Swedish governmental inquiry did not propose significant public policy effort for promoting the sharing economy, although it stated that consumer protection legislation and informative measures might be necessary to protect users (Finansdepartementet, 2017). The European Commission, while generally positive (calling it a 'collaborative economy'), has stressed the need for social protection and to carefully consider tax legislation (European Commission, 2016). Thus, the sustainability promise of the sharing economy is uncertain, and there have been few attempts to 'steer' it in a more sustainable direction by governments or the European Commission.

The circular economy complements current energy–climate policy by focusing on natural resources and materials.[8] The most widely used definition is:

> [...] an industrial system that is restorative or regenerative by intention and design. It replaces the end-of-life concept with restoration, shifts towards the use of renewable energy, eliminates the use of toxic chemicals, which impair reuse, and aims for the elimination of waste through the superior design of materials, products, systems, and, within this, business models. (Ellen MacArthur Foundation, 2012: 7)

In its Action Plan on the circular economy, the European Commission refers to a '[...] circular economy, where the value of products, materials and resources is maintained in the economy for as long as possible, and the generation of waste minimised' (European Commission, 2015: 2). Murray et al. (2017) state that the circular economy represents the most recent attempt to conceptualize the integration of economic activity with environmental and resource concerns. In other words, the concept of circular economy combines older, established notions of resource efficiency with economic aspects.

Unlike the sharing economy, the circular economy is considered a sustainability-related vision that requires many policy interventions (Milios, 2017). The EU Action Plan (European Commission, 2015) outlines existing and new policies for supporting this transition (Figure 9.1).

As can be seen in Figure 9.1, the regulatory agenda is quite ambitious, targeting several actors and life cycle phases. The main problem with the circular economy concerns its implementation: progress requires vision, new business models and, most notably, stringent policies. The policies outlined in the Action Plan are ambitious, but most are only proposals. From a sustainable consumption perspective, it is interesting that these circular economy documents stress product-oriented policies, like ecodesign and various labels: these will now be discussed.

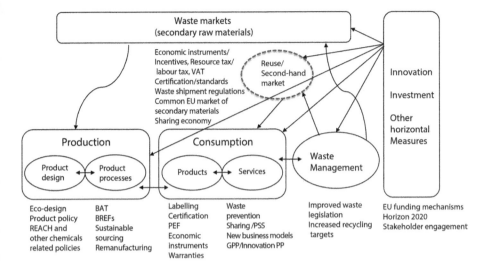

Source: Milios 2017

Figure 9.1   EU policy landscape for the circular economy

5.   Product policies to combat obsolescence

5.1   The emerging palette of European product regulations

While early environmental policies focused on production activities, in recent decades there have been an increasing number of regulations addressing the different life cycle phases of products, for example: (1) chemicals in products, (2) collection and recycling of used products and (3) energy efficiency of products (Faure and Dalhammar, 2018). New policies are emerging to address conflict minerals and product durability.[9] Policies can be both compulsory and voluntary, and be adopted both at the EU level and national level (Faure and Dalhammar, 2018; Maitre-Ekern and Dalhammar, 2016; Svensson et al., 2018). Table 9.4 outlines the main European policies.

European policymakers are currently very interested in incentivizing longer product life cycles and in supporting repair services, especially for consumer products. This can be done in several ways (see Maitre-Ekern and Dalhammar, 2016). Table 9.4 illustrates the different approaches applied in the EU and at member state level, including:

- Direct regulation of durability through the Ecodesign Directive. Regulations have set durability requirements for vacuum cleaners and lighting.[10] Further similar regulation is expected.
- Planned obsolescence has been criminalized in France.[11]
- Scheme in France to promote availability of spare parts.[12]
- Public procurement of remanufactured computers and furniture is taking

Table 9.4   Product-related policies in Europe

Type of environmental aspect	European Union law and policy	Examples of Member State policies
Chemical and material content	Horizontal legislation (e.g. REACH) Conflict minerals Sector oriented laws on chemical restrictions (e.g. Packaging, electronics)	Green public procurement criteria for, e.g. chemicals and conflict minerals Eco-labels Taxes on chemicals
Collection and recycling of waste products	General rules and guidelines (e.g. Waste Framework Directive) Sector oriented EPR laws (e.g. WEEE Directive; Waste and Packaging Waste Directive)	Waste-related taxes Infrastructure for re-use and recycling Re-use parks/shops for re-used products/repair activities Mandatory re-use obligations for white goods (Spain)
Energy efficiency	Mandatory energy performance standards (MEPS) (set under the Ecodesign Directive) Mandatory energy labelling (set under the Energy Labelling Directive) Voluntary labelling (Energy Star)	Eco-labels Green public procurement criteria The use of life cycle costing (LCC) in public procurement
Durability, lifetime and reparability	*Direct incentives:* Mandatory lifetime requirements set under the Ecodesign Directive Vacuum cleaners, lighting products Proposal: providing information about expected lifetime to consumers through mandatory information set under the Energy Labelling Directive Voluntary eco-design agreement, imaging equipment *Indirect incentives:* Minimum rules on consumer guarantees	*Direct incentives:* Banning planned obsolescence (France) *Indirect incentives:* Incentivizing the provision of spare parts (France) National rules on longer consumer guarantees and/ or changed rules for burden of proof is transferred from seller to consumer (several EU Member States) Lower VAT on repairs Public procurement of remanufactured furniture and computers (Sweden)

Source: Amended from Faure and Dalhammar, 2018.

place in some EU member states (for example, computers in Sweden; see Crafoord et al. 2018).

- National consumer legislation in several EU countries has introduced longer compulsory consumer warranties than the minimum requirements stipulated in EU law.
- Reduced value added tax (VAT) for some repair services has been introduced in some countries, for instance in Sweden.

These policies are quite different in nature and include both compulsory legal requirements and market-based approaches. Interestingly, some of the policies clearly signal that markets cannot be trusted to deliver durability even if consumers want it, and that governmental intervention is needed. Governments are starting to take serious action when they suspect corporations are undertaking measures that promote obsolescence. One case that received a great deal of media attention is the investigation of French prosecutors into Apple iPhones and whether there was evidence of planned obsolescence (BBC, 2018). While this can be hard to prove, the signals that governments send to markets are important, and this is likely to affect industrial practices such as standardization. That is why these new regulations have the potential to become real game changers.

We also note that several states in the USA have proposed laws that mandate producers to support independent repairs with tools and manuals for repair, which can make repairs more economically attractive for consumers (Svensson et al., 2018).

Currently, there is discussion at EU level on whether there should be consumer labelling on the expected life cycle of products so that consumers will be able to benchmark products (Maitre-Ekern and Dalhammar, 2016). This type of labelling could be compulsory or voluntary; compulsory labelling would of course have a greater effect. Such labelling could trigger innovation among manufacturers to compete around the issue of durability. However, designing such labelling is complex (Dalhammar and Richter, 2017).

It seems that some 'policy experimentation' is likely to take place in the coming years. Reversing current trends probably requires an effective policy mix, with many components that include:

- Ecodesign rules that force manufacturers to make products easy to disassemble, repair and reassemble.
- Forcing manufacturers to provide spare parts and repair tools at reasonable cost.
- Reducing VAT for the repair sector.
- Providing information for consumers about the environmental impact of electronics and environmental gains from repairs.
- Supporting to do-it-yourself activities like repair cafés.

5.2   Policies addressing product obsolescence

Planned obsolescence consists in 'instilling in the buyer the desire to own something a little newer, a little better, a little sooner than is necessary' (Stevens, 1954, cited in Adamson, 2003: 129). *Oxford Dictionaries* defines planned obsolescence as 'a policy of producing consumer goods that rapidly become obsolete and so require replacing, achieved by frequent changes in design, termination of the supply of spare parts, and the use of non-durable materials'. Thus, obsolescence can be triggered by several different factors.

Planned obsolescence cannot be viewed only as a business strategy but also as a way of life, associated with the 'throwaway society' (see Slade, 2007). For instance, consumer electronics are today replaced more and more frequently and one of the main reasons for this seems to be consumer preferences (Prakash et al., 2015). Consumer tastes and choices are being shaped in order to encourage rapid product replacement. This psychological aspect is deeply embedded in our society. Obsolescence is especially complex in the case of information and communications technology as consumers must match hardware and software (Basulto, 2012).

Product durability and prolonging the life cycle of products are promising strategies for saving resources. Consumer preferences lead to a chicken-and-egg dilemma with regard to obsolescence: if there is constant innovation, with new models constantly appearing, consumers are persuaded to change models often. If a producer designs a more durable product with a longer life cycle, this could lead to wasted resources ('over-engineering') if consumers nevertheless change the model before the product breaks down. Here producers have little incentive to ensure longer product life cycles. Interviewee studies with producers, however, indicate that if producers were forced to design long-lasting, expensive, high-quality products, they would probably consider changing not only product design practices but also business models (Dalhammar, 2016). Here it could make sense to make a product that can be upgraded and leased out to consumers, thus focusing on the service and functionality.

In the case of consumer electronics, it is especially relevant to use them for longer periods, as most life cycle environmental impacts come from the raw material, production and waste phases (Prakash et al., 2015). However, the trend has gone in the opposite direction. This is due to several factors, including the continuous output of products with novel functions, the failure of vital product components (e.g. batteries) that break down before other product components, software updates that can inhibit functionality, and the fact that repair is not an attractive option due to labour costs, expensive spare parts and lack of guarantees (which new products have). Labour costs are high in countries like Sweden (where products can be repaired) but lower in areas where new consumer electronics are produced (mainly Asia). Low raw material costs are also a factor. Thus companies with a 'circular' business model that is based on remanufacturing or leasing find it difficult to compete with companies with 'linear' business models. However, there are now a number of policies that have the potential to incentivize longer product life cycles as they influence product design and make product repairs a more attractive option compared to product replacement when a product breaks down. In a truly circular economy there is no place for cheap products: products and materials must be high quality and durable, and repairable.

6.   Concluding remarks and need for further research

The development of an agenda for sustainable consumption progresses (see Chapter 2 in this volume) is not keeping pace with that required to maintain the integrity of our ecosystems. It would appear we need a new consumption paradigm, based on a 'grand dialogue' related to lifestyles, rights, markets and consumption. However, there seems to be little appetite for this among politicians and citizens. Also, a new paradigm might not result from a grand dialogue but instead from several more minor policies that – taken together – could influence mindsets and markets over time.

This chapter has aimed to point towards a less progressive but perhaps more immediate path forward. It has looked at relevant developments that could lead to greater changes over time. Recent EU policies and national policies in EU member states regarding products have been noted as an especially promising development, as these policies challenge the current logic of the market. Adopting policies to prolong product life cycles challenges the current way markets operate where only some manufacturers compete on quality and durability. This issue is gaining traction also because some new proposed policies – most notably policies aiming to incentivize design for durability and repairability, and policies that makes repair accessible and economically attractive – are supported by the general public and consumer non-governmental organizations (Svensson et al., 2018). However, buying quality products costs more, and everyone – private consumers as well as the public sector – will need to learn to pay more for quality if we are going to move towards a circular economy.

Several avenues are relevant for future research. First of all the elements in new policy areas that have potential for real changes in consumption habits need to be defined, along with an analysis of how these elements could be strengthened and supported. Furthermore, it is necessary to identify policies that have real 'leverage' and could lead to greater systemic change. Research into the design of new policies and new policy packages specifically targeting markets and consumption activities is required; this could include schemes to communicate information about product durability to consumers. Such policies will be contentious as they alter the power dynamics of the market (Svensson et al., 2018). Therefore the research task is a challenging one. Nevertheless, to revisit the title of this chapter, it is too early to give up just yet.

Acknowledgements

This research was supported by the Mistra REES (Resource Efficient and Effective Solutions) programme, funded by Mistra (The Swedish Foundation for Strategic Environmental Research).

NOTES

1 Fairphone is a mobile phone with modular design where ethical considerations have been integrated into the design and supply chain; see https://www.fairphone.com/en.

2 Rebound effects are behavioural responses to changes in technology or policy that offset some of the environmental gains. For instance, if cars become more fuel efficient, the response may be to drive longer distances: direct rebound effect. If the response is not to drive less, the consumer may use the savings to consume other goods and services: an indirect rebound effect.

3 One example is the efforts of municipalities in Sweden to work with selected families to decrease their carbon emissions through 'carbon dieting': change in diets and travelling habits (Håkansson, 2012).

4 'Prosumer' is a relatively new term in the energy field – it usually refers to consumers who both produce and consume electricity.

5 This claim is based on discussions with researchers and staff at Swedish municipalities. The issue is highlighted in research related to prosumers (Lavrijssen, 2017).

6 See Bradford, 2013; Selin and VanDeveer, 2006.

7 This includes pollution reductions due to changes in production techniques and fuels, but there are of course also instances when pollution levels have decreased due to outsourcing of industrial production from Europe to other jurisdictions.

8 Strategies related to resource efficiency can greatly contribute to climate mitigation (see Sitra et al., 2018).

9 'Conflict resources', or 'conflict minerals', are natural resources extracted in a conflict zone and sold to perpetuate the fighting.

10 Regulation 666/2013/EU of 8 July 2013 Implementing Directive 2009/125/EC of the European Parliament and of the Council with regard to Ecodesign Requirements for Vacuum Cleaners [2013] OJ L192/24; Regulation 1194/2012 of 12 Dec. 2012 Implementing Directive 2009/12/EC of the European Parliament and of the Council with Regard to Ecodesign Requirements for Directional Lamps, Light Emitting Diode Lamps and Related Equipment (2012) OJ L342/1.

11 Article L. 213-4-1 of the Consumer Code FR490.

12 Article L. 111-3 of the Consumer Code FR490.

References

Adamson, G. (2003), *Industrial Strength Design: How Brooks Stevens Shaped Your World*, Cambridge, MA: MIT Press.

Alcott, B. (2010), 'Impact caps: Why population, affluence and technology strategies should be abandoned', *Journal of Cleaner Production*, **18** (6), 552–60.

Alcott, B. (2018), 'Environmental caps as a solution to rebound effects', in R. Mastini (ed.), *Sufficiency – Moving beyond the Gospel of Eco-Efficiency*, Brussels: Friends of the Earth Europe.

Basulto, D. (2012), 'Welcome to the new planned obsolescence', *Washington Post*, 9 November, accessed 20 December 2018 at https://www.washingtonpost.com/blogs/innovations/post/welcome-to-the-new-planned-obsolescence/2012/11/09/6d6188f4-2901-11e2-aaa5-ac786110c486_blog.html?noredirect=on&utm_term=.3a51e071fc3b.

BBC (2018), 'Apple investigated by France for "planned obsolescence"', 8 January, accessed 15 September 2018 at http://www.bbc.com/news/world-europe-42615378.

Berglund, C. and S. Matti (2006), 'Citizen and consumer: The dual role of individuals in environmental policy', *Environmental Politics*, **15** (4), 550–71.

Binswanger, M. (2001), 'Technological progress and sustainable development: What about the rebound effect?', *Ecological Economics*, **36** (1): 119–32.

Bradford, A. (2013), 'The Brussels effect', *Northwestern University Law Review*, **107** (1), 1–68.

Brinkmann, S. (2017), *Stand Firm: Resisting the Self-Improvement Craze*, Cambridge: Polity Press.

Brown L., C. Dalhammar and O. Mont (2010), 'The right to consume: Exploring the legitimacy of sufficiency policies' (Working paper 2010:1), IIIEE, Lund University.

Carter, N. (2007), *The Politics of the Environment: Ideas, Activism, Policy*, Cambridge: Cambridge University Press.

Confino, J. (2010), 'Sustainability depends on breaking free of our consumerist fixation', *The Guardian*, 2 December, accessed 13 October 2018 at https://www.theguardian.com/sustainable-business/consumerism-sustainability-short-termism.

Crafoord, K., C. Dalhammar and L. Milios (2018), 'The use of public procurement to incentivize longer lifetime and remanufacturing of computers', *Procedia CIRP*, **73**, 137–41.

Dalhammar, C. (2016), 'Industry attitudes towards ecodesign standards for improved resource efficiency', *Journal of Cleaner Production*, **123** (1):155–66.

Dalhammar, C. and J.L. Richter (2017), 'Options for lifetime labeling: design, scope and consumer interfaces', paper presented at the Product Lifetimes and the Environment conference (PLATE), Delft University of Technology.

Defila, R., A. Di Giulio and C. R. Schweizer (2018), 'Two souls are dwelling in my breast: Uncovering how individuals in their dual role as consumer–citizen perceive future energy policies', *Energy Research & Social Science*, **35**, 152–62.

Ellen MacArthur Foundation (2012), *Towards the Circular Economy, vol. 1. Economic and Business Rationale for an Accelerated Transition*, Cowes, UK: Ellen MacArthur Foundation.

European Commission (2009), 'Europeans' attitudes towards the issue of sustainable consumption and production', Analytical report, Brussels: The Gallup organisation, Hungary and the European Commission.

European Commission (2015), 'Closing the loop – An EU action plan for the circular economy', Communication, COM 614 final, Brussels: European Commission.

European Commission (2016), 'A European agenda for the collaborative economy', Communication, COM(2016) 356 final, Brussels: European Commission.

European Environment Agency (2015), 'The European environment: State and outlook', Synthesis report, Copenhagen: European Environment Agency.

Faure, M. and C. Dalhammar (2018), 'Principles for the design of a policy framework to address product life cycle impacts', in E. Maitre-Ekern, C. Dalhammar and H.C. Bugge (eds), *Preventing Environmental Damage from Products – Analyses of the Policy and Regulatory Framework in Europe*, Cambridge: Cambridge University Press, pp. 57–86.

Finansdepartementet (2017), 'Delningsekonomi på användarnas villkor' (SOU 2017:26), Stockholm: Stadens offentliga utredningar.

Håkansson, M. (2012), 'Koldioxidbantning – Vilken roll skulle det kunna spela i den kommunala klimatpolitiska styrningen?', paper, Lund University, Sweden.

Hamilton, C. (2010), 'Consumerism, self-creation and prospects for a new ecological consciousness', *Journal of Cleaner Production*, **18** (6), 571–5.

Hardin, G. (1968), 'The tragedy of the commons', *Science* **162** (3859), 1243–8.

Jackson, T. (2005), *Motivating Sustainable Consumption*, Guildford, UK: Centre for Environmental Strategy, University of Surrey.

Jackson, T. (2009), *Prosperity without Growth: Economics for a Finite Planet*, London: Earthscan.

Jackson, T. (2013), 'Angst essen Seele auf – Escaping the "iron cage" of consumerism', *Wuppertal Spezial* **48**, Wuppertal Institute for Climate, Environment and Energy.

Jackson, T. and L. Michaelis (2003), 'Policies for sustainable consumption', a report to the Sustainable Development Commission, Centre for Environmental Strategy, University of Surrey with Environmental Change Institute, Oxford University.

Latouche, S. (2010), 'Degrowth', *Journal of Cleaner Production*, **18** (6), 519–22.

Lavrijssen, S. (2017), 'Power to the energy consumers', *European Energy and Environmental Law Review*, **26** (6), 172–87.

London, B. (1932), *Ending the Depression through Planned Obsolescence*, New York.

Maitre-Ekern, E. and C. Dalhammar (2016), 'Regulating planned obsolescence: A review of legal approaches to increase product durability and reparability in Europe', *Review of European, Comparative & International Environmental Law (RECIEL)*, **25** (3), 378–94.

Milios, L. (2017), 'Advancing to a circular economy: Three essential ingredients for a comprehensive policy mix', *Sustainability Science*, **13** (3), 861–78.

Mont, O. and C. Dalhammar (2005), 'Sustainable consumption: At the cross-road of environmental and consumer policies', *International Journal of Sustainable Development*, **8** (4), 258–79.

Mont, O. and C. Dalhammar (2008), 'Public policy for sustainable consumption', in S.J. Evans (ed.), *Public Policy Issues Research Trends*, Hauppauge, NY: NOVA Science Publishers.

Mont, O., E. Heiskanen, K. Power et al. (2013), 'Improving Nordic policymaking by dispelling myths on sustainable consumption', *TemaNord* (2013:553), Denmark: Nordic Council of Ministers.

Mont, O., Lehner, M. and E. Heiskanen (2014), 'Nudging – A tool for sustainable behaviour?' (Report 6643), Stockholm: Swedish Environmental Protection Agency.

Murray A., K. Skene and K. Haynes (2017), 'The circular economy: An interdisciplinary exploration of the concept and application in a global context', *Journal of Business Ethics*, **140** (3) 369–80.

Perez, C. (2016), 'Capitalism, technology and a green global golden age: The role of history in helping to shape the future', in M. Jacobs and M. Mazzucato (eds), *Rethinking Capitalism*, Hoboken, NJ: Wiley Blackwell.

Prakash, S., G. Dehoust, M. Gsell et al. (2015), 'Einfluss der Nutzungsdauer von Produkten auf ihre Umweltwirkung: Schaffung einer Informationsgrundlage und Entwicklung von Strategien gegen "Obsoleszenz"', Report, Dessau-Roßlau: Umweltbundesamt.

Rinne, A. (2018), 'The dark side of the sharing economy', World Economic Forum, accessed 25 May 2018 at https://www.weforum.org/agenda/2018/01/the-dark-side-of-the-sharing-economy.

Röhne, J. (2018), 'Svenskar vill inte dela', *Aktuell Hållbarhet*, 3 March, accessed 28 April 2018 at https://www.aktuellhallbarhet.se/svenskar-vill-inte-dela.

Rosanvallon, P. (2009), *Demokratin som problem*, Hägersten, Sweden: TankeKraft Förlag.

Sanne, C. (2002), 'Willing consumers – or locked-in? Policies for a sustainable consumption', *Ecological Economics* **42** (1–2), 273–87.

Sax, D. (2017), 'Our love affair with digital is over', *New York Times*, 18 November, accessed 7 July 2018 at https://www.nytimes.com/2017/11/18/opinion/sunday/internet-digital-technology-return-to-analog.html.

Selin, H. and S. VanDeveer (2006), 'Raising global standards: Hazardous substances and e-waste management in the European Union', *Environment Science and Policy for Sustainable Development*, **48** (10), 6–18.

Selin, H. and S.D. VanDeveer (2015), 'Broader, deeper and greener: European Union environmental politics, policies, and outcomes', *Annual Review Environment and Resources*, **40**, 309–35.

Sen, A. (2004), 'An essay on entitlement and deprivation: Why we should preserve the spotted owl', *London Review of Books*, **26** (3), 10–11.

Shove, E. (2003), 'Changing human behaviour and lifestyle: A challenge for sustainable consumption?', in I. Ropke and L. Reisch (eds), *Consumption: Perspectives from Ecological Economics*, Cheltenham, UK and Northampton, MA, USA: Edward Elgar Publishing, pp. 111–32.

Sitra, the Finnish Innovation Fund, European Climate Foundation, Climate-KIC et al. (2018), 'The circular economy – A powerful force for climate mitigation', Report, Stockholm: Material Economics Sverige.

Slade, G. (2007), *Made to Break: Technology and Obsolescence in America*, Cambridge, MA: Harvard University Press.

Steffen, W., W. Broadgate, L. Deutsch et al. (2015), 'The trajectory of the Anthropocene: The great acceleration', *The Anthropocene Review*, **2** (1), 81–98.

Stiglitz, J. (2018), 'Post-Davos Depression', *Project Syndicate*, 1 February, accessed 19 March 2018 at https://www.project-syndicate.org/commentary/davos-ceos-tax-cuts-trump-by-joseph-e--stiglitz -2018-02.

Svensson, S., J.L. Richter, E. Maitre-Ekern et al. (2018), 'The emerging "right to repair" legislation in the EU and the US', paper presented at Going Green – Care Innovation conference, Vienna, Austria, 26–8 November.

Thaler, R. and C. Sunstein (2009), *Nudge: Improving Decisions about Health, Wealth, and Happiness*, New York: Penguin Group.

von Wright, G.H. (1993), *Myten om framsteget*, Stockholm: Albert Bonniers Förlag.

10 Editing out unsustainability from consumption: From information provision to nudging and social practice theory

Eva Heiskanen and Senja Laakso

1. Introduction

Human actions have already exceeded many planetary boundaries (Steffen et al., 2015). In order to stay within the safe operating space, both decarbonization and dematerialization by a factor of ten or more are deemed necessary (Bringezu, 2015; Jackson, 2009; Tukker et al., 2010). These targets require changes in consumption patterns: the utilization of products, services and infrastructure, from acquisition and use to disposal (Girod et al., 2014).

This chapter illustrates the journey from 'mainstream paradigms' of studying and steering consumption towards sustainability (Keller et al., 2016), to a critique of these approaches, and the latest ideas on how to make consumption more sustainable.

The traditional approach to sustainable consumption draws on cognitive approaches, viewing consumers as choice-makers whose decisions are supported by improved information and product labelling (Heiskanen et al., 2014). More recently, behavioural models have gained traction following increased policy interest in behavioural economics. These models have provided stimuli for designing better choice architectures that 'nudge' consumers to behave in accordance with the conservation of public goods, such as the global environment (Nagatsu, 2015; Schubert, 2017).

Most of the work drawing on economic and psychological models is methodologically individualist: it views consumers as isolated actors, rather than members of a consumer society. A more sociological approach looks beyond individual consumers to the historical, structural and cultural factors shaping consumer society (Shove and Spurling, 2013). Social practice theory represents the newest entrant into the field of sustainable consumption research and policy discourse, and investigates how daily practices are shaped by established services and technologies, by shared norms, conventions and capabilities, as well as by organizational, institutional and political rules (for example, Geels et al., 2015; Shove, 2014).

We review the contributions of these three fields of research on sustainable consumption, with examples from residential energy use. We consider the contribution of each paradigm to 'strong sustainable consumption', emphasizing the need for a reduction in overall resource use rather than in the environmental impacts of individual products (Fuchs and Lorek, 2005). Furthermore, strong sustainable consumption considers people not only as consumers but also as citizens, and emphasizes the social embeddedness of consumption (Lorek and Fuchs, 2013). Since sustainable consumption is not only an academic field, we also focus on policy relevance and policy implications. Given its rising prominence, we devote more attention to social practice theory than to the other perspectives. By doing so, we aim to provide an analysis of not only the promise, but also the policy challenges of social practice theory as a framework for 'editing out' unsustainability and reconfiguring consumer society.

2.   The traditional approach to promoting sustainable consumption: Empowerment through information

Sustainable consumption emerged at a time when neoliberalism was gaining ground, and markets were seen as the solution to virtually every problem. The 1980s saw a rise of green consumer guides, green marketing and the first eco-labelling schemes. Green consumption was seen as a way of moving consumption patterns towards less unsustainable alternatives, for example, by reducing the chemicals in detergents. The promotion of household energy and resource conservation has an even longer pedigree, dating back to the oil crises of the 1970s (Geller and Attali, 2005). The overall aim has been to correct market failures by providing consumers with more and better information in order to raise awareness of environmental issues (for instance, understanding the environmental consequences of their actions) and facilitate pro-environmental choices in practice through task-related information.

These approaches, based on attitude–behaviour models (Ajzen, 1991; Ajzen and Fishbein, 2000) and value–belief–norm models (Stern, 2000) have dominated the research on both energy conservation and green consumption for several decades. The underlying assumption in such models is that consumers lack awareness of the environmental implications of their consumption patterns and that providing such information would to lead to behavioural changes. There is some – though not very strong – evidence to justify this expectation. Meta-analyses (Bamberg and Möser, 2007; Klöckner, 2013) show that awareness of environmental problems and the environmental consequences of actions explains about 4–5% of the variations in (self-reported) behaviour, whereas attitudes towards particular environmentally relevant behaviours (for example, recycling, energy conservation) explain about 13–18% of the variations in (self-reported) behaviour.[1]

A focus on enabling consumers to steer the market towards sustainability via information is still very evident, in European Union (EU) energy policies and the discourses related to the Energy Union and smart power grids, for example. In its 2015

Summer Package, the European Commission argued that 'citizens must be at the core of the Energy Union', which will be accomplished by 'helping consumers save money and energy through better information, giving consumers a wider choice of action when choosing their participation in energy markets and maintaining the highest level of consumer protection' (European Commission, 2015: 1). Similarly, in its proposal for a directive on an internal market for electricity, the European Commission relies on the power of information:

> Fully integrating industrial, commercial and residential consumers into the energy system can avoid significant costs for 'backup' generation; costs which consumers would otherwise end up paying. It even allows consumers to benefit from price fluctuations and to earn money through participation in the market. Activating consumer participation is therefore a prerequisite for managing the energy transition successfully and in a cost-effective way. (European Commission, 2016: 4)

The proposal that consumers can be empowered is obvious in energy markets where the earlier set-up of the market made enlightened consumer participation virtually impossible. Consumers have been excluded from active participation for decades and competition is a fairly recent phenomenon. The product itself is difficult to understand and billing practices have only recently begun to reflect underlying consumption patterns through quarter-yearly real-time billing rather than billing based on estimates with an annual settling of actual consumption (Burke and Stephens, 2017; Heiskanen and Matschoss, 2016).

From the perspective of strong sustainable consumption, the evidence concerning improved metering and billing is only slightly encouraging. A meta-analysis by Delmas et al. (2013) indicated that information strategies reduced residential energy consumption by 7% on average, though with variable results from one study to another. Given the scale of the strong sustainable consumption challenge, this is a good start, but insufficient. However, current efforts to provide more information (for example, via smart meters) and enable active energy citizenship are positive in the sense that they enable consumers to gain agency – for example, by joining energy cooperatives (European Commission, 2015). The concern is that only a small group of pioneering consumers are enthusiastic enough about energy for such active engagement, whereas most consumers are not particularly interested in their energy consumption on a daily basis due to other pressing concerns (Heiskanen and Matschoss, 2016).

3.   Beyond rationality: The promise and limitations of behavioural economics and 'nudges'

Decades of research on the 'energy efficiency gap' (Gillingham and Palmer, 2014) indicate that consumers' behaviour is far from rational, if rationality is defined in a narrow, calculative sense. The fact that people consistently underinvest in energy conservation, as well as other observations from behavioural economics, have gained increasing prominence in the public debate, not the least thanks to best-selling books like *Nudge* (Thaler and Sunstein, 2008) and *Thinking Fast and Slow* (Kahneman, 2011). Due to the overall political status of economics, and the behavioural economists' focus on empirical observation and evidence-based policy, behavioural economics has made a breakthrough into sustainable consumption policy – it probably can be said to represent the current mainstream policy paradigm (Organisation for Economic Co-operation and Development, 2017).

The underlying argument of 'nudges' is that most or our daily behaviour is based on 'fast' (less-conscious) thinking (Kahneman, 2011), and thus is prone to a host of biases and errors. Consumers are unable to make rational choices, either in self-interest or in accordance with their (pro-environmental, pro-social) preferences. The solution thus is to design better 'choice architectures', that is, decision settings and environments that 'alter people's behaviour in a predictable way without forbidding any options or significantly changing their economic incentives' (Thaler and Sunstein, 2008: 6). This definition could include the provision of information (Ölander and Thøgersen, 2014), but nudges typically attempt to bypass higher-order information processing. Typical nudge tools (Lehner et al., 2016; Thaler and Sunstein, 2008) include:

- *Simplification and framing of information* that aims to influence fast, unreflective thinking. For example, instead of kilowatt hours, electricity bills feature a graphic comparison to previous months and typical peer consumption, and smiley faces if consumption has decreased.
- *Changes to the physical environment* that aim to steer unreflective behaviour rather than overloading people with information. For example, people are directed to use the stairs with arrows painted on the floor, or are prompted to choose vegetarian options via cafeteria design.
- *Changes to default settings* that build on people's propensity to stick with the status quo or the situation that requires the least effort (or to consider the default as some kind of official endorsement; see Schubert, 2017). For example, green electricity can be offered by default. Consumers can de-select this if they prefer the conventional options.
- *The use of descriptive social norms* that builds on people's desire to behave 'normally' (some behavioural economists call this herding bias). For example, residents are informed with door-hangers that people in their county typically use fans instead of air conditioning to keep cool.

There is evidence that some individual nudges are indeed quite effective: in particular, changes to default settings (Lehner et al., 2016). In a natural experiment, 95–99% of customers kept a 'green electricity default' rather than switching to 'black electricity' (Pichert and Katsikopoulos, 2008) and reducing plate size in hotels while providing social cues led to 20% less food waste (Kallbekken and Sælen, 2013). Other than defaults, one of the most effective nudges that Lehner et al. (2016) found was an experiment by Wansink (2007) that reduced the consumption of Pringles crisps by 50% by dyeing every seventh crisp red (thus allowing consumers to monitor how many crisps they had eaten). Such quantitative evidence is highly attractive to policymakers who feel they have finally found a tool for sustainable consumption policy (Jones et al., 2014).

However, these examples also illustrate one of the severest limitations to the use of behavioural economics in sustainable consumption policy. Delivering each of these effective nudges described above on a large scale requires great effort, often with more modest results than those described above. The large-scale rollout of informative energy bills, for example, offering the type of simplification and framing described above, reduced energy consumption by about 2% (Allcott and Mullainathan, 2010). Moreover, influencing the myriad choices that consumers fail to 'get right' requires the collaboration of market players such as energy companies, hotels and manufacturers. Such collaboration might in some cases be in their interest – that is, hotels may indeed desire to reduce food waste – but the opposite could also be the case (for example, the Pringles example above). From a policymaker's perspective, using nudges to promote strong sustainable consumption on a large scale would require a huge administrative effort in the micromanagement of consumers' choice architectures (Lehner et al., 2016; Wilson and Dowlatabadi, 2007).

There are also discussions about the legitimacy of nudges. While our consumer society is replete with subliminal marketing, it is not obvious that such tools are legitimate for policymakers in democratic societies (Goodwin, 2012). Concern has also been raised that covert nudges might alienate people from the sustainable consumption agenda if the means used are seen as illegitimate (Felsen et al., 2013; Lehner et al., 2016). Some psychologists have questioned the basic argument of libertarian paternalism – the notion of cognitive biases – and emphasize the inevitability and benefits of cognitive heuristics instead (Gigerenzer and Gaissmaier, 2011). However, this in itself would not call into question the use of nudges in a sustainable consumption context where nudges can be deemed non-paternalistic: that is, their aim is to promote social welfare and internalize environmental externalities rather than guide people towards their own (presumed) interests (Nagatsu, 2015; Schubert, 2017).[2] From this perspective, social nudges are no different from other types of institutions that solve social dilemmas (Nagatsu, 2015).

From the perspective of strong sustainable consumption, evidence concerning the effectiveness of nudges and other behavioural interventions is not clear cut. Spectacular individual success stories do exist, but these interventions were very carefully designed and focused on particular behaviours, each only representing a small portion of consumption patterns. From the perspective of treating consumers as citizens, moreover, the picture concerning nudges is mixed. Schubert (2017) has argued that when implemented in a transparent and democratic fashion, nudges might enhance citizen awareness of the hidden commercial manipulation shaping our decisions. Yet as a social engineering solution, nudging also runs the risk of depoliticizing and individualizing sustainability and thus overlooking the deeper socio-cultural roots of environmental and social problems (Schubert 2017).

4.   The academic shift beyond behaviour change: From consumption choices to social practices

Parallel to the rise of behavioural economics in the sustainable consumption discussion, criticism of the individualist focus of consumption research has gained ground in the sustainable consumption community. It follows on from an interest in 'ordinary consumption' (Gronow and Warde, 2001) in the sociology of consumption. This has been reinforced by a growing realization in the sustainable consumption community that we should focus on overall resource use and on re-evaluating how priority areas such as food, housing and mobility are provided (Fuchs and Lorek, 2005; Heiskanen and Pantzar, 1997; Lorek and Fuchs, 2013).

Social practice theory makes two important arguments for sustainable consumption. First, it addresses some deficiencies of the methodologically individualist stance in most previous research on consumption (Heiskanen et al., 2010) and moves the focus from isolated behaviours towards socially shared practices, that is, embodied habits, institutionalized or otherwise shared knowledge, meanings and engagements, and materials and technologies (see for example, Gram-Hanssen, 2015; Schatzki, 2002). Cultural conventions define appropriate ways of consumption: what a decent home is like, how people should dress and what and when they should eat (Shove, 2003), and consumption patterns are further shaped by shared infrastructures, such as building, energy and information and communications technology (ICT) systems, and by (often commercial) provision systems, like the available supply of goods in supermarkets. These place material constraints on changes towards sustainable consumption, while also communicating particular symbolic meanings to consumers.

Second, social practice theory moves the focus from efforts towards changing particular types of behaviours (like energy conservation) to the root causes of unsustainable consumption. People do not consume energy as such, but rather perform different kinds of practices that, in different ways, entail energy use. So, for example, rather than considering how to get people to purchase energy-efficient washing machines, social practice theory investigates how and why Europeans wash so much laundry each year (Mylan and Southerton, 2017; Shove, 2003). Rather than trying to get consumers to engage with energy conservation, for example, social practice theory asks how energy consumption is driven by changes in daily routines such as showering, and shared conventions such as expectations concerning cleanliness or thermal comfort (Gram-Hanssen, 2017; Shove and Walker, 2014). While some consumers might be willing to make changes in their lives, such changes can be exceedingly difficult if they run counter to shared cultural, infrastructural and market conventions and expectations (Heiskanen et al., 2010).

Much of recent research on mundane consumption has indeed been based on social practice theory. It embraces the idea that energy usage is configured through complex relations between people's personal, routinized lives and the wider development of material and social structures, and that these relations should be in focus on understanding (increasing) consumption (see Gram-Hanssen, 2015; Røpke, 2009; Shove, 2014; Shove and Walker, 2010). Within energy consumption research, attention has also been focused on what happens inside and outside the home. Such research explores how people live their lives in relation to other people, things and places, and what the role is of 'unconventional' or 'non-human' energy consumers, such as 'babies, pets, pests and pool pumps' (Butler et al., 2016; Strengers et al., 2016). It also explores how new technologies (like mobile phones, computers, cars and heating systems) extend and change the boundaries of our homes (Wallenborn and Wilhite, 2014).

Social practice theory thus challenges what Keller et al. (2016) call the 'mainstream paradigms' of sustainable consumption. A focus on providing information alone is not enough since daily practices create complex systems. Skilful performances are negotiated in relation to other people and systems, and nudging individual behaviours does not go far enough in addressing escalating societal expectations regarding 'cleanliness, comfort and convenience' (Shove, 2003). Despite an increasing interest in social practice theory in academic research, the implications for policy have remained quite general. This is the case even though many policies already have implications for daily practices and their transformation (Shove and Walker, 2010). Much of the research on social practices highlights their complexity, contextuality and diversity – aspects that often present policymakers with 'don't' rather than 'do' types of implications. However, there are some examples of practical policy implications drawing from social practice theory. Shove (2014) and Spurling et al. (2013) argue that policy makers should:

1. Focus on transforming collective conventions, working simultaneously at transforming or 're-crafting' meanings, competencies and material foundations. For example, they could provide support for changing to renewable heating systems, together with the development of common meanings (like self-sufficiency and autonomy) and the development of competencies and identities as communities having a more active role in energy (Jalas et al., 2017; Raven et al., 2008).

2. Deliberately reconfigure the relations between competing practices, such as heating space versus heating people, thus setting in motion positive feedback effects to support the favoured practice over the non-favoured, unsustainable one. For example, adaptive heating practices – that is, systems where users adapt to changes in temperature, rather than expect steady-state thermal comfort always and everywhere – entail different material products (Kuijer, 2014), building systems standards (Taleghani et al., 2013), and user competencies and meanings (Strengers and Maller, 2011) compared to practices based on steady-state thermal comfort. The more people (consumers, building engineers, regulators) engage with adaptive thermal comfort, the greater the political and technical support for such adaptive systems.

3. Modify the ways practices interlock to make the system of practices as a whole more sustainable. For example, the required size of homes depends in part on the number of goods and activities that need space in the home (Heiskanen and Jalas, 2003).

4. Look beyond behavioural change and environmental policy at the diverse drivers of escalating consumption. For example, in the case of housing, there is a need to reconsider policies that offer tax advantages for speculating on real estate, housing and building standards, thus leading to increased use of space and health policies that promote increased energy use (Strengers and Maller, 2011).

Until now, many of the studies on more or less sustainable consumption practices have focused on qualitative, in-depth analyses of day-to-day activities (that is, practices-as-performances; see Schatzki, 2002). The small-scale interventions and experiments to reveal and change daily performances in households have been insightful (for example, Devaney and Davies, 2017; Jack, 2013; Kuijer, 2014; see also Laakso and Heiskanen, 2017). Although disruptions in routines are often inconvenient or even severe, they nevertheless entail opportunities to explore and learn about new practice configurations (Laakso, 2017; Wallenborn and Wilhite, 2014). However, there are still few clear proposals for scaling up these changes to transform practices-as-entities (Hui et al., 2017; Laakso, 2017). From the perspective of strong sustainable consumption, social practice theory thus provides promising avenues by moving attention towards root causes of consumption. However, challenges remain in translating these insights into policy measures.

5.   Where do we stand in terms of moving towards more sustainable practices?

Strong sustainable consumption emphasizes the need for a reduction in overall resource use (Fuchs and Lorek, 2005), and studies show that alternatives exist to decarbonize and dematerialize consumption. Girod et al. (2014), for instance, have reviewed the carbon emissions of products in the consumption categories of food, shelter, travel, goods and services, and identified options compatible with the greenhouse gas intensity required in 2050 to limit global warming within 2°C above pre-industrial levels. Lettenmeier et al. (2014) suggest that a sustainable level of resource use is achievable while providing for nutrition, housing, household goods, mobility, leisure activities, other purposes and public services. Research has demonstrated how households are able to significantly reduce the environmental impacts of their consumption, at least temporarily (Laakso, 2017). On the other hand, studies also show how and where the greatest impediments lie to achieving a sustainable level by individual actions alone (Hirvilammi et al., 2013). The challenge is thus to transform practices-as-entities: shared patterns of consumption shaped by collective rules, infrastructures and systems of provision. This can (and should) occur in two ways: through a scaling up of local change initiatives and through adjustment of society's macrostructures, that is, policies that shape the conditions for more or less sustainable consumption.

Civil society movements have been the originators of many more sustainable practices that are currently mainstream, such as recycling (Lounsbury et al., 2003) and local renewable energy production (Jamison, 2001). It is encouraging that cities and local governments have taken an active role recently in trying out new practices that support more sustainable consumption patterns, particularly in the case of housing and mobility (Bulkeley and Castán Broto, 2013). Local experiments can nurture legitimacy and create a sense of familiarity, while challenging norms and conventions (Heiskanen et al., 2015), and open up the contextual and cultural aspects of consumption (Lutzenhiser, 2014; Shove, 2018). They can also shift power to the local people and empower them towards a more active role in the energy system. This also entails the development of new competencies, which are not only about the provision of information, but also about developing localized and mutually aligned capabilities between consumers and local service providers (Heiskanen et al., 2017; Neij et al., 2017). A close analysis of such 'learning by doing' can also shed light on the 'fossilization' of practices, that is, processes during which a practice becomes outmoded (Watson, 2013).

The challenge is that sustainable consumption cannot be 'strong' unless it is adopted by the majority of consumers. Lessons concerning the conditions for scaling up more sustainable practices can be drawn from practice/theoretical analyses of how, for example, Nordic walking became a recognized form of exercise that travelled across continents (Pantzar and Shove, 2010) and how DIY home improvements caught on among previously unskilled consumers (Watson and Shove, 2008). Relevant lessons can also be drawn from research on sociotechnical change: for example, how local solar initiatives grew into a global industry (Dewald and Truffer, 2011), how early passive house experiments led to standards and legislation (Ornetzeder and Rohracher, 2009), and how local organic food initiatives turned into a mainstream industry (Smith, 2007). Finally, research on institutional entrepreneurship (Levy and Scully, 2007) and change in strategic action fields (Fligstein and McAdam, 2012) illustrates the conditions under which local initiatives can grow to challenge dominant institutions and interests.

A common thread in previous research on how local innovative practices become mainstream is that mainstreaming is uncertain, contingent and takes a long time. Since we cannot afford to wait decades for strong sustainable consumption to emerge from the grassroots, top-down change through policy reform is equally necessary. In this context, social practice theory suggests that we seriously consider how current policies – beyond explicitly environmental policies – shape consumption. The increased interest in regulatory impact assessment (Radaelli, 2005) could helpfully be informed by a deeper understanding of the interconnections between practices. How, for example, do tax breaks for real estate investment influence urban form[3] and the related expectations concerning housing, or how is housing influenced by educational or labour market policies? Sustainable consumption policy cuts across policy sectors and requires much greater policy coordination than single-sector policies (Heiskanen et al., 2014).

As already illustrated in many examples by Spurling et al. (2013) and Shove (2015), policies that transform practices already exist. The most progressive transport policies are already considering how materials, meanings and competencies are linked in moving towards more sustainable mobility practices (Dowling and Kent, 2015; Larsen, 2017). In contrast, there is no similar understanding of different uses of the home (and thus different energy-related practices at home). A practice-theoretical approach could provide some tools in answering questions such as how to move from maintaining the present practices to questioning what energy is for and what kind of services it provides (Shove, 2018), what a home is, how different aspects of the home are related to energy use and where the boundaries of control and cooperation are drawn (Gram-Hanssen and Darby, 2018; Wallenborn and Wilhite, 2014), and what kinds of expectations and diversification of consumption are created by new technologies (Pantzar and Shove, 2010; Røpke and Christensen, 2013).

When considering residential energy use from this perspective, one particularly sensitive question relates to the increasing amount of living space per person in Europe, largely due to the growing number of single households. One-third of all households in the EU-28, for example, are composed of a single person and this has been the fastest growing group during the past ten years (Eurostat, 2017). In Sweden, over half of all households are single-person households, followed by more than 40% in Lithuania, Denmark, Finland and Germany. Whereas living alone is often related to situations in life, the ideal of having one's own, private space or feelings attached to a particular place, this trend nevertheless has implications for energy use due to the increasing number of household appliances and the increasing amount of space to be heated. Considering whether some products (for example, sports equipment) and activities (for example, bathing) could be located outside the home, for example, via shared services (for example, rental, public baths, libraries) and enabled by careful town planning, could offer options for reducing the growth of the floor space of private homes (Fremstad et al., 2018).

The above-mentioned questions undeniably require new, more comprehensive expertise and collaboration among various actors. Transitions in consumption practices require parallel transitions in practices of governing, manufacturing, investing, and so on (Watson, 2013). Whereas expertise in technological improvements such as renewable energy and smart home solutions can be achieved through education, there is no such expertise in changing the meanings attached to home – who is to say how much space people need and what kind of space and facilities are required by different needs? Practice-based living laboratories can be one way to facilitate collaborative processes in which knowledge is co-created among various actors to find new ways of consumption that are more sustainable (Laakso et al., 2017). Such transdisciplinary approaches can provide means to tackle the complexity, contextuality and diversity that are embedded in social practices (Heiskanen et al., 2018), while deliberation based on practical experience can open discussions on the politics of practices (Sayer, 2013). A strong sustainable consumption approach suggests that such considerations are not only useful, but will also be unavoidable when current consumption patterns and the current economic system hit the wall of planetary boundaries.

6.   Conclusion and implications: Prospects of providing solid policy advice for sustainable consumption

We have shown that the three research areas reviewed here make a contribution to sustainable consumption. However, information interventions and nudges fall short in terms of addressing natural resource consumption in its totality (for instance, strong sustainable consumption), whereas the promise of social practice theory to address escalating expectations in consumer society is still embryonic in terms of policy implications. We have outlined some bottom-up and top-down policy pathways that could be pursued in parallel, yet these would definitely require significant changes in how sustainable consumption policy is practised.

Such change is likely to be evolutionary rather than revolutionary. At first sight, the bodies of research reviewed above entail contradictory policy implications, which policymakers are likely to experience as a barrier to utilization of research (Heiskanen et al., 2014). This, however, does not mean that findings could not be integrated. Several proposals advocating policy mixes for sustainable consumption (for example, Nissinen et al., 2015) could be integrated (practically, if not ontologically and epistemologically) with a practice approach. Similarly, while some academics might take issue with behavioural economists' notions of cognitive biases, few would disagree with the idea of changing default settings or changing the physical environment in order to promote sustainable consumption. Information about the environmental impacts of consumption and the available alternatives to growing resource consumption might not change behaviour, but is critical for the engagement of citizens.

A more problematic issue for policy uptake is the disciplinary division within the policy sectors responsible for (un)sustainable consumption. The notion of 'editing out' unsustainable consumption implies all-powerful policymakers sitting outside the society they are attempting to change (Shove and Walker, 2010), rather than the real-life policymakers who are embroiled in the practices they are attempting to change. This is evident if we take seriously the proposal from social practice theory to reform policies that are not explicitly 'environmental', yet have indirect impact by driving unsustainable consumption. These policies cut across several sectors that would need to be engaged in a common search for better solutions.

One proposal that policymakers themselves have advocated is to engage in closer co-construction of knowledge, for example through action research and real-life experimentation (Heiskanen et al., 2014). Creating networks of policy actors, co-creating knowledge on practices and their potential for change, and experimenting in real life could provide avenues for research, policy and citizens to jointly engage in discussions on why there is growing consumption of, for example, appliances and living space (Gram-Hanssen, 2015; Heiskanen et al., 2014). Through hands-on engagement in change initiatives, policymakers cannot remain distant 'editors' of unsustainable consumption patterns, but are faced with the need to change their own policy practices. Strong sustainable consumption is still an issue that political discourse prefers to avoid, since current policies are geared to questions of efficiency rather than sufficiency. This, however, does not mean that this state of affairs is inevitable, given the pressing needs of climate change and global environmental degradation.

Acknowledgements

The research presented here has received funding from the European Union's H2020 Research and Innovation programme under grant agreement number 727642. The sole responsibility for the content of this paper lies with the authors.

NOTES

1 Kormos and Gifford (2014) have shown that self-reports only explain about 21% of the variance in observed behaviours, yet their meta-analysis failed to identify a social desirability bias – that is, according to their meta-analysis, people simply do not remember their behaviour, or survey instruments are not sufficiently perceptive.

2 While Thaler and Sunstein (2008) anchor the concept of nudge within the philosophy of libertarian paternalism, it has been argued that pro-social nudges used for sustainable consumption do not require a paternalist stance to individual autonomy. Social nudges encourage the voluntary provision of public goods (Nagatsu, 2015), that is, provide a way to avoid social dilemmas.

3 'Urban form is defined as the physical characteristics that make up built-up areas, including the shape, size, density and configuration of settlements. It can be considered at different scales: regional, urban, neighbourhood, block and street. Urban form evolves constantly in response to social, environmental, economic and technological developments; planning, housing and urban policies; and health, transport and economic policies (Williams, 2014).

References

Ajzen, I. (1991), 'The theory of planned behavior', *Organizational Behavior and Human Decision Processes*, **50**, 179–211.

Ajzen, I. and M. Fishbein (2000), 'Attitudes and the attitude-behavior relation: Reasoned and automatic processes', *European Review of Social Psychology*, **11** (1), 1–33.

Allcott, H. and S. Mullainathan (2010), 'Behavior and energy policy', *Science*, **327** (5970), 1204–5.

Bamberg, S. and G. Möser (2007), 'Twenty years after Hines, Hungerford and Tomera: A new meta-analysis of psycho-social determinants of pro-environmental behaviour', *Journal of Environmental Psychology*, **27** (1), 14–25.

Bringezu, S. (2015), 'Possible target corridor for sustainable use of global material resources', *Resources*, **4** (1), 25–54.

Bulkeley, H. and V. Castán Broto (2013), 'Government by experiment? Global cities and the governing of climate change', *Transactions of the Institute of British Geographers*, **38** (3), 361–75.

Burke, M.J. and J.C. Stephens (2017), 'Energy democracy: Goals and policy instruments for sociotechnical transitions', *Energy Research and Social Science*, **33**, 35–48.

Butler, C., K.A. Parkhill and N.F. Pidgeon (2016), 'Energy consumption and everyday life: Choice, values and agency through a practice theoretical lens', *Journal of Consumer Culture*, **16** (3), 887–907.

Delmas, M.A., M. Fischlein and O.I. Asensio (2013), 'Information strategies and energy conservation behavior: A meta-analysis of experimental studies from 1975 to 2012', *Energy Policy*, **61**, 729–39.

Devaney, L. and A.R. Davies (2017), 'Disrupting household food consumption through experimental HomeLabs: Outcomes, connections, contexts', *Journal of Consumer Culture*, **17** (3), 823–44.

Dewald, U. and B. Truffer (2011), 'Market formation in technological innovation systems – diffusion of photovoltaic applications in Germany', *Industry and Innovation*, **18** (3), 285–300.

Dowling, R. and J. Kent (2015), 'Practice and public–private partnerships in sustainable transport governance: The case of car sharing in Sydney, Australia', *Transport Policy*, **40**, 58–64.

European Commission (2015), 'Transforming Europe's energy system – Commission's energy summer package leads the way' (Press release), accessed 6 November 2018 at http://europa.eu/rapid/press-release_IP-15-5358_en.htm.

European Commission (2016), 'Proposal for a Directive of the European Parliament and of the Council on common rules for the internal market in electricity (recast)', COM (2016) 864 final/2, accessed 6 November 2018 at https://eur-lex.europa.eu/legal-content/EN/TXT/?uri=COM:2016:0864:FIN.

Eurostat (2017), 'Household composition statistics', accessed 6 November 2018 at http://ec.europa.eu/eurostat/statistics-explained/index.php/Household_composition _statistics.

Felsen, G., N. Casteloy and P.B. Reiner (2013), 'Decisional enhancement and autonomy: public attitudes towards overt and covert nudges', *Judgement and Decision Making*, **8** (3), 202–13.

Fligstein, N. and D. McAdam (2012), *A Theory of Fields*, Oxford and New York: Oxford University Press.

Fremstad, A., A. Underwood and S. Zahran (2018), 'The environmental impact of sharing: Household and urban economies in CO_2 emissions', *Ecological Economics*, **145**, 137–47.

Fuchs, D.A. and S. Lorek (2005), 'Sustainable consumption governance: A history of promises and failures', *Journal of Consumer Policy*, **28** (3), 261–88.

Geels, F.W., A. McMeekin, J. Mylan et al. (2015), 'A critical appraisal of sustainable consumption and production research: The reformist, revolutionary and reconfiguration positions', *Global Environmental Change*, **34**, 1–12.

Geller, H. and S. Attali (2005), *The Experience with Energy Efficiency Policies and Programmes in IEA Countries: Learning from the Critics*, Paris: IEA.

Gigerenzer, G. and W. Gaissmaier (2011), 'Heuristic decision making', *Annual Review of Psychology*, **62**, 451–82.

Gillingham, K. and K. Palmer (2014), 'Bridging the energy efficiency gap: Policy insights from economic theory and empirical evidence', *Review of Environmental Economics and Policy*, **8** (1), 18–38.

Girod, B., D.P. van Vuuren and E.G. Hertwich (2014), 'Climate policy through changing consumption choices: Options and obstacles for reducing greenhouse gas emissions', *Global Environmental Change*, **25** (1), 5–15.

Goodwin, T. (2012), 'Why we should reject "nudge"', *Politics*, **32** (2), 85–92.

Gram-Hanssen, K. (2015), 'Housing in a sustainable consumption perspective', in L.A. Reisch and J. Thøgersen (eds), *Handbook of Research on Sustainable Consumption*, Cheltenham, UK and Northampton, MA, USA: Edward Elgar Publishing, pp. 178–91.

Gram-Hanssen, K. (2017), 'New needs for better understanding of household's energy consumption – behaviour, lifestyle or practices?', *Architectural Engineering and Design Management*, **10** (1–2), 91–107.

Gram-Hanssen, K. and S. J. Darby (2018), '"Home is where the smart is"? Evaluating smart home research and approaches against the concept of home', *Energy Research and Social Science*, **37**, 94–101.

Gronow, J. and A. Warde (eds) (2001), *Ordinary Consumption*, Abingdon, UK: Routledge.

Heiskanen, E. and M. Pantzar (1997), 'Toward sustainable consumption: Two new perspectives', *Journal of Consumer Policy*, **20** (4), 409–42.

Heiskanen, E. and M. Jalas (2003), 'Can services lead to radical eco-efficiency improvements? – A review of the debate and evidence', *Corporate Social Responsibility and Environmental Management*, **10** (4), 186–98.

Heiskanen, E. and K. Matschoss (2016), 'Consumers as innovators in the electricity sector? Consumer perceptions on smart grid services', *International Journal of Consumer Studies*, **40** (6), 665–74.

Heiskanen, E., M. Johnson, S. Robinson et al. (2010), 'Low-carbon communities as a context for individual behavioural change', *Energy Policy*, **38** (12), 7586–95.

Heiskanen, E., O. Mont, and K. Power (2014), 'A map is not a territory – making research more helpful for sustainable consumption policy', *Journal of Consumer Policy*, **37** (1), 27–44.

Heiskanen, E., M. Jalas, J. Rinkinen et al. (2015), 'The local community as a "low-carbon lab": Promises and perils', *Environmental Innovation and Societal Transitions*, **14**, 149–64.

Heiskanen, E., K. Hyvönen, S. Laakso et al. (2017), 'Adoption and use of low-carbon technologies: Lessons from 100 Finnish pilot studies, field experiments and demonstrations', *Sustainability*, **9** (5), (847).

Heiskanen, E., S. Laakso, K. Matschoss et al. (2018), 'Articulating theories of change to design real-world laboratories for the reduction of residential energy use', *GAIA*, **27** (S1), 60–67.

Hirvilammi, T., S. Laakso, M. Lettenmeier et al. (2013), 'Studying well-being and its environmental impacts: A case study of minimum income receivers in Finland', *Journal of Human Development and Capabilities*, **14** (1), 134–54.

Hui, A., T. Schatzki and E. Shove (eds) (2017), *The Nexus of Practices: Connections, Constellations, Practitioners*, Abingdon, UK: Routledge.

Jack, T. (2013), 'Nobody was dirty: Intervening in inconspicuous consumption of laundry routines', *Journal of Consumer Culture*, **13** (3), 406–21.

Jackson, T. (2009), *Prosperity without Growth? The Transition to a Sustainable Economy*, London: Earthscan.

Jalas, M., S. Hyysalo, E. Heiskanen et al. (2017), 'Everyday experimentation in energy transition: A practice-theoretical view', *Journal of Cleaner Production*, **169**, 77–84.

Jamison, A. (2001), *The Making of Green Knowledge: Environmental Politics and Cultural Transformation*, Cambridge: Cambridge University Press.

Jones, R., J. Pykett and M. Whitehead (2014), 'The geographies of policy translation: How nudge became the default policy option', *Environment and Planning C: Government and Policy*, **32** (1), 54–69.

Kahneman, D. (2011), *Thinking, Fast and Slow*, London: Macmillan.

Kallbekken, S. and H. Sælen (2013), '"Nudging" hotel guests to reduce food waste as a win–win environmental measure', *Economics Letters*, **119** (3), 325–7.

Keller, M., B. Halkier and T. Wilska (2016), 'Policy and governance for sustainable consumption at the crossroads of theories and concepts', *Environmental Policy and Governance*, **26**, 75–88.

Klöckner, C.A. (2013), 'A comprehensive model of the psychology of environmental behaviour – A meta-analysis', *Global Environmental Change*, **23** (5), 1028–38.

Kormos, C. and R. Gifford (2014), 'The validity of self-report measures of proenvironmental behavior: A meta-analytic review', *Journal of Environmental Psychology*, **40**, 359–71.

Kuijer, L. (2014), 'Implications of social practice theory for sustainable design', PhD thesis, Delft, Netherlands: Technical University of Delft.

Laakso, S. (2017), 'A practice approach to experimental governance: Experiences from the intersection of everyday life and local experimentation', PhD thesis, Helsinki: University of Helsinki.

Laakso, S. and E. Heiskanen (2017), 'Good practice report: Capturing cross-cultural interventions', ENERGISE – European Network for Research, Good Practice and Innovation for Sustainable Energy, Deliverable 3.1.

Laakso, S., E. Heiskanen and K. Matschoss (2017), 'Living Labs background report', ENERGISE – European Network for Research, Good Practice and Innovation for Sustainable Energy, Deliverable 3.2.

Larsen, J. (2017), 'The making of a pro-cycling city: Social practices and bicycle mobilities', *Environment and Planning A*, **49** (4), 876–92.

Lehner, M., O. Mont and E. Heiskanen (2016), 'Nudging – A promising tool for sustainable consumption behaviour?', *Journal of Cleaner Production*, **134**, 166–77.

Lettenmeier, M., C. Liedtke and H. Rohn (2014), 'Eight tons of material footprint – suggestion for a resource cap for household consumption in Finland', *Resources*, **3** (3), 488–515.

Levy, D. and M. Scully (2007), 'The institutional entrepreneur as modern prince: The strategic face of power in contested fields', *Organization Studies*, **28**, 971–91.

Lorek, S. and D. Fuchs (2013), 'Strong sustainable consumption governance – precondition for a degrowth path?', *Journal of Cleaner Production*, **38**, 36–43.

Lounsbury, M., M. Ventresca and P.M. Hirsch (2003), 'Social movements, field frames and industry emergence: a cultural–political perspective on US recycling', *Socio-Economic Review*, 1 (1), 71–104.

Lutzenhiser, L. (2014), 'Through the energy efficiency looking glass', *Energy Research and Social Science*, 1, 141–51.

Mylan, J. and D. Southerton (2017), 'The social ordering of an everyday practice: The case of laundry', *Sociology*, 52 (6), 1134–51.

Nagatsu, M. (2015), 'Social nudges: Their mechanisms and justification', *Review of Philosophy and Psychology*, 6 (3), 481–94.

Neij, L., E. Heiskanen and L. Strupeit (2017), 'The deployment of new energy technologies and the need for local learning', *Energy Policy*, 101, 274–83.

Nissinen, A., E. Heiskanen, A. Perrels et al. (2015), 'Combinations of policy instruments to decrease the climate impacts of housing, passenger transport and food in Finland', *Journal of Cleaner Production*, 107, 455–66.

Ölander, F. and J. Thøgersen (2014), 'Informing versus nudging in environmental policy', *Journal of Consumer Policy*, 37 (3), 341–56.

Organisation for Economic Co-operation and Development (2017), *Behavioural Insights and Public Policy: Lessons from Around the World*, Paris: OECD.

Ornetzeder, M. and H. Rohracher (2009), 'Passive houses in Austria: The role of intermediary organizations for the successful transformation of a socio-technical system', conference paper, France: ECEEE 2009 Summer Study.

Pantzar, M. and E. Shove (2010), 'Understanding innovation in practice: A discussion of the production and re-production of Nordic Walking', *Technology Analysis and Strategic Management*, 22 (4), 447–61.

Pichert, D. and K.V. Katsikopoulos (2008), 'Green defaults: Information presentation and pro-environmental behaviour', *Journal of Environmental Psychology*, 28 (1), 63–73.

Radaelli, C.M. (2005), 'Diffusion without convergence: How political context shapes the adoption of regulatory impact assessment', *Journal of European Public Policy*, 12 (5), 924–43.

Raven, R.P., E. Heiskanen, R. Lovio et al. (2008), 'The contribution of local experiments and negotiation processes to field-level learning in emerging (niche) technologies: meta-analysis of 27 new energy projects in Europe', *Bulletin of Science, Technology and Society*, 28 (6), 464–77.

Røpke, I. (2009), 'Theories of practice – New inspiration for ecological economic studies on consumption', *Ecological Economics*, 68 (10), 2490–97.

Røpke, I. and T.H. Chrisensen (2013), 'Transitions in the wrong direction? Digital technologies and daily life', in E. Shove and N. Spurling (eds), *Sustainable Practices: Social Theory and Climate Change*, London: Routledge, pp. 49–68.

Sayer, A. (2013), 'Power, sustainability and well-being: An outsider's view', in E. Shove and N. Spurling (eds), *Sustainable Practices: Social Theory and Climate Change*, London: Routledge, pp. 167–80.

Schatzki, T.R. (2002), *The Site of the Social: A Philosophical Account of the Constitution of Social Life and Change*, University Park: Pennsylvania State University Press.

Schubert, C. (2017), 'Green nudges: Do they work? Are they ethical?', *Ecological Economics*, 132, 329–42.

Shove, E. (2003), *Comfort, Cleanliness and Convenience: The Social Organization of Normality*, Oxford: Berg Publishers.

Shove, E. (2014), 'Putting practice into policy: Reconfiguring questions of consumption and climate change', *Contemporary Social Science*, 9 (4), 415–29.

Shove, E. (2015), 'Linking low carbon policy and social practice', in Y. Strengers and C. Maller (eds), *Social Practices, Intervention and Sustainability. Beyond Behaviour Change*, London: Routledge, pp. 31–44.

Shove, E. (2018), 'What is wrong with energy efficiency?', *Building Research and Information*, 46 (7), 779–89.

Shove, E. and N. Spurling (eds) (2013), *Sustainable Practices: Social Theory and Climate Change*, Abingdon, UK: Routledge.

Shove, E. and G. Walker (2010), 'Governing transitions in the sustainability of everyday life', *Research Policy*, **39** (4), 471–6.

Shove, E. and G. Walker (2014), 'What is energy for? Social practice and energy demand', *Theory, Culture and Society*, **31** (5), 41–58.

Smith, A. (2007), 'Translating sustainabilities between green niches and socio-technical regimes', *Technology Analysis and Strategic Management*, **19** (4), 427–50.

Spurling, N., A. McMeekin, E. Shove et al. (2013), 'Interventions in practice: Re-framing policy approaches to consumer behaviour', Sustainable Practices Research Group Report.

Steffen, W., K. Richardson, J. Rockström et al. (2015), 'Planetary boundaries: Guiding human development on a changing planet', *Science*, **347** (6240), 1217.

Stern, P.C. (2000), 'New environmental theories: Toward a coherent theory of environmentally significant behavior', *Journal of Social Issues*, **56** (3), 407–24.

Strengers, Y. and C. Maller (2011), 'Integrating health, housing and energy policies: social practices of cooling', *Building Research and Information*, **39** (2), 154–68.

Strengers, Y., L. Nicholls and C. Maller (2016), 'Curious energy consumers: Humans and nonhumans in assemblages of household practice', *Journal of Consumer Culture*, **16** (3), 761–80.

Taleghani, M., M. Tenpierik, S. Kurvers et al. (2013), 'A review into thermal comfort in buildings', *Renewable and Sustainable Energy Reviews*, **26**, 201–15.

Thaler, R.H. and C.R. Sunstein (2008), *Nudge: Improving Decisions about Health, Wealth, and Happiness*, New Haven: Yale University Press.

Tukker, A., M.J. Cohen, K. Hubacek et al. (2010), 'The impacts of household consumption and options for change', *Journal of Industrial Ecology*, **14** (1), 13–30.

Wallenborn, G. and H. Wilhite (2014), 'Rethinking embodied knowledge and household consumption', *Energy Research and Social Science*, **1**, 56–64.

Wansink, B. (2007), 'Helping consumers eat less', *Food Technology*, **61**, 34–8.

Watson, M. (2013), 'Building future systems of velomobility', in E. Shove and N. Spurling (eds), *Sustainable Practices: Social Theory and Climate Change*, London: Routledge, pp. 117–31.

Watson, M. and E. Shove (2008), 'Product, competence, project and practice: DIY and the dynamics of craft consumption', *Journal of Consumer Culture*, **8** (1), 69–89.

Williams, K. (2014), 'Urban form and infrastructure: A morphological review', Technical Report, Government Office for Science, accessed 18 December 2018 at http://eprints.uwe.ac.uk/24989.

Wilson, C. and H. Dowlatabadi (2007), 'Models of decision making and residential energy use', *Annual Review of Environment and Resources*, **32**, 169–203.

11 The role of local governments in governing sustainable consumption and sharing cities

Jenny Palm, Nora Smedby and Kes McCormick

1. Introduction

Municipalities are key actors in their role as planners for sustainable urban development, and also have the responsibility to transform ambitious national and global goals and visions into local practices (McCormick et al., 2013). The role of municipalities in relation to enhancing sustainable consumption patterns has been increasingly highlighted by policymakers and in research. Creating sustainable societies and shaping their consumption patterns has become an everyday activity for municipalities. This is also the case for the Nordic countries and not least for Sweden, which will be used as an example in this chapter. The Nordic countries have the ambition of becoming sustainable leaders and enabling sustainable consumption (Mont et al., 2013).

Sweden has a long tradition of public ownership and centralized technical infrastructure, along with municipal autonomy, including self-governing of a large budget, taxation-rights and a high level of authority in spatial planning; the so-called planning monopoly (Palm, 2006). Municipalities will continue to play a central role in sustainable development, but in recent decades stakeholder participation has turned into an important prerequisite for municipal activities. In order to ensure sustainable development, municipalities need to adopt working methods and approaches that include external stakeholders in their processes. Municipalities can use both traditional forms of authority and new partnerships or processes to achieve effective governance (Bulkeley and Kern, 2006).

Achieving sustainable consumption demands a reinterpretation of the role of municipalities, businesses and citizens, and generates complex challenges and institutional contradictions for governance. This leads municipalities to explore new modes of governing. Several authors have developed theories and conceptual models to substantiate governance arrangements (for example, Evans et al., 2006; Hajer, 2011; Hoppe et al., 2014).

In this chapter we will discuss the model by Bulkeley and Kern (2006) where they formulated a typology of four different modes of governing in local climate governance that is based on the type of capacity used by the municipality in its different roles (see also Kern and Alber, 2008). These four models are: *self-governing (or governing by example)*, which relies on the organizational capacity of the municipality to manage its own operations; *governing by provision*, which is related to the municipal role as provider of different goods and services; and *governing by authority*, which concerns the ability of a municipality to make specific behaviours compulsory and impose sanctions if this is not done. Finally, the authors discuss *governing by enabling*, which refers to the municipality's capacity to persuade and encourage through the use of positive incentives such as subsidies, information campaigns or the facilitation of different types of initiatives.

The typology has been extended by Bulkeley et al. (2009) with *governing by partnership*, which we include here. Compared with governing by enabling, governing by partnership is characterized by a more equal relationship between the municipality and other actors. Development of this kind of governance structure is seen as a consequence of the increased need to mobilize resources from actors outside formal control in order to formulate and implement public policy. In this network, the government is one of several actors and has no formal steering power over the other members (Peters and Pierre, 1998; Rhodes, 1997). Public and private actions and resources are coordinated and given a common direction and meaning.

In municipalities, consumption is related to local actors by managing available resources and dealing with limitations, which municipalities govern through both policy formation and policy implementation. To deepen the understanding of how municipalities govern sustainable consumption, we also need to scrutinize the development of different functions and strategies in municipalities. What can municipalities, in practice, achieve with different governing modes and is this engagement from a municipality always beneficial for sustainable consumption? This will be discussed below.

2.   Different modes of governing in relation to authority and control

Policymaking today can be characterized by a process of the opening up of government towards broader governance comprising partnerships and network-oriented decision-making in an intricate interplay between public, private and non-profit organizations. The role of the municipality changes – it becomes one actor among many. Yet municipalities need to mobilize external actors (and their resources) for the formulation and implementation of public policy (Considine, 2005; Palm and Thoresson, 2014). Municipalities still need to carry out their compulsory duties and fulfil their responsibilities for providing welfare services to their citizens. Most of the tasks of municipalities are regulated in special legislation and these are managed by formal government processes.

This traditional government approach is characterized by the formal steering chain of public organizations and top-down hierarchal decision-making by political actors. 'Government' implies that this governing takes place within governments and their formal institutions and the state's monopoly on the use of legitimate coercion is focused on this (Boyer, 1990; Stoker, 1998). In contrast, 'governance' refers to networks that are self-organizing and not fully accountable to governmental bodies. Cooperation and coordination are key processes and legitimacy is gained through the interplay of legal interpretations, common understanding and trust (Börzel, 1998; Peters and Pierre, 2004; Rhodes, 1997; Wihlborg and Palm, 2008).

This leads to implications for how municipalities govern consumption and the outcomes that a governing mode can be expected to achieve. In this chapter we will elaborate on the four governing modes in relation to three scenarios where the policy process is characterized by greater or less government involvement.

When a process or issue is initiated within a municipality, this is characterized as governmental. The results can be defined at the beginning, all decisions are made within the municipality, the municipality is responsible for implementation and the municipality also governs the whole process.

When a process or issue is initiated in collaboration with others, this is characterized as governance. When the municipality tries to predict results, these can take the form of different scenarios and the outcome is more open and can be different from predictions made during governmental processes. Decision-making is done in networks of public–private partnerships, implementation is done in collaboration and the municipality is one partner among many.

When a process is characterized as being mainly in the private or voluntary sector (for instance, outside the public sphere), from the municipality's point of view, this means that results are uncertain and cannot be predicted by the municipality. Decision-making is in the hands of the initiator – the private or volunteer actor – and implementation is carried out by the partners involved. The role of the municipality is mainly to support or facilitate these processes.

These three characterizations of a policy process will be discussed in relation to the governing modes identified in earlier research. Then we will present experiences from Sweden where different governing modes have been applied by municipalities. We will then discuss the role of municipalities and whether the examples illustrate a governmental, governance or private/volunteer process and what implications this could have for the municipality for governing sustainable consumption.

3.   Experiences from Sweden of different governance modes

We will now discuss examples from Sweden where different governing modes have been used. These illustrate how municipalities have contributed to sustainable consumption practices, and we will use these examples for an initial discussion about the suitability of these approaches.

3.1   Self-governing

Self-governing (or governing by example) is strongly connected to government policy processes and a municipality's own role as a consumer. When a public organization buys a product (goods or services or a combination) with public funds, this is called public procurement and a large share of municipal consumption takes place within this framework. Since municipalities constitute a significant share of public procurement, municipalities have strong capacities in this area.

Public authorities are major consumers. In Europe, public authorities consume 16% of GDP in the 28 EU countries, which means that the public sector holds both great influence on sustainable consumption and has significant purchasing power (European Commission, 2011; Organisation for Economic Co-operation and Development, 2009). Public spending ranges from the purchase of medical equipment to the construction of roads and hospitals. Thus public procurement is an important regulation of public consumption. Sustainable Public Procurement (SPP) and Green Public Procurement (GPP) have been in focus recently. These concepts aim to capture the process used to secure the acquisition of goods and services in a way that minimizes damage to the environment (Meehan and Bryde, 2011; Michelsen and de Boer, 2009).

Research indicates that local and regional actors are becoming increasingly involved in projects that emphasize sustainable procurement. One reason for this is the proximity of the local level to citizens and the fact that the local level can detect unmet needs and act as an enabler of innovative sustainable measures (Dale-Clough, 2015). In Sweden, municipalities and municipal enterprises represented 68% of the number of public procurements advertised (National Agency for Public Procurement and the Swedish Competition Authority, 2016). Through public procurement, cities can incrementally limit their own environmental impact by purchasing 'greener' options, such as more energy-efficient vehicles.

Due to the large amounts purchased, municipalities also have the opportunity to contribute to technological change by purchasing niche products, such as biogas cars instead of more energy efficient vehicles (Palm and Backman, 2017a). Furthermore, public procurement can foster not only technological innovation, but also the innovation of new business models associated with more sustainable consumption, for example, hiring a car instead of purchasing one so that the vehicle can be driven by others when not in use by the municipality. Knowledge is, however, limited regarding to what extent this involvement has an effect on consumption (Lember et al, 2011). Earlier studies have shown that SPP or GPP is not used to its full potential in municipalities; this is explained by the existence of conflicting policies that create uncertainty with regard to the procurement process (Sporrong and Kadefors, 2014).

Another way of self-governing is through different organizational policies, such as travel policies for the municipality's staff (see Elofsson et al., 2018). Such a policy can either steer the employee travels in a more sustainable direction, or limit the amount of travelling done. For example, Västerås Municipality has a travel policy that encourages virtual meeting formats as opposed to meeting in person (Elofsson et al., 2018). On the other hand, however, some municipalities in Sweden have travel policies that explicitly propose flying as the first option, such as in Trelleborg in the case of journeys where flying would decrease travel time compared to a train journey, and thus avoid the need for an overnight stay (Trelleborg Municipality, 2017). While such a travel policy appears counterproductive from an environmental perspective, it does highlight the difficulty in negotiating between different priorities within a municipality.

In Gothenburg, a self-proclaimed forerunner in terms of consumption governance, the 2018 budget contained several targeted goals for local administration units that focus on how the city can use its common resources more efficiently: for example, by renting out more of the municipal property premises that are empty for part of the day or longer periods.

3.2   Governing by provision

Municipalities can influence what is consumed within their geographical boundaries. In governing by provision, production and consumption usually takes place within the municipality and, therefore, production and consumption governance coincide to a large extent. Heating is one area where municipalities, or municipally owned companies, often have the ability to influence the consumption of residents (Magnusson, 2016). In Sweden, the provision of district heating, and the provision of heating produced by renewable resources as part of district heating networks, has played an important role in limiting the carbon emissions associated with heat consumption in cities (Di Lucia and Ericsson, 2014).

Governing by provision may also be about non-provision, for example, if gas is not provided via a gas grid, heating buildings with gas is thus not an option and solutions based on low heat demand in combination with electric heating could become more attractive. This was the case in a sustainability focused development in Egedal Municipality in Denmark (Smedby and Quitzau, 2016).

Municipally owned companies are often central in governing by provision, both in more traditional forms and in more innovative initiatives. In Eskilstuna Municipality, Sweden, a municipally owned waste and energy company runs a shopping centre called Retuna, which looks like a mainstream shopping centre but primarily sells reused and remanufactured products (Hedegård et al., 2016). The shopping centre opened in 2016 and is still at an early stage of development – it is, thus, too soon to assess its success.

3.3   Governing by authority

Municipalities have limited powers to govern by authority in relation to sustainable consumption. There are examples where municipalities have the right to regulate certain types of consumption. An example from the Swedish context is to limit the time for stationary cars leaving their engines running. However, these are relatively isolated areas with limited impact. Another more commonly used regulation is to lower parking quotas for new buildings. Thus municipalities can influence consumption indirectly through different technical regulations, but here too, authority is limited.

In some countries, municipalities have the right to set their own energy performance standards on buildings, for example, when the city owns municipal land to be developed (see for example, Bulkeley and Kern, 2006; Smedby and Quitzau, 2016; Tambach and Visscher, 2012). Another way to exercise authority is as an inspection body for certain national regulations, like building regulations. Depending on the administrative context, municipalities can choose to be more or less stringent with regard to ensuring such regulations are applied and, in this way, can exercise some form of agency.

In 2015, Växjö Municipality won a court case that permitted them to force residential buyers of municipal land to connect their houses to the municipal district heating system, which, of course, will have a huge impact on the future heat consumption of these homeowners. The judgement was appealed by the Swedish competition authority, which, however, decided to withdraw this appeal in 2016 as the chance of winning was marginal.

3.4   Governing by enabling

In terms of governing by enabling, that is, through positive incentives, information and facilitation, municipalities have many avenues for promoting sustainable consumption. In particular, various types of information campaigns can be used to foster behavioural change. Municipalities can also support different types of grassroots initiatives for sustainable consumption, which is also a form of governing by enabling.

One example of governing by enabling is when a municipality, through the planning permission procedure, negotiates the minimum numbers of parking spaces required for new developments (SALAR, 2013). For example, in Malmö, if a developer makes an agreement with a car pooling company to offer their services to the residents of a new housing development, the number of parking spaces can be decreased. This is a way of enabling more sustainable forms of transport consumption and promoting business models at an early stage of development. This case also illustrates how different modes of governing are combined: governing by authority through the parking space requirement in planning permission, and governing by enabling through the option of flexible negotiation.

A different example that relies more on information than on negotiation is the various campaigns run by cities to encourage more sustainable forms of mobility. Again, Malmö serves as example with their campaign 'No ridiculous car journeys', which aimed to discourage car use for journeys shorter than five kilometres (Malmö

City Council, 2014). The campaign used both traditional forms of information such as advertising in newspapers and around the city, as well as more innovative forms, including campaign cyclists moving around in the city and a competition for the most ridiculous car journey. The campaign reached a broad audience (50% of the municipality) and of those residents who became aware of the campaign, 15% stated that it had persuaded them drive less (Hörlén et al., 2008).

The STPLN Open Maker Space in Malmö, an arts and community centre that hosts a co-working facility, a space for exhibitions and performances, and several do-it-yourself workshops for textile printing, sewing, knitting, carpentry, digital production, bicycle service and construction, and creative reuse/recycling, is an example of how the sharing economy can be supported. It is targeted at people of all ages active within the arts, technology, innovation, design and crafts. In most cases, people can use STPLN for free and, in return give their time and knowledge. The STPLN building is owned by Malmö City Council, which also provides basic financial support. STPLN offers new work and leisure opportunities for all Malmö citizens, encouraging more sustainable lifestyles, enhancing social cohesion, allowing for new ways of interaction, and providing learning and exchange of skills.

Other examples or sharing where municipalities are involved in minimizing consumption include different kinds of 'libraries', such as traditional book libraries but also, for example, 'tool libraries' or 'tool pools' where city dwellers can borrow tools at low or no cost. While the direct environmental benefit may be limited, it is often highlighted as innovative in a city's consumption governance (see also Chapter 7 in this volume). For example, in the district of Hammarby Sjöstad in Stockholm, the municipality enables different sharing activities via a cycle sharing infrastructure, tool and equipment sharing programmes and coordination of waste and recycling collection between tenants and owner associations to reduce the number of contractors and vehicles.

Sege Park in Malmö is planned to become one of the leading residential areas in the world based around the sharing economy. At the time of writing, discussion about construction was at an early stage: plans include a shared parking garage, with different auxiliary facilities to facilitate sharing, such as bicycle pools, car pools and laundry services, providing a physical structure where governing by design can enable sharing.

A further example of governing by design comes from the city of Umeå in northern Sweden. Access to green spaces is an important issue in a growing city in order to manage sustainable urban development. The Norrland University Hospital in Umeå is currently looking for green spaces that would be conducive to the recovery of patients, as well as providing recreational space for staff, students and residents. Demand for such space is expected to grow, not least because the number of residents will increase since the area around the city is becoming more densely populated. Today green structures near the hospital are mostly used by students and are thus utilized less often during the summer months. Umeå City Council had the idea of developing trial activities for sharing the green spaces and increasing their attractiveness, as well as ensuring greater utilization of the park around the hospital via collaboration between property owners and tenants.

3.5   Governing by partnership

Climate change and sustainable consumption are developing within a context of increased globalization, deregulation and neoliberal ideology; this requires network-oriented decision-making processes that are based on an intricate inter-play of public, private and non-profit organizations and the coordination of their resources. Horizontal cooperation between a municipality and its partners from communities, industry, interest organizations and local businesses is usually neces-sary for successful implementation.

One such example is that Swedish municipalities have started addressing energy efficiency in local businesses in order to achieve local and national energy reduc-tion goals. This is done by creating a network of companies with the declared aim of reducing energy consumption in these companies. The networks usually involve around ten companies, but there are also examples of 60 companies coming together to improve energy efficiency (Palm and Backman, 2017b).

Another example is from Malmö where contracts from the City Council allocat-ing land to real estate developers include the requirement for participation in a dialogue process. The aim is to identify investment that would contribute to social, ecological and economic sustainability. Large sections of the physical space in cities are not under the control of municipalities and thus real estate developers and property owners need to be involved and engaged in sustainable urban plan-ning processes so that the ambitious objectives regarding sustainability can be implemented.

4.   Discussion

Swedish municipalities have a great deal of autonomy and have the power to act on many issues. The four different governing modes indicate that municipalities also find ways to circumvent any lack of power by choosing a specific governing mode. If, for example, they do not have the power to influence energy efficiency in local businesses, they can choose a partnership mode that opens up opportunities for governing in this area. Consumption governance is an area where municipali-ties often govern at the limits of their jurisdiction and/or their traditional area of governing.

Governing by example is a clear case of the process being defined by government. The municipality can decide on an objective and then use its own organization to implement and control the outcome of the process. The other clear governmental example is governing by authority, where the municipality can impose regulations in an area and thus enforce sustainable consumption patterns.

When operating in a border area like sustainable consumption where public, private and voluntary sectors interweave, it is rare that municipalities control the whole process from the setting of the agenda to implementation. In these cases, the choice of governing mode(s) becomes even more important for ensuring implementation. Governing by partnership is such a case where the formulation of contracts is crucial to attaining the successful implementation of sustainable goals (compare Palm and Wihlborg, 2006; Wihlborg and Palm, 2008). Governing through enabling has also become common in connection with sustainable consumption.

With regard to recent developments in the sharing economy, municipalities have engaged in processes that enable sharing. Sharing has many possibilities for contributing to more sustainable consumption: fewer resources are needed if a product or a space can be shared between many actors. However, this is not the point we aim to make here. The issue we would like to reflect upon is that of the role of municipalities in sharing. As noted above, municipalities in Sweden have invested in different solutions to enable their citizens to share more often. One critical issue that must be discussed in this connection is whether engaging in the sharing economy is the task of municipalities. Sweden has a long tradition of municipalities planning and implementing local sustainable solutions (Palm, 2006). Citizens *participate* in municipal planning, but seldom initiate it or take the leading role (Fenton et al., 2015; 2016).

One possible interpretation of engagement in the sharing economy is that municipalities are more effective than volunteer groups and thus disempower them from acting and engaging in a bottom-up movement that could contribute to a new kind of sharing economy under the municipality's 'radar'. When taking a leading role in developing a sharing economy, municipalities might also misunderstand or misinterpret which elements of consumption citizens actually want to share. This could result in many sharing points or hubs where no one actually participates in the sharing practice. As discussed, when a policy process is characterized as being both in the private and volunteer sector, from the perspective of the municipality this process has an uncertain character and an outcome that cannot be controlled. The question must then be asked as to whether the municipality should initiate and manage such a process.

All the governing modes, but especially those with a governmental character, contain a strong collaborative element. Depending on the municipality's collaboration partners, this has implications for the type of consumption governance taking place. If, as argued by Khan (2013), for example, these collaborative arrangements are dominated by existing elites, then they are likely to foster win–win commercial solutions for selected sustainability problems. In relation to urban consumption governance, the umbrella of smart cities captures many such solutions, for example, those related to energy efficiency and demand response management (Bulkeley et al., 2009). In these cases, municipalities contribute to new technologies that could result in more sustainable consumption patterns. However, at the same time, this could entail the drawback of the municipality supporting solutions from established regime actors at the expense of grassroots initiatives and thus reinforcing unequal power relations.

Collaborative urban consumption responses, such as those gathered under the umbrella of Sharing Cities (McLaren and Agyeman, 2015) could also include solutions that are both compatible and incompatible with current market logic. A current trend is the development of more commercial forms of innovation in relation to collaborative consumption. For example, Sweden's largest car sharing cooperative announced in January 2018 that they would terminate their activities, stating that it was difficult to collaborate with the growing commercial actors in the area of car sharing (P4 Göteborg, 2018).

Nevertheless, we would like to note that being engaged in all different governing modes could be a suitable activity for a municipality. Enabling a sustainable solution could shape practices and expectations that could feed into future policy formation. For example, the introduction of reduced parking space allocation could lead to changing the cultural norm of car ownership, thus opening up opportunities for even more radical non-car-based mobility policies for cities. This interplay between policy implementation and policy formation is key to the increasingly experimental nature of local sustainability governance (Bulkeley and Castán Broto, 2012; Hoffmann, 2011; Smedby and Quitzau, 2016). The intention of raising critical issues in relation to the use of different governing modes is to emphasize the need for many actors to initiate and govern processes leading to sustainable consumption.

5.   Conclusions

Changing patterns of consumption significantly demands connecting and strengthening both a diversity of activities in the sharing economy and sustainable consumption itself. As discussed, municipalities have many options for governing local consumption, yet it is important to maintain critical reflection and also to discuss when municipalities have gone beyond their mandate and their designated role. Municipalities have limited budgets and must prioritize. It is important that they do not do this in a way that rejects good ideas and initiatives from the private and voluntary sectors. These ideas and initiatives are often overshadowed by enthusiastic and ambitious projects run by municipalities. Yet this is also why collaboration in projects like Sharing Cities, to take just one example, is critical.

All governing modes will most likely require a sustainable transition; they also fulfil different functions in the process of achieving sustainable consumption. However, there is no clear picture of all ongoing governing processes. Given the lack of evaluation of these processes, it would be difficult to know whether the sum of all activities had led to a sustainable outcome. The activities will no doubt require coordination as well as a comparison of goals and the identification of conflicts between these goals in order to define the most effective way for municipalities to contribute to sustainable consumption. More research also needs to be done on how to measure progress when a municipality is working in different areas, with diverse challenges that sometimes cut across various sectors and where the starting point in every sector is profoundly different. The infrastructure and planning of cities also needs to change in order to facilitate sustainable consumption and the sharing economy, but defining how and when this is to be done would necessitate further research.

References

Börzel, T.A. (1998), 'Organizing Babylon – on the different conceptions of policy networks', *Public Administration*, **76** (2), 253–73.

Boyer, W.W. (1990), 'Political science and the 21st century: From government to governance', *PS: Political Science and Politics*, **23** (1), 50–54.

Bulkeley, H. and K. Kern (2006), 'Local government and the governing of climate change in the UK', *Urban Studies*, **43** (12), 2237–59.

Bulkeley, H. and V. Castán Broto (2012), 'Government by experiment? Global cities and the governing of climate change', *Transactions of the Institute of British Geographers*, **37**, 361–75.

Bulkeley, H., H. Schroeder and K. Janda et al. (2009), 'Cities and climate change: The role of institutions, governance and urban planning', paper presented at the World Bank Urban Research Symposium: Cities and Climate Change, Marseille, France.

Considine, M. (2005), *Making Public Policy*, Cambridge: Polity Press.

Dale-Clough, L. (2015), 'Public procurement of innovation and local authority procurement: Procurement modes and framework conditions in three European cities', *Innovation*, **28** (3), 220–42.

Di Lucia, L. and K. Ericsson (2014), 'Low-carbon district heating in Sweden – Examining a successful energy transition', *Energy Research and Social Science*, **4**, 10–20.

Elofsson, A., N. Smedby, J. Larsson et al. (2018), 'Local governance of greenhouse gas emissions from air travel', *Journal of Environmental Policy and Planning*, **20** (5), 578–94.

European Commission (2011), 'Public Procurement Indicators 2010', accessed 14 February 2018 at http://ec.europa.eu/internal_market/publicprocurement/docs/indicators2010_en.pdf.

Evans, B., M. Joas, S. Sundback et al. (2006), 'Governing local sustainability', *Journal of Environmental Planning and Management*, **49** (6), 849–67.

Fenton, P., S. Gustafsson, J. Ivner et al. (2015), 'Sustainable energy and climate strategies: Lessons from planning processes in five municipalities', *Journal of Cleaner Production*, **98**, 213–21.

Fenton, P., S. Gustafsson, J. Ivner et al. (2016), 'Stakeholder participation in municipal energy and climate planning – experiences from Sweden', *Local Environment*, **21** (3), 272–89.

Hajer, M. (2011), *The Energetic Society: In Search of a Governance Philosophy for a Clean Economy*, The Hague: Netherlands Environmental Assessment Agency.

Hedegård, L., M. Paras and E. Gustafsson (2016), 'Contradictions in reuse-based fashion retail – the ReTuna Mall', paper presented at Global Fashion, Stockholm.

Hoffmann, M.J. (2011), *Climate Governance at the Crossroads: Experimenting with a Global Response after Kyoto*, New York: Oxford University Press.

Hoppe, T., M.M. van den Berg and F.H. Coenen (2014), 'Reflections on the uptake of climate change policies by local governments: Facing the challenges of mitigation and adaptation', *Energy, Sustainability and Society*, **4** (1), 8.

Hörlén, A, S. Forslund and P. Nilsson (2008), 'No ridiculous car journeys evaluation report, ['Inga löjliga bilresor]', Civitas SMILE, Malmö City Council.

Kern, K. and G. Alber (2008), 'Governing climate change in cities: Modes of urban climate governance in multi-level systems', paper presented at the OECD International Conference on Competitive Cities and Climate Change, Milan, Italy.

Khan, J. (2013), 'What role for network governance in urban low carbon transitions?', *Journal of Cleaner Production*, **50**, 133–9.

Lember, V., T. Kalvel and R. Kattel (2011), 'Urban competitiveness and public procurement for innovation', *Urban Studies*, **48** (7), 1373–95.

Magnusson, D. (2016), 'Who brings the heat? – From municipal to diversified ownership in the Swedish district heating market post-liberalization', *Energy Research and Social Science*, **22**, 198–209.

Malmö City Council (2014), 'No ridiculous car trips' ['Inga löjliga bilresor'], film, accessed 15 January 2018 at https://vimeo.com/125160935.

McCormick, K., L. Neij, S. Anderberg et al. (2013), 'Advancing sustainable urban transformation', *Journal of Cleaner Production*, **50**, 1–11.

McLaren, D. and Agyeman, J. (2015), *Sharing Cities: A Case for Truly Smart and Sustainable Cities*, Cambridge, MA: MIT Press.

Meehan, J. and D. Bryde (2011), 'Sustainable procurement practice', *Business Strategy and the Environment*, **20** (2), 94–106.

Michelsen O. and L. de Boer (2009), 'Green procurement in Norway: A survey of practices at the municipal and county level', *Journal of Environmental Management*, **91** (1), 160–67.

Mont, O., E. Heiskanen, K. Power et al. (2013), 'Nordic policy brief: Improving Nordic policymaking by dispelling myths on sustainable consumption', *TemaNord*, **2013** (566), DOI: https://doi.org/10.6027/TN2013-566.

National Agency for Public Procurement and the Swedish Competition Authority (2016), 'Statistics on public procurement 2016', accessed 15 January 2018 at https://www.upphandlingsmyndigheten.se/globalassets/publikationer/rapporter/rapport-2016-2-statistik-om-offentlig-upphandling-2016.pdf.

Organisation for Economic Co-operation and Development (2009), 'The innovation value chain', accessed 29 January 2018 at http://www.oecd.org/innovation/inno/43726748.pdf.

P4 Göteborg (2018), Sveriges Radio, 31 January, 'One of Sweden's largest car cooperatives terminates' ['Ett av Sveriges största bilkooperativ läggs ned'], accessed 15 February 2018 at https://sverigesradio.se/sida/artikel.aspx?programid=104&artikel=6873352.

Palm, J. (2006), 'Development of sustainable energy systems in Swedish municipalities: A matter of path dependency and power relations', *Local Environment*, **11**, 445–57.

Palm, J. and F. Backman (2017a), 'Public procurement of electric vehicles as a way to support a market: Examples from Sweden', *International Journal of Electric and Hybrid Vehicles*, **9** (3), 253–68.

Palm, J. and F. Backman (2017b), 'Policy network creation as a driver of energy-efficient industry', *International Journal of Energy Sector Management*, **11** (1), 143–57.

Palm, J. and J. Thoresson (2014), 'Strategies and implications for network participation in regional climate and energy planning', *Journal of Environmental Policy and Planning*, **16** (1), 3–19.

Palm, J. and E. Wihlborg (2006), 'Governed by technology? Urban management of broadband and 3G systems in Sweden', *Journal of Urban Technology*, **13** (2), 71–89.

Peters, G. and J. Pierre (1998), 'Governing without government: Rethinking public administration', *Journal of Public Administration and Theory*, **8**, 223–42.

Peters, G. and J. Pierre, (2004), 'Multi-level governance and democracy: A Faustian bargain?', in I. Bache and M. Flinders (eds), *Multi-Level Governance*, New York: Oxford University Press, pp. 75–91.

Rhodes, R.A.W (1997), *Understanding Governance: Policy Networks, Governance, Reflexivity and Accountability*, Milton Keynes, UK: Open University Press.

SALAR [Swedish Association of Local Authorities and Regions] (2013), 'Parking for sustainable urban development' ['Parkering för hållbar stadsutveckling'], accessed 14 February 2018 at https://webbu tik.skl.se/sv/artiklar/parkering-for-hallbar-stadsutveckling.html.

Smedby, N. and M.B. Quitzau (2016), 'Municipal governance and sustainability: The role of local governments in promoting transitions', *Environmental Policy and Governance*, **26**, 323–36.

Sporrong, J. and A. Kadefors (2014), 'Municipal consultancy procurement: New roles and practices', *Building Research and Information*, **42** (5), 616–28.

Stoker, G. (1998), 'Governance as theory: Five propositions', *International Social Science Journal*, **50**, 17–28.

Tambach, M. and H. Visscher (2012), 'Towards energy-neutral new housing developments: Municipal climate governance in the Netherlands', *European Planning Studies*, **20** (1), 111–30.

Trelleborg Municipality (2017), 'Guidelines for meetings and travels for Trelleborg Municipality' ['Riktlinjer för möten och resor för Trelleborgs kommun'], decided by the municipal council 25 April 2016, revised by the municipal executive board 27 September 2017, §195.

Wihlborg, E. and J. Palm (2008), 'Who is governing what? Governing local technical systems – an issue of accountability', *Local Government Studies*, **34**, 349–62.

12 From worktime reduction to a post-work future: Implications for sustainable consumption governance

Maurie J. Cohen

1. Introduction

The proposition of reduced working hours has received notable but inconsistent attention in research on sustainable consumption governance over the past two decades (Schor, 1998; 2005; Sanne, 2002; Kallis et al., 2013; Nässén and Larsson, 2015; Mont, 2016). This ambivalence can be attributed to a material-centric world-view among scholars, policymakers, and advocates that emphasizes biophysical flows and tends to disregard human labour and the resultant incomes that enable and reproduce commercial provisioning activities. Moreover, the pursuit of sustainable consumption has been premised on a discernible conceit – one that is contrary to the historical record and in all likelihood mostly mistaken – that consumer-led innovation rather than novel producer capabilities constitutes the leading edge of social change. Nonetheless, the notion that limiting worktime could lead to a lowering of greenhouse gas emissions and contribute to other environmental and social improvements remains an important tenet of sustainable consumption governance (Fuchs and Lorek, 2005; Keller et al., 2016). While prominent exceptions exist, systematic efforts to pursue worktime reduction as a way to decrease resource throughput have, to date, been constrained by a lack of willingness by policymakers to act on this knowledge (Coote et al., 2010; Knight et al., 2013; Pullinger, 2014).

In the face of this reticence to curtail working hours, the last couple of years have given rise to profound anxiety about the disruptive effects of new digital automation technologies and the prospect of sweeping downsizing in the availability of work (McClure, 2018; Naastepad and Mulder, 2018). Specifically, societal diffusion of artificial intelligence, general-purpose robots and self-driving vehicles is threatening to sharply diminish demand for labour and lead to a future of large-scale unemployment. These circumstances force us to expand the vista of how to think about sustainable consumption governance and to conceptualize anew the associated challenges in terms that go beyond incrementally limiting fossil fuel use and attenuating ecological footprints. The emergent need to address the problems stemming from the scarcity of wage labour, to reconceive the relationship between work and consumption and to re-envisage the ways in which households will access goods and services compels consideration of how to manage the transition to a reconfigured system of social organization. In other words, it is not hyperbolic to suggest that we stand on the threshold of revolutionary changes that are tantamount to the ruptures that gave birth first to industrialism and subsequently brought forth the onset of consumerism (Landes, 1969; Leach, 1994; Trentmann, 2017).

In formulating an agenda for sustainable consumption governance, this chapter assembles several different threads of contemporary scholarship on how acquisition of the means to consume is likely to evolve in the future. First, existing literature on the environmental and social benefits of worktime reduction is summarized. Second, the chapter reviews recent assessments on the rising wave of digital automation and contrasts forecasts about the degree to which these technologies will displace human workers. Third, the provocations advanced by a group of social theorists who have taken up the theme of a 'post-work' society are discussed. Finally, the chapter highlights three issues that will likely become salient in coming years as the challenges of sustainable consumption governance evolve in new directions.

2.   Worktime reduction and sustainable consumption

The case for policies that shorten working hours to reduce greenhouse gas emissions and to curb other sources of ecological degradation is compelling. Juliet Schor (2005: 38) articulated the fundamental issue more than a decade ago:

> [I]n the global North a successful path to sustainability must confront our commitment to growth and will ultimately entail a stabilization of consumption through reductions in hours of work. Indeed, it is difficult to imagine a globally ethical, timely, and politically feasible resolution to the global ecological crisis in which populations in the North do not reduce the number of hours worked per capita.

The key contention is that improvements in labour productivity can be used either to decrease worktime (hence increasing leisure and opportunities for non-working activities) or to enhance consumption volumes. From the latter decades of the nineteenth century through the first third of the twentieth century, combinations of social mobilization and legislative reform led to a decrease in working hours across most of Western Europe and North America (Negrey, 2013; Ehmer and Lis, 2016). This trend continued after World War II and was especially marked in Sweden, Norway, Denmark and the Netherlands because of political commitment to more equitable distribution of available employment (Eichengreen, 2008). Accordingly, a month or more of paid leave came to be the norm in these nations and female workers were typically entitled to separate and extended periods of compensated time off after giving birth.

This decline in working hours began to stagnate by the end of the 1970s in virtually all countries of the Organisation for Economic Co-operation and Development (OECD) and in some significant cases – notably the United States – average per person worktime increased during the 1980s and 1990s. More recent evidence suggests that a pattern of extreme working hours has become manifest in a larger number of nations over the past decade, though France and Scandinavia are notable exceptions (Burger, 2015). In other words, ongoing productivity gains have, overall, not facilitated greater leisure or created opportunities for non-wage vocations but instead have been channelled to offset languishing incomes and to augment household consumption.

Furthermore, rigidities in labour markets have made it difficult for workers to negotiate with employers for fewer hours (with proportional reduction in earnings), even if they prefer shorter schedules. As a result, the situation today in the United States (and to a somewhat lesser extent in other OECD countries) compels people to favour consumption over leisure even if a goods-intensive lifestyle is contrary to personal inclinations. While the widespread availability of prepared – and largely unhealthy – 'convenience' meals and the seemingly ceaseless proliferation of 'on-demand' services are obvious expressions of this condition, other putative consequences include the heightened levels of stress and strained domestic relationships associated with long working hours (Weil, 2014; Fleming, 2017). Proponents of worktime reduction thus claim that a reduction in working hours could contribute to broad improvements in life satisfaction, societal well-being and environmental sustainability (Buhl and Acosta, 2016; Borowy and Aillon, 2017).

Despite the ostensible appeal of a shift toward fewer hours of paid work, it has been difficult to organize political constituencies to successfully press the case (Knight et al., 2013; Pullinger, 2014). Resistance is partly attributable to the fact that people are locked into fixed consumption routines and are disinclined to favour less time in compensated employment (and the lower income that would result). Interestingly, though, there is evidence that preferences change when attention is focused on the future rather than the present (Schor, 2005; Grözinger et al., 2010). Another serious obstacle is that trade unions in most OECD countries have experienced significant decline and particularly in the United States organized labour has been rendered mostly irrelevant in all but a few sectors (Arnowitz, 2015; Geoghegan, 2016). The slackening of the labour market after the 2008 financial crisis further eroded negotiating leverage, but more recent tightening of conditions holds the prospect for at least a modest reversal. At the same time, the weakening or possible elimination of newly instituted regulatory controls on freewheeling bankers suggests that the next meltdown may not be too far away (Hilary, 2013; Wolfe, 2016).

Onset of the next economic collapse will likely accelerate diffusion of the digital automation technologies discussed in the following section. If developments unfold at the pace that some analysts are ominously forecasting, it will obviate most efforts to curtail worktime as a credible sustainability strategy and shift emphasis to different and more immediate priorities. More specifically, we can expect that sustainable consumption governance will be required to expand beyond its predominant emphasis on contracting fossil fuel use consistent with the Paris Climate Agreement and fostering progress on the United Nations 2030 Agenda (Alfredsson et al., 2018; Bengtsson et al., 2018). Policymakers will instead need to pursue a wider mandate centred on assuring sufficient livelihoods for the swelling ranks of former workers who have lost access to previously reliable forms of wage labour (Ashford et al., 2012). As such, the social dimensions of sustainability will come to play a much more prominent role than is presently the case.

3.   Work in the era of digital automation

We are currently witnessing early deployment of three overlapping categories of extremely powerful and disruptive digital automation technologies. First, artificial intelligence systems driven by machine learning are upending entire industries and promise to become a new and unprecedented general purpose technology (Bresnahan and Trajtenberg, 1995; Bekar et al., 2018). Applications extend from IBM's *Watson*, which vaulted to worldwide attention when it defeated two all-time champions of *Jeopardy!* (a US television game show that tests contestants' encyclopaedic knowledge) to more mundane applications for improving clerical and managerial efficiency. A compelling example of the latter type is being developed by a company called WorkFusion and is evocatively described by author and entrepreneur Martin Ford (2015: 95) in the following terms:

> The WorkFusion software initially analyzes the project to determine which tasks can be directly automated, which can be crowd sourced, and which must be performed by inhouse professionals. It can then automatically post job listings to websites like Elance or Craigslist and manage the recruitment and selection of qualified freelance workers. Once the workers are on board, the software allocates tasks and evaluates performance. It does this in part by asking freelancers to answer questions to which it already knows the answer as an ongoing test of the workers' accuracy. It tracks productivity metrics like typing speed, and automatically matches tasks with the capabilities of individuals. If a particular person is unable to complete a given assignment, the system will automatically escalate that task to someone with the necessary skills.

Other modes of artificial intelligence include voice-activated virtual assistants like Apple's *Siri* and Amazon's *Alexa* that are rapidly gaining popular acceptance and herald the extent to which similar electronic tools will become embedded across a spectrum of applications.

Second, high-capability and readily adaptable robots are being developed for industrial and consumer activities. Specific devices range from drones that collect data and undertake surveillance to Rethink Robotics' manufacturing automaton called Baxter to iRobot's autonomous vacuum cleaner. Japan, due to the country's ageing population, chronic labour shortage, technophilic culture and dogged search for economic advantage is leading the way in the commercialization of social robots (Robertson, 2017; Sone, 2017).

Finally, driverless vehicles, enabled by complex arrays of environmental sensors, visioning tools and control systems are increasingly able to navigate traffic-congested roads without the aid of a human operator. Information technology paragons (Google), legacy automobile manufacturers (Ford Motor Company), ride-sharing start-ups (Uber) and others have been vying to establish themselves at the forefront of this hugely lucrative industry. Autonomous cars will eliminate the need for drivers, while concomitantly improving performance and safety and perhaps even overturning the necessity for widespread automobile ownership. One conception of how implementation would develop anticipates users summoning a small electric-powered mobile unit with a smartphone. Vehicles would be dispatched from a centralized staging facility (for example, an underground parking garage), retrieve the passenger and convey her to a selected destination. The car would then either return to a storage depot or proceed to collect the next passenger. While this scenario provides an entrancing vision, initial uptake of autonomous capabilities will likely be by fleet operators that provide relatively routinized activities involving security patrols, goods delivery and municipal services (Markoff, 2016).

The adoption of digital automation technologies creates potential for significant displacement of labour across a vast number of sectors (Brynjolfsson and McAfee, 2014; Ford, 2015). While we must acknowledge that the future is unknowable and that it is extremely difficult to discern how these systems will ultimately evolve, current debates centre on two binary options. On the one hand, there is an optimistic expectation that they will prompt creation of entirely new employment opportunities (perhaps managing self-driving vehicles or servicing social robots). On the other hand, we face acute anxiety that the onrushing changes will give rise to more portentous outcomes that could precipitate mass joblessness.

Most economists and allied travellers embrace the former outlook and contend that if we harken back to the early Industrial Revolution it is apparent that society has gone through numerous phases of technological change. At each juncture, pessimists have anticipated sweeping employment losses, but these outcomes have never materialized. Purveyors of these sunny prognoses are apt to observe that innovation eliminates some jobs, but it also triggers the creation of new – and frequently better and more remunerative – opportunities. A corollary is that it is futile to resist technological advancement and the best strategy is to get ahead of the disruption through a combination of cleverness and guile.

A contrasting stance emanates out of analyses such as the prominent study by Frey and Osborne (2017). This work anticipates that nearly half of all available jobs in the United States are susceptible to replacement by digital automation within the next two decades and there are likely to be fewer ways to reabsorb displaced workers than during prior upheavals. Big losers will be white-collar occupations, for example, underwriters, lawyers and telemarketers. Such assessments anticipate a future of expanding labour informality, economic precarity and social vulnerability (Standing, 2011; Breman and van der Linden, 2014). In its darker expressions, this perspective imagines a future where companies that own the algorithms will propel society toward a techno-feudal system of post-industrial social organization (Ford, 2015; Kostakis et al., 2016).

While popular consideration of different possibilities tends to shuttle between these diametric visions, the menu of prospective alternatives is, of course, much richer and more diverse. It would be just as foolish to fall into the economists' trap of bountiful opportunity as it would be to preclude that we are inescapably headed toward robot-impelled repeasantization. We have capacity to manage the opportunities afforded by the extraordinary technologies that are currently unfolding by establishing political priorities and making careful policy decisions. It is, though, a very open question of whether we will choose wisely. The next section offers some guidance that might help to increase our likelihood for success.

4.   Towards a post-work future?

Over the past two decades, a community of scholars has coalesced around the notion of a 'post-work' future in which wage labour declines in social and economic significance (Gorz, 1999; Hayden, 1999; Weeks, 2011; Hunnicutt, 2013; Frayne, 2015; Frase, 2016). While there are important differences among authors regarding how comprehensively jobless this world might be, the basic idea is that the decentring of paid work will enable realization of the leisurely lifestyles that have been imagined since the days of classical economists like Adam Smith and John Stewart Mill. Most famously, this prospect was foretold by John Maynard Keynes (1932 [1930]) in an essay entitled 'Economic possibilities for our grandchildren' in which he projected ahead seventy years and predicted that the average working week would be scaled back to just fifteen hours. In formulating this vision, the foremost economist of the twentieth century coined the term 'technological unemployment' and described it as 'a new disease of which some readers may not yet have heard the name, but of which they will hear a great deal in the years to come' (Keynes, 1932 [1930]: 364).

The post-work authors regard productivity improvements, along with a lack of meaningful non-financial rewards from work, as the impetus for abandoning long-standing policy commitments to full employment. They consider the groundswell of digital automation as a historic opportunity to prepare for a time when, as Keynes (1932 [1930]: 369) put it: 'the accumulation of wealth is no longer of high social importance' and we will be able to devote ourselves to pursuits that engender more credible forms of personal satisfaction. While this claim is partly attributable to the currently bewildering pace of change, it is also being propelled by concerns that the pending instability, driven by potent machine-learning algorithms, is more likely this time around to overturn the fortunes of people who work in offices than their counterparts who toil on factory floors. In short, the politics of post-work will be propelled to an outsized degree by the apprehensions of middle-class households.

The question that immediately emerges is how, in the absence of regularized employment, will people create viable livelihoods for themselves? Over the last few years, a common response has been to invoke the idea of a universal basic income (UBI) that would be provided to all societal members without a conditional work requirement and regardless of socio-demographic, income or other factors (Reich,

2016; van Parijs and Vanderborght, 2017). Friedrich Hayek and Milton Friedman separately advanced this proposition during the 1970s and it attracted support from political figures as diverse as Richard Nixon and Martin Luther King, Jr. In recent years, numerous experiments have been launched to test the viability of UBI in a number of countries including Finland and Kenya and in 2016 it was the focal point of a national referendum in Switzerland (Dörre, 2017; Kangas et al., 2017). Additionally, the Silicon Valley-based social accelerator, Y Combinator, carried out a pilot project in Oakland, California in 2017 and has plans to expand the initiative by recruiting 2 000 people and distributing to each of them US$1 000 per month for three to five years (McFarland, 2017).

A major challenge for proponents of UBI is how to generate the necessary revenue, which will need to be considerable if the disbursements are to be maintained over an extended period of time. Interesting from the standpoint of sustainable consumption governance is that several models are being discussed and, at least in one case, there is significant experience, while other alternatives are still at the conceptual stage (Cohen, 2017a). First, the Alaska Permanent Fund has a proven record of accumulating the public proceeds from the state's oil production and then annually distributing a portion to all residents as a citizen's dividend (Barnes, 2014; Berman, 2018). Second, UBI could be funded through a so-called common asset trust that imposes a user charge on exploitation of local resources as compensation for appropriation of collectively held assets like groundwater (and potentially applicable to the climate) (Barnes et al., 2008; Farley et al., 2015). Finally, an old idea that has recently been rediscovered calls for a carbon tax that would be partly returned to households as a monthly or annual dividend (Baker et al., 2017; Roberts, 1994).

While these strategies engender significant political challenges, they are typically construed as offering a practicable means of supplementing wage income with alternative sources and could confer a measure of economic security as customary employment contracts. However, some post-work proponents advance the bolder idea of moving toward 'full automation'. Dubbed the accelerationists, these advocates comingle a heady admixture of Marxism, libertarianism and anarchism with unbridled technological utopianism. The aim is to speed up capitalism to a point at which it becomes possible to achieve a kind of liberatory escape velocity and thereby break free of the strictures of the contemporary system (Mackay and Avanessian, 2014; Pitts and Dinerstein, 2017). In a recent review article, Andy Beckett (2017) writes:

> Accelerationists argue that technology, particularly computer technology, and capitalism, particularly the most aggressive variety, should be massively sped up and intensified – either because this is the best way forward for humanity, or because there is no alternative. Accelerationists favour automation. They favour the further merging of the digital and the human. They often favour the deregulation of business, and drastically scaled-back government. They believe that people should stop deluding themselves that economic and technological progress can be controlled. They often believe that social and political upheaval has a value in itself.

The accelerationist philosophy cuts across the conventional left–right political divide while simultaneously injecting into the current frayed discourse a riotous and irreverent fervour. Proponents argue that the long-standing mistake of would-be revolutionaries has been to try to overturn capitalism, when the more appropriate strategy is to get the digital wheels spinning so fast that the system destructs on its own accord. A more recent expression, so-called 'left accelerationism' advanced by Nick Srnicek and Alex Williams (2015), embraces shattering forms of technological innovation and claims that we need to achieve 'full automation' with all possible haste but to complement it with policies to reduce working hours and achieve UBI.

Important questions, though, remain as to whether UBI in any form constitutes a sufficient policy for forestalling economic instability and offsetting precarity among workers released from paid labour by the impending wave of technological innovation (Battistoni, 2017; Heller, 2018). After all, relying on public tax revenue to fund an auxiliary income, regardless of its particular revenue-raising mechanism, is unlikely to alter the balance of power between robot owners and the unemployed multitudes. Under these circumstances, UBI is essentially a transfer payment that is similar to contemporary forms of social welfare. We can also anticipate that the size of the disbursements and the eligibility requirements would be recurrent points of debate with the outcome at any moment determined by shifting political winds. While an unconditional income might provide a financial salve to ease certain sources of instability in the short term, it does not address the underlying problems of structural inequality that will be compounded in the era of increasing digital automation.

A complementary strategy would enable the dwindling number of human workers to acquire the financial proceeds of productivity improvements through ownership of robot-related stock. At present, in the United States, only 52 per cent of the population owns shares and the wealthiest 1 per cent of households possesses 38 per cent of total market valuation (McCarthy, 2016). Improving this situation requires reshaping the contours of asset ownership through implementation of policies to encourage broad-based stock ownership (BBSO) (Blasi et al., 2013; Cohen, 2017b). Distributing more widely the ability to garner dividends and capital gains could diminish structural inequalities caused by the fading availability of formal employment and the decline of wage income.

Analysts who contend that it is unrealistic to extend policy support for BBSO should note that as recently as 2007 the proportion of Americans invested in the stock market was 65 per cent with most individuals of modest means participating primarily through their pension or retirement plans. It is furthermore instructive to adopt a still longer historical perspective, anchored in long-standing efforts to encourage expansive societal participation in a different asset class, namely acquisition of a house. In the United States, only 44 per cent of the population were homeowners in 1940, with the majority living at the time in rental accommodation (Fishback et al., 2013). While it is important not to overlook the inequities that all too frequently have been associated with their design and implementation, vigorous and coordinated policies over several decades successfully raised national homeownership to a peak in 2004 of 69 per cent (it has since declined to a current level of 64 per cent) (United States Census Bureau, 2018).

Largely due to the effectiveness of facilitating programmes (including extremely generous subsidies delivered through the tax system), for many households, the family residence currently serves as their lone significant asset. It moreover remains the case that the United States is not the only country to assign priority to homeownership and rates are even higher across parts of Europe (Doling and Ford, 2003; van Gent, 2010). The lesson here is that robust policies to encourage stock acquisition could be created along similar lines if there was interest in expanding prevailing political commitments beyond the acquisition of real property.

5. Conclusion

The governance challenges associated with sustainable consumption will likely evolve in coming years as digital automation technologies undermine the availability of wage labour and usher in an increasingly jobless future. Contemporary emphasis on decoupling economic growth from resource utilization will be supplemented by the need to simultaneously facilitate the ability of households to maintain materially adequate livelihoods as the familiar relationship between wage labour and consumerist lifestyles further erodes. Meanwhile, difficult ecological problems are not going to quietly recede. Climate change, as well as more ordinary and yet unresolved dilemmas such as air pollution, groundwater depletion and soil toxicity will continue to undermine health and well-being. Although many of the specifics remain indeterminate, what is probable is that in a post-work future sustainable consumption will become more multi-faceted and complex. Household procurement of goods and services will in the future be less routinized and instead predicated on a more diverse portfolio of activities. As is evermore the case in many other domains, clear distinctions between the provisioning practices of countries at differing levels of affluence will become less distinguishable (Breman and van der Linden, 2014; Deaton, 2018).

Recognition that people will need to forge more adaptable lifestyles opens up a range of prospective issues for sustainable consumption governance. The first task will be to redesign conventional educational systems (Aoun, 2017; Davidson, 2017). Schools remain largely geared to delivering vocational training and to preparing students for a world of work. But what happens when industrial and post-industrial forms of employment have disappeared? Even today, many formerly employed or underemployed people struggle to find satisfying pursuits because the necessity to generate cash income is the predominant consideration and everything else comes to a grinding halt when financially compensated opportunities vanish. The chief objective of post-work education will be, by contrast, to offer instruction on how to live well with more unstructured time and to cultivate interests consistent with personal proclivities and ambitions.

Second, sustainable consumption governance will need to focus on modifying urban infrastructure – especially buildings and transportation systems – for post-work lifestyles. As noted at the outset, this process is expected to be at least as transformational as prior transitions from agrarianism to industrialism and subsequently from manufacturing to post-industrial systems of social organization. While there is no shortage of technological innovations that promise to enhance the sustainability of 'smart cities', it is important to recognize that many of these applications are principally intended to improve efficiency, to foster economic competitiveness and to quicken the pace of overall busyness (Bellezza et al., 2017; Bibri and Krogstie, 2017; Martin et al., 2018). Since the various technical interventions that constitute this policy programme do not typically address the confounding relationship between affluence and consumption, the most likely outcome will be the sparking of perverse rebound effects that undermine in whole or part any resultant improvements in urban productivity (Wiedenhofer et al., 2018).

Even iconic technologies of nominally 'green' urban living like bicycle-sharing systems are generally embraced by users not out of a commitment to less resource-consumptive lifestyles but because they are cheaper or, at least in some cities, provide a more stylish alternative to existing mobility options (Tironi, 2015; Zademach and Musch, 2018). This paradox stems from the preparedness of policymakers to embrace 'weak' sustainability prescriptions but to dismiss recommendations capable of achieving absolute reductions in energy and materials utilization (Fuchs and Lorek, 2005; Spangenberg, 2014; Fuchs et al., 2016).

Fortunately, it is possible to point to several early experiments in how to put into practice the notion of 'sufficient lifestyles' (Princen, 2005; Gorge et al., 2015; Spengler, 2016; Daoud, 2018). One interesting area of application is focused on innovative co-working/co-living arrangements that enable the malleability that fluid and less materially invested livelihoods require (Grozdanic, 2016; Kadat, 2017). A property developer in San Francisco, for example, has recently begun constructing dormitories for adults that replicate many of the features of intentional communities without imposing onerous moral requirements and similar projects are springing up in New York and other cities (Kaysen, 2015; Bowles, 2018). It is, of course, premature to formulate a clear understanding of how these adaptive responses will develop over time and become arrayed into patterns that enable people to forge flourishing lifestyles, but numerous processes of learning are currently under way and useful knowledge is being accumulated and demonstrated.

Finally, an archetype of the post-work future may be the acclaimed digital nomad who has no fixed home and seamlessly combines work, leisure and travel, often relocating every few months to a different locale to partake in the novel experiences on offer (Reichenberger, 2017). While this kind of peripatetic and multitasking existence may be both appealing and achievable for ardently cosmopolitan millennials or semi-retired professionals, for less interculturally proficient individuals the future is liable to entail not globetrotting adventure but rather impoverished and unrooted migration, an itinerant existence plagued by weak communal connections and continuous economic insecurity. In the absence of uplifting interventions, these people will remain trapped in a listless drift through a fraught workscape that provides only temporary and low-skill jobs that have yet to be consigned to the robots (Bruder, 2017).

For still others unfortunate to be subjected to the cruel realities of internecine conflict, chronic resource scarcity or perpetual environmental degradation (or perhaps all of these adversities at the same time), the second half of the twenty-first century is apt to be even harsher. Indeed, the treacherous journeys that seemingly more and more people around the world have been prepared to undertake in recent years could be a discordant harbinger of what is yet to come. In the absence of practicable arrangements for the provisioning of essential supplies and services – and this may prove to be the ultimate challenge of sustainable consumption governance – it is not difficult to envisage a future of truly dire and overwhelming proportions.

References

Alfredsson, E., M. Bengtsson, H. Brown et al. (2018), 'Why achieving the Paris Agreement requires reduced overall consumption and production', *Sustainability: Science, Practice and Policy*, **14** (1), 1–5.

Aoun, J. (2017), *Robot-Proof: Higher Education in the Age of Artificial Intelligence*, Cambridge, MA: MIT Press.

Arnowitz, S. (2015), *The Death and Life of American Labor: Toward a New Workers' Movement*, New York: Verso.

Ashford, N., R. Hall and R. Ashford (2012), 'The crisis in employment and consumer demand: Reconciliation with environmental sustainability', *Environmental Innovations and Societal Transitions*, **2**, 1–22.

Baker, J., M. Feldstein, T. Halstead et al. (2017), *The Conservative Case for Carbon Dividends*, Washington, DC: Climate Leadership Council.

Barnes, P. (2014), *With Liberty and Dividends for All: How to Save Our Middle Class When Jobs Don't Pay Enough*, San Francisco, CA: Berrett-Koehler.

Barnes, P., R. Costanza, P. Hawken et al. (2008), 'Creating an Earth atmosphere trust', *Science*, **319** (5864), 724.

Battistoni, A. (2017), 'The false promise of universal basic income', *Dissent*, **64** (2), 51–62.

Beckett, A. (2017), 'Accelerationism: How a fringe philosophy predicted the future we live in', *The Guardian*, 11 May, accessed 21 January 2018 at https://www.theguardian.com/world/2017/may/11/accelerationism-how-a-fringe-philosophy-predicted-the-future-we-live-in.

Bekar, C., K. Carlaw and R. Lipsey (2018), 'General purpose technologies in theory, application and controversy: A review', *Journal of Evolutionary Economics*, **28** (5), 1005–33.

Bellezza, S., N. Paharia and A. Keinan (2017), 'Conspicuous consumption of time: When busyness and lack of leisure time become a status symbol', *Journal of Consumer Research*, **44** (1), 118–38.

Bengtsson, M., E. Alfredsson, M. Cohen et al. (2018), 'Transforming systems of consumption and production for achieving the sustainable development goals: Moving beyond efficiency', *Sustainability Science*, **13** (6), 1533–47.

Berman, M. (2018), 'Resource rents, universal basic income and poverty among Alaska's Indigenous peoples', *World Development*, **106**, 161–72.

Bibri, S. and J. Krogstie (2017), 'Smart sustainable cities of the future: An extensive interdisciplinary literature review', *Sustainable Cities and Society*, **31**, 183–212.

Blasi, J., R. Freeman and D. Kruse (2013), *The Citizen's Share: Reducing Inequality in the 21st Century*, New Haven, CT: Yale University Press.

Borowy, I. and J.-L. Aillon (2017), 'Sustainable health and degrowth: Health, health care and society beyond the growth paradigm', *Social Theory and Health*, **15** (3), 346–68.

Bowles, N. (2018), 'Dorm living for professionals comes to San Francisco', *The New York Times*, 4 March, accessed 21 January 2019 at https://www.nytimes.com/2018/03/04/technology/dorm-living-grown-ups-san-francisco.html.

Breman, J. and M. van der Linden (2014), 'Informalizing the economy: The return of the social question at the global level', *Development and Change*, **45** (5), 920–40.

Bresnahan, T. and M. Trajtenberg (1995), 'General purpose technologies: "engines of growth"?', *Journal of Econometrics*, **65** (1), 83–108.

Bruder, J. (2017), *Nomadland: Surviving America in the Twenty-First Century*, New York: W.W. Norton.

Brynjolfsson, E. and A. McAfee (2014), *The Second Machine Age: Work, Progress and Prosperity in a Time of Brilliant Technologies*, New York: W.W. Norton.

Buhl, J. and J. Acosta (2016), 'Work less, do less? Working time reductions and rebound effects', *Sustainability Science*, **11** (2), 261–76.

Burger, A. (2015), *Extreme Working Hours in Western Europe and North America: A New Aspect of Polarization*, LSE 'Europe in Question', Discussion Paper Series.

Cohen, M. (2017a), 'Workers – and consumers of the world unite! Opportunities for hybrid co-operativism', in J. Michie, J. Blasi and C. Borzaga (eds), *The Oxford Handbook of Mutual, Co-operative and Co-owned Business*, Oxford: Oxford University Press, pp. 374–85.

Cohen, M. (2017b), *The Future of Consumer Society: Prospects for Sustainability in the New Economy*, Oxford: Oxford University Press.

Coote, A., J. Franklin and A. Simms (2010), *21 Hours*, London: New Economics Foundation.

Daoud, A. (2018), 'Unifying studies of scarcity, abundance and sufficiency', *Ecological Economics*, **147**, 208–17.

Davidson, C. (2017), *The New Education: How to Revolutionize the University to Prepare Students for a World in Flux*, New York: Basic Books.

Deaton, A. (2018), 'The U.S. can no longer hide from its deep poverty problem', *The New York Times*, 24 January, accessed 21 January 2019 at https://www.nytimes.com/2018/01/24/opinion/poverty-united-states.html.

Doling, J. and J. Ford (2003), *Globalisation and Home Ownership: Experiences in Eight Member States of the European Union*, Amsterdam: IOS Press.

Dörre, P. (2017), 'The promise of Kenya's experiment with universal basic income', *World Politics Review*, 5 December, accessed 21 January 2019 at https://www.worldpoliticsreview.com/articles/23750/the-promise-of-kenya-s-experiment-with-universal-basic-income.

Ehmer, J. and C. Lis (2016), *The Idea of Work in Europe from Antiquity to Modern Times*, New York: Routledge.

Eichengreen, B. (2008), *The European Economy since 1945: Coordinated Capitalism and Beyond*, Princeton, NJ: Princeton University Press.

Farley, J., R. Costanza, G. Flomenholft et al. (2015), 'The Vermont Common Assets Trust: An institution for sustainable, just and efficient resource allocation', *Ecological Economics*, **109**, 71–9.

Fishback, P., J. Rose and K. Snowden (2013), *Well Worth Saving: How the New Deal Safeguarded Home Ownership*, Chicago, IL: University of Chicago Press.

Fleming, P. (2017), *The Death of Homo Economicus: Work, Debt and the Myth of Endless Accumulation*, London: Pluto Press.

Ford, M. (2015), *Rise of the Robots: Technology and the Threat of a Jobless Future*, New York: Basic Books.

Frase, F. (2016), *Four Futures: Life after Capitalism*, New York: Verso.

Frayne, D. (2015), *The Refusal of Work: The Theory and Practice of Resistance to Work*, London: Zed Books.

Frey, C. and M. Osborne (2017), 'The future of employment: How susceptible are jobs to computerisation?', *Technological Forecasting and Social Change*, **114**, 254–80.

Fuchs, D. and S. Lorek (2005), 'Sustainable consumption governance: A history of promises and failures', *Journal of Consumer Policy*, **28** (3), 261–88.

Fuchs, D., A. DiGiulio, K. Glaab et al. (2016), 'Power: The missing element in sustainable consumption and absolute reductions research and action', *Journal of Cleaner Production*, **132**, 298–307.

Geoghegan, T. (2016), *Only One Thing Can Save Us: Why America Needs a New Kind of Labor Movement*, New York: New Press.

Gorge, H., M. Herbert, N. Özçağlar-Toulouse et al. (2015), 'What do we really need? Questioning consumption through sufficiency', *Journal of Macromarketing*, **35** (1), 11–22.

Gorz, A. (1999), *Reclaiming Work: Beyond the Wage-Based Society*, Cambridge: Polity Press.

Grozdanic, L. (2016), 'Space as a service: Business models that change how we live and work', *Archipreneur*, 24 March, accessed 21 January 2019 at https://archipreneur.com/space-as-a-service-business-models-that-change-how-we-live-and-work.

Grözinger, G., W. Matiaske and V. Tobsch (2010), 'Employee-friendly labour time: A key element to a sustainable pattern of production and consumption', *International Journal of Public Policy*, **5** (4), 357–72.

Hayden, A. (1999), *Sharing the Work, Sparing the Planet: Work-Time, Consumption and Ecology*, London: Zed Books.

Heller, N. (2018), 'Who really stands to win from universal basic income?', *The New Yorker*, 9 July, accessed 21 January 2019 at https://www.newyorker.com/magazine/2018/07/09/who-really-stands-to-win-from-universal-basic-income.

Hilary, J. (2013), *The Poverty of Capitalism: Economic Meltdown and the Struggle for What Comes Next*, London: Pluto Press.

Hunnicutt, B. (2013), *Free Time: The Forgotten American Dream*, Philadelphia, PA: Temple University Press.

Kadat, A. (2017), 'The shortest commute: Where co-working and co-living collide', *The Wall Street Journal*, 15 August, accessed 21 January 2019 at https://www.wsj.com/articles/the-shortest-commute-where-co-working-and-co-living-collide-1502805600.

Kallis, G., M. Kalush, H. O'Flynn et al. (2013), '"Friday off": Reducing working hours in Europe', *Sustainability*, **5** (4), 1545–67.

Kangas, O., M. Simanainen and P. Honkanen (2017), 'Basic income in the Finnish context', *Intereconomics: Review of European Economic Policy*, **52** (2), 87–91.

Kaysen, R. (2015), 'The Millennial commune', *The New York Times*, 31 July, accessed 21 January 2019 at https://www.nytimes.com/2015/08/02/realestate/the-millennial-commune.html.

Keller, M., B. Halkier and T.-A. Wilska (2016), 'Policy and governance for sustainable consumption at the crossroads of theories and concepts', *Environmental Policy and Governance*, **26** (2), 75–88.

Keynes, J. (1932 [1930]), *Essays in Persuasion*, New York: Harcourt, Brace and Company.

Knight, K., E. Rosa and J. Schor (2013), 'Could working less reduce pressures on the environment? A cross-national panel analysis of OECD countries, 1970-2007', *Global Environmental Change*, **23** (4), 691–700.

Kostakis, V., A. Roos and M. Bauwens (2016), 'Towards a political ecology of the digital economy: Socio-environmental implications of two competing value models', *Environmental Innovation and Societal Transitions*, **18**, 82–100.

Landes, D. (1969), *Prometheus Unbound: Technological Change and Industrial Development in Western Europe from 1750 to the Present*, Cambridge: Cambridge University Press.

Leach, W. (1994), *Land of Desire: Merchants, Power and the Rise of a New American Culture*, New York: Vintage.

Mackay, R. and A. Avanessian (eds) (2014), *#Accelerate#: The Accelerationist Reader*, Falmouth: Urbanomic Media.

Markoff, J. (2016), 'Want to buy a self-driving car? Big-rig trucks may come first', *New York Times*, 17

May, accessed 21 January 2019 at https://www.nytimes.com/2016/05/17/technology/want-to-buy-a-self-driving-car-trucks-may-come-first.html.

Martin, C., J. Evans and A. Karvonen (2018), 'Smart and sustainable? Five tensions in the visions and practices of the smart-sustainable city in Europe and North America', *Technological Forecasting and Social Change*, **133**, 269–78.

McCarthy, J. (2016), 'Just over half of Americans own stocks, matching record low', *Gallup*, 20 April, accessed 21 January 2019 at https://news.gallup.com/poll/190883/half-americans-own-stocks-matching-record-low.aspx.

McClure, P. (2018), '"You're fired", says the robot: The rise of automation in the workplace, technophobes and fears of unemployment', *Social Science Computer Review*, **36** (2), 139–56.

McFarland, K. (2017), 'Y Combinator releases proposal for expanded study of basic income', *Basic Income Earth Network*, 8 October, accessed 21 January 2019 at https://basicincome.org/news/2017/10/united-states-y-combinator-releases-proposal-expanded-study-basic-income.

Mont, O. (2016), 'The changing landscape of worktime reduction: The past and the future', in M. Koch and O. Mont (eds), *Sustainability and the Political Economy of Welfare*, New York: Routledge.

Naastepad, C. and J. Mulder (2018), 'Robots and us: Towards an economics of the "Good Life"', *Review of Social Economy*, **76** (3), 302–34.

Nässén, J. and J. Larsson (2015), 'Would shorter working time reduce greenhouse gas emissions? An analysis of time use and consumption in Swedish households', *Environmental Planning C*, **33**, 726–45.

Negrey, C. (2013), *Work Time: Conflict, Control and Change*, Malden, MA: Polity Press.

Pitts, F. and A. Dinerstein (2017), *Postcapitalism, Basic Income and the End of Work: A Critique and Alternative*, Bath: University of Bath.

Princen, T. 2005. *The Logic of Sufficiency*, Cambridge, MA: MIT Press.

Pullinger, M. (2014), 'Working time reduction in a sustainable economy: Criteria and options for its design', *Ecological Economics*, 103, 11–19.

Reich, R. (2016), *Saving Capitalism for the Many, Not the Few*, New York: Vintage.

Reichenberger, I. (2017), 'Digital nomads: A quest for holistic freedom in work and leisure', *Annals of Leisure Research*, **21** (3), 364–80.

Roberts, P. (1994), 'Systems and the problematique: The case of a carbon tax', *Futures*, **26** (7), 730–40.

Robertson, J. (2017), *Robo Sapiens Japanicus: Robots, Gender, Family and the Japanese Nation*, Berkeley, CA: University of California Press.

Sanne, C. (2002), 'Willing consumers – or locked-in? Policies for a sustainable consumption', *Ecological Economics*, **42** (1–2), 273–87.

Schor, J. (1998), *The Overspent American: Why We Want What We Don't Need*, New York: Harper Perennial.

Schor, J. (2005), 'Sustainable consumption and worktime reduction', *Journal of Industrial Ecology*, **9** (1–2), 37–50.

Sone, Y. (2017), *Japanese Robot Culture: Performance, Imagination and Modernity*, New York: Palgrave Macmillan.

Spangenberg, J. (2014), 'Institutional change for strong sustainable consumption: sustainable consumption and the degrowth economy', *Sustainability: Science, Practice and Policy*, **10** (1), 62–77.

Spengler, L. (2016), 'Two types of "enough": Sufficiency as minimum and maximum', *Environmental Politics*, **25** (5), 921–40.

Srnicek, N. and A. Williams (2015), *Inventing the Future: Postcapitalism and a World without Work*, New York: Verso.

Standing, G. (2011), *The Precariat: The New Dangerous Class*, New York: Bloomsbury.

Tironi, M. (2015), '(De)politicizing and ecologising bicycles: The history of the Parisian Vélib system and its controversies', *Journal of Cultural Economy*, **8** (2), 166–83.

Trentmann, F. (2017), *Empire of Things: How We Became a World of Consumers, from the Fifteenth Century to the Twenty-First*, New York: Harper Perennial.

United States Census Bureau (2018), 'Table 16: Quarterly Homeownership Rates for the U.S. and Regions. Housing Vacancies and Homeownership', United States Census Bureau, accessed 21 January 2019 at https://www.census.gov/housing/hvs/data/histtabs.html.

van Gent, W. (2010), 'Housing policy as a lever for change? The politics of welfare, assets and tenure', *Housing Studies*, **25** (5), 735–53.

van Parijs, P. and Y. Vanderborght (2017), *Basic Income: A Radical Proposal for a Free Society*, Cambridge, MA: Harvard University Press.

Weeks, K. (2011), *The Problem with Work: Feminism, Marxism, Antiwork Politics and Postwork Imaginaries*, Durham, NC: Duke University Press.

Weil, D. (2014), *The Fissured Workplace: Why Work Became So Bad for So Many and What Can Be Done to Improve It*, Cambridge, MA: Harvard University Press.

Wiedenhofer, D., B. Smetschka, L. Akenji et al. (2018), 'Household time use, carbon footprints and urban form: A review of the potential contributions of everyday living to the 1.5° climate target', *Current Opinion in Environmental Sustainability*, **30**, 7–17.

Wolfe, R. (2016), *Capitalism's Crisis Deepens: Essays on the Global Economic Meltdown*, New York: Haymarket Books.

Zademach, H.-M. and A.-K. Musch (2018), 'Bicycle-sharing systems in an alternative/diverse economy perspective: A sympathetic critique', *Local Environment*, **23** (7), 734–46.

Index